Navigating Comp
International Development

Praise for this book

'Burns and Worsley bring an acute understanding of the practitioner's art and science of development. Intangibles like participation, learning, and network development are at the core of ownership and appropriate action for social change for the poor. Navigating Complexity in International Development unlocks the analysis and dialogue needed to impact sustainable large-scale change. An important contribution for all of us working at the front end of development.'

Steve Hollingworth, President and CEO, Freedom from Hunger

'This book makes an important case for engaging complex systems, and contributes theory and practice for those researching and intervening to improve the conditions of the poor. It challenges current linear development thinking and offers new methods to effectively engage complexity. Its reflective case studies give rise to a new hope that, with the right approach, development can do better.'

Frank Rijsberman, CEO, CGIAR consortium

'The timely message of the book then is that we must adopt a collaborative systems orientation anchored in the realities of human participation when dealing with the complexity inherent in international change endeavours.'

Hilary Bradbury, Professor, Division of Management, Oregon Health and Science University, and Editor, Action Research

'This book presents powerful and persuasive case-based evidence to show how systemic change can be achieved at scale.'

Robert Chambers, Research Associate and Professor Emeritus, Institute of Development Studies, University of Sussex

'One of the most thoughtful explorations on the nature of complexity in the development sector. A rare example of a book where the writing is accessible without trivializing the underlying theory. It provides a great platform from which the participative action research and complexity theory communities can develop an exciting new body of both theory and practice.'

Dave Snowden, Founder & Chief Scientific Officer, Cognitive Edge Pte Ltd

'It is courageous to think in terms of complexity in an era where linear thinking and accountability set the tone. In my experience, working together, coping with power differences, energy, trial, error, reflection and learning, keeping an eye on the parts as well as the whole, using data as well as your senses – are a few essential elements to make change processes developmental. The book is inspiring since it captures both practice and theoretical reflections.'

Annemiek Jenniskens, ex-director, SNV/Netherlands Development Organisation

'For too long, development problems have been articulated as technical issues – reframed in ways that remove politics, power imbalances and economics from the analysis. In contrast, this valuable book draws upon original studies to demonstrate the case for taking account of complexity, emphasizing the importance of participatory action and reflection whilst recognizing the need to link bottom-up approaches with wider strategies for social change.'

Marjorie Mayo, Emeritus Professor of Community Development,
Goldsmith's College, University of London

'A very readable and valuable contribution to the growing body of literature on change in complex situations, underscoring the futility of linear approaches based on the prediction of measurable results. With diverse examples of systemic action research, Burns and Worsley show how ownership, adoption and building relationships can lead to sustainability and scale with appropriate development interventions. Deserves to be read by practitioners – and twice by development investors.'

Richard Hawkins, International Centre for development oriented Research
in Agriculture, Wageningen, the Netherlands

'There are different ways to navigate complexity in development. One way is to attempt to model it quantitatively, in the hope that new and better analytical techniques can help resolve the tension between our current modus operandi – steeped as it is in neo-Newtonian thinking – and the challenges we increasingly face. Another way is to engage multiple stakeholders, and draw in different perspectives and mentalities, facilitating processes of social learning that can help better collective understanding and action. This book articulates how participatory methods can be used to effectively understand and engage with complexity. As such it provides an important bridge between these two approaches, and a vital step in showing how complexity thinking can be made practical and useful for those on the front line of development interventions, and – most importantly – for the communities they seek to support.'

Ben Ramalingam, Leader, Digital & Technology Cluster, Institute of
Development Studies, and author, Aid on the Edge of Chaos

Navigating Complexity in International Development

Facilitating sustainable change at scale

Danny Burns and Stuart Worsley

PRACTICAL ACTION
Publishing

Practical Action Publishing Ltd
The Schumacher Centre
Bourton on Dunsmore, Rugby,
Warwickshire CV23 9QZ, UK
www.practicalactionpublishing.org

A catalogue record for this book is available from the British Library.

A catalogue record for this book has been requested from the Library of Congress.

ISBN 9781853398513 Hardback
ISBN 9781853398520 Paperback
ISBN 9781780448510 Library Ebook
ISBN 9781780448527 Ebook

Citation: Burns, D., and Worsley, S., (2015) Navigating Complexity
in International Development, Rugby, UK: Practical Action Publishing,
<http://dx.doi.org/10.3362/9781780448510>

Since 1974, Practical Action Publishing has published and disseminated books and
information in support of international development work throughout the world.
Practical Action Publishing is a trading name of Practical Action Publishing Ltd
(Company Reg. No. 1159018), the wholly owned publishing company of Practical
Action. Practical Action Publishing trades only in support of its parent charity
objectives and any profits are covenanted back to Practical Action
(Charity Reg. No. 247257, Group VAT Registration No. 880 9924 76).

Cover design by Andrew Corbett
Indexed by Elizabeth Ball
Typeset by vPrompt eServices, India
Printed by Hobbs the Printers Ltd., UK

Dedications

To my children Caitlin, Nico, and Aaron – this book is in service
of the better world that I hope you will inherit.

—Danny

To my children Sohrab and Seraj – this book can guide you to be
smart in how you approach complex life. It's about finding
a way to make great things happen.

—Stuart

Gill,

As a very longstanding friend
and colleague thank you for
all the insights that you have
given to me over the years.

I hope this book is useful to
you in your work at Blundge
and beyond.

Take good care

Danny.

Contents

Figures, Boxes and Tables

Figures

Boxes

Tables

Preface

The story of the book

This book is the result of two life trajectories that came together to create something new. Danny came from a world of community development, social activism, and organizational change. Stuart came from a world of international development and aid, where he had worked to address poverty. Both had discovered that participation was the essential foundation for sustainable change. In 2005, Stuart was appointed to work for SNV in South Sudan, a new country within which a new government was being formed under international guidance. He reached out to Danny at the University of the West of England, having read *Auditing Community Participation* (Burns and Taylor, 2000), to see if Danny was interested in contributing to a process of advising the formation of county councils. While this work did not continue given unexpected turmoil in South Sudan, this first conversation opened up a connection between the two of us – to deepen mutual understanding and knowledge on participation in international development.

Joint work started in earnest with Stuart in the role of country director for SNV in Kenya and Southern Sudan, and Danny as Professor of Social and Organisational Learning at the University of the West of England, where he co-led the Social and Organisational Learning as Action Research (SOLAR) centre. Both of us were interested in operationalizing bottom-up approaches to development within a systemic understanding of change. In the ensuing years we worked together seeding ideas, facilitating workshops, and gradually changing the culture of SNV in Kenya. Some of the examples in this book come from our experiences before meeting, from joint work, and from subsequent individual work. The journey that the alliance has formed has been instructive and revealing as it has transformed both of our lives. This book makes sense of an approach to international development that is based on the stimulation of learning-based movement, where the action of people that live with the consequences of poverty is facilitated to inquire into ways and means of unlocking critical problems. Over time, and with proper facilitation, we have found that such processes enable transformation at scale.

We conducted a number of successful experiments and piloted emergent processes which began to model how we might operationalize participatory and complexity-based approaches to change. This book describes our individual and joint experiences to illustrate an alternative development paradigm, and frames a development philosophy, approach, and method that we think is critical to success.

The focus and structure of the book

The world and its systems are complex, dynamic, and unpredictable. Yet development approaches are largely fixed, and tied firmly to preordained plans and change theories. As a result, development interventions often fail and are very rarely sustainable. We do not believe that this needs to be the case. By explicitly developing approaches to engage with complex systems, interventions can and have been shown to work. This book is about how this can be done.

In Chapters 1, 2, and 3, we look at the failures of large-scale planning models to effectively engage with complexity. We explain this in relation to a failure to understand how change happens in complex systems and we propose a model of prerequisites for sustainable change. In Chapter 4 we look at two ways of seeing systems and complexity. This is what allows us to navigate. In Chapters 5 and 6, we explore a number of case studies of change, and focus on systemic action research and on nurtured emergent development processes. Finally, Chapters 7 and 8, look at power and participation in emergent development, and Chapter 9 concludes with a short summary of the development implications.

We have faced some dilemmas about how best to pitch this book. For example Chapter 2 on 'How change happens' goes into some depth on complexity theory because we think it is important that readers understand exactly why we need to engage differently. Complexity theorists will find this has a fairly light touch; practitioners might find it heavy going. Similarly, in Chapter 4, we have gone into some detail about how to do system mapping. This might seem like a diversion in the narrative to some readers but we think it is important because there is so little literature out there which shows 'how' to do this work. So we encourage you to take what you need from the different parts of the book according to who you are and what you are trying to do.

The book is written for thinking development practitioners, policymakers and researchers; however, it is also important as an articulation of development theory. It suggests that we change the way in which we think, provides the means to put this into practice, and offers the real possibility of sustainable change at scale.

Reference

Burns, D. and Taylor, M. (2000) *Auditing Community Participation: An Assessment Handbook*, Bristol: Policy Press and York: Joseph Rowntree Foundation.

Acknowledgements

Danny

Susan Weil for setting up SOLAR which became a home for my early thinking on these issues, and which was formative to my work. Yoland Wadsworth as pioneer of systemic action research.

Joanna Wheeler, for her courage and good judgement in joining with me on the 'Participate' journey and co-creating such a vibrant and exciting initiative. Thea Shahrokh, Erika Lopez Franco, Jo Howard, Catherine Setchell, Marion Clarke, Vivi Benson, Amy Pollard, Neva Frecheville, and all of the amazing people who were part of the global Participatory Research Group which set up and facilitated the Participate Initiative. There are too many of you to name but you are all inspiring.

The 'we can also make change team' of disabled and older people in Dhaka and Cox Bazaar, Bangladesh, who became the most inspirational ground-level participatory research team that I have engaged with.

Colleagues at IDS who have kept me believing that what we are doing is worth doing. Stephen Wood for supporting me and our team through turbulent times. Linda Waldman who is one of the most thoughtful, caring, and supportive people I have ever met. Pauline Oosterhoff who always reminds me that process is not enough and that there is no point in doing these things if they don't have an impact. Petra Bongartz for making sure that the heart and body and mind are always present in our work.

Violeta Vajda, Jody Aked, Elizabeth Hacker, Simon Lewis, Alexandra Picken, Valerio Clamonte and Katy Turner for the great work that you did on the VSO Valuing Volunteering project.

Peter Coleman, Rob Ricigliano, and all of my other friends in the Systemic Conflict Transformation network from whom I have probably learned the most these last years. Stephen Gray and Josefine Roos for opening up an extraordinary space for community-based research in Myanmar.

Hilary Bradbury, Dave Snowden, Elise Wach, Robert Chambers, and Petra Bongartz, for your helpful comments on all or parts of this manuscript.

Jo Kreiter, Ginny Bauman, Elise Wach, Alan Hirons, Robin Hambleton, and Paul Hoggett, for your enduring friendship.

Stuart

SNV (an international development organization based in the Netherlands), for transforming to become a reflective, process-oriented development organization that would continually struggle to find better ways to facilitate development.

Donna Copnall for introducing me to the complex space of peace building and being an early shaper of my thinking that development change could be so profound through facilitation of processes.

Paul Barker for overseeing my work in CARE Afghanistan, and leading through profoundly difficult moments where there was no choice but to engage with complexity. Paul recognized parent power and fought off resistance to 'give-up on Home Schools'. His foresight has given us a great example of participation and emergence.

Abdul Raouf Nazhand who led the interface between CARE and the various Afghan authorities and provided key insights into the telling of the Home Schools story.

Ahmad Farouk, Semir Sedky, Gebril Mahjoub, Hussein Raafat, Ahmad Roushdy, Ameyni Fathi, and all the committed members of the CARE Egypt FarmLink team. Together, we discovered that farmers were the smartest articulators of technology demand and were applying a wide range of complexity approaches, back in the days before we knew about them.

Thomas Were and Dido Sabdiyo Bashuna for their work to transform remote livestock markets in North Kenya.

Many people have influenced my thinking over the years and you all have had an influence on the way that I grew and shaped my thinking. You are many, and it would take another book to honour you all. I must mention Dan Coster (Doc), Mike DeVries, Geoffrey Chege, Asif Rahimi, Sally Austin, Kees Zevenbergen, Worku Behonegne, Rudolph Glotzbach, Mary Njuguna, Harm Duiker, Remi and Linda Gauthier, James Fennel, Jim Sumberg, Jonathan Bartsch, and Robert de Jong.

Participatory research projects

Throughout this book we refer in detail to a number of research and capacity development projects. We refer to these by the names that follow. For ease of reference these are as follows.

The Lake Victoria Water and Sanitation project 2009-10

Funded by the United Nations Human Settlement Programme (UN-Habitat), this project was designed to ensure clean water and sanitation could be delivered to small towns in Uganda, Tanzania, and Kenya on the shores of Lake Victoria. Stuart directed an SNV-lead consortium to provide an inquiry-based capacity development programme to run alongside the implementation process and input into it. Danny was the methodological advisor to the programme.

VSO Valuing Volunteering 2011-14

This was a three-year action research programme directed by Danny Burns and Joanna Wheeler at the Institute of Development Studies (IDS). It was funded by Voluntary Service Overseas (VSO) and facilitated by four VSO volunteers selected for their qualitative research experience. They each facilitated action research on the role of volunteers in sustainable development over a two-year period in Mozambique, Kenya, Nepal, and the Philippines.

The Participate Initiative 2012-13

A major two-year programme funded by the UK Department for International Development (DFID). It was co-directed by Danny Burns and Joanna Wheeler at IDS and brought together 18 participatory research groups who were carrying out ground-level participatory research to feed into the global process on what was to follow the Millennium Development Goals (MDGs).

'We can also make change' project, Bangladesh 2012

Facilitated by Danny Burns and Katy Oswald and funded by Sightsavers, Action on Disability in Development (ADD), and HelpAge this project worked with disabled people in Bangladesh, supporting them to become participatory researchers and analyse their own life experience and that of their peers.

Myanmar community-based research for peace 2013-15

Directed by Stephen Gray and Josephine Roos and supported by Danny Burns. This is an action research programme based in Northern Myanmar that has engaged local civil society organizations in a story analysis process and is now underpinning a local action research process, which will generate both local action and knowledge to feed into the Myanmar peace process.

Slavery and Bonded Labour programme 2015-18

Funded by the Freedom Fund. Danny Burns and Pauline Oosterhoff, working in partnership with the Praxis Institute for Participatory Practices, have been directing a participatory research process which involves working with 18 non-governmental organizations (NGOs) across Bihar and Uttar Pradesh in India. The process has involved a participatory story analysis process with eight NGOs, a participatory statistics process generating data across more than 60 villages, and an action research process. The work is currently being extended to Nepal.

Acronyms

ADD	Action on Disability in Development
APTU	Anti-poll tax union
BEFARe	Basic Education for Afghan
BUWASA	Bukoba Water and Sewerage Supply Authority
CBE	Community-based education
CBO	Community-based organization
CGIAR	Consortium of International Agricultural Research Centers
CIDA	Canadian International Development Agency
CLTS	Community Led Total Sanitation
COPE	Community Organised Primary Education project
CSO	Civil Society Organization
DFID	Department for International Development, UK
DLMA	District Livestock Marketing Association, Kenya
DPHE	Department of Public Health Engineering, Bangladesh
ELDOWAS	Eldoret Water and Sanitation Company
FAO	Food and Agriculture Organization
GCRN	Ghana Community Radio Network
GDP	Gross domestic product
GLP	Ground Level Panel
GTZ	The German Technical Cooperation Agency
HLP	High Level Panel
HRDGG	Human Rights, Democratisation and Good Governance policy (Canada)
IDP	Internally displaced people
IDS	Institute of Development Studies at Sussex University
IHHS	Individual household hardware subsidy
ILRI	International Livestock Research Institute
IMF	International Monetary Fund
INGO	International non-governmental organization
KLMC	Kenya Livestock Marketing Council
LGBT	Lesbian, gay, bisexual, and transgender
LMA	Livestock Marketing Association
LVWATSAN	Lake Victoria Water and Sanitation programme
MDG	Millennium Development Goal
MSF	Multi-stakeholder forum
MVP	Millennium Villages Project

NED	Nurtured emergent development
NGO	Non-governmental organization
NRA	National Rifle Association (US)
ODF	Open defecation free
ODI	Overseas Development Institute
OECD	Organisation for Economic Co-operation and Development
OECD - DAV	Organisation for Economic Co-operation and Development – Development Co-operation Directorate
OHCHR	Office of the High Commission for Human Rights
PACE-A	Partnership for Advocating Community Education in Afghanistan
PAR	Participatory action research
PCI	Pastoralist Communication Initiative
PRA	Participatory rural appraisal
PRSP	Poverty Reduction Strategic Plan
PSI	Participatory systemic inquiry
RANIR	Civil society network in Kachin Myanmar
RBA	Rights-based approach
REF	Research Excellence Framework
SAR	Systemic action research
SCC	Samburu County Council
SIDA	Swedish International Development Cooperation Agency
SIDEP	Samburu Integrated Development Programme
SLTS	School-led Total Sanitation
SNV	International development organization based in the Netherlands
SOLAR	Social and Organisational Learning as Action Research
TYLCV	Tomato yellow leaf curl virus
UN DESA	United Nations Department of Economic and Social Affairs
UNDP	United Nations Development Programme
UNEP	United Nations Environment Programme
UN-Habitat	United Nations Human Settlement Programme
UNICEF	United Nations Children's Fund
USAID	United States Agency for International Development
UNV	United Nations Volunteers
USIP	United States Institute for Peace
VERC	Village Education Resource Centre, Bangladesh
VSO	Voluntary Service Overseas
WASH	Water, Sanitation and Hygiene
WHO	World Health Organization
WSP	Water and Sanitation Programme

CHAPTER 1
Failures of top-down development planning

International development is not working. Externally defined expert-driven plans continue to override the reality of the local context and intervene in ways that are either irrelevant or damaging. This chapter examines iconic strategic planning approaches: big push thinking (Millennium Villages) technically driven programming (Green Revolution), good governance programming, and rights-based approaches, and concludes that lasting results have been elusive because our approach to development is rooted in flawed assumptions.

Keywords: planning failure; top-down development; big push; Green Revolution; good governance

Defining development 'problems'

Across the world, people and nations are facing huge challenges. Our climate is changing and temperatures are rising, principally as a result of human activities. This affects water supply, food production, health, and peace. Mitigation and adaption will be required at local, national, and international levels. Increasing urbanization is creating unprecedented concentrations of deprivation whose hallmark is poverty and social unrest. Whole cultures are being threatened by powerful new governance systems, with ancient systems such as pastoralism now facing an uncertain future. War is becoming more prevalent, with social and political unrest in the Middle East spreading at an alarming rate. Pandemics are becoming more common, with new diseases and new resistances. Water scarcity affects more people than ever before. The need for development interventions that enable humankind to meet these challenges is more critical now than at any time in our history.

Development organizations have tried to bring about lasting and sustainable change to improve people's lives. Vast sums of money are spent on reducing poverty, promoting rights, stimulating economic growth, reducing inequity, reversing environmental damage, and promoting good governance. According to the Organisation for Economic Co-operation and Development – Development Co-operation Directorate (2014), in 2013 almost US$135 billion official development assistance was spent, yet much of this has had minimal impact on the lives of marginalized people and those living in poverty.

To make improvements happen, development practitioners and investors analyse poverty, try to determine its root causes, define causal pathways and design interventions to fix these. Linear intervention logic is used to offer solutions that address critical problems in the causal pathway and thereby

http://dx.doi.org/10.3362/9781780448510.001

reduce or reverse bad effects. *Impact* is seen to be a direct result of intervention. Like other contemporary commentators such as Ramalingam (2013), we will argue that this does not make sense as change happens through far more complex processes. By failing to understand how change happens, development interventions are likely to be ineffectual or damaging.

A central feature of all development programmes is the definition of problems that need to be fixed, and the positioning of technical solutions to address these. Viewed by experts, development issues occur within a defined and subjectively bounded domain. Boundaries are set by ideological frameworks that determine what is seen to be beneficial and what is not. Over time, development agendas change. In the years since the Marshall Plan, they have evolved to cover food production, industrialization, good governance, human rights, democracy, basic services, free markets, peace and security, gender equity, and much more. Now there is particular focus on creating security, economic growth, more food, and sustainable energy while apparently antithetical narratives such as mitigation of environmental damage are growing simultaneously. At the beginning of this century, the Millennium Development Goals (MDGs) were enshrined by the United Nations as a unifying mantra.

Consensus on what constitutes progress has changed as global discourse has meandered through new philosophies and ideologies, and the world experiences new events. We will refer to the ideas that bound and shape development investment and intervention as 'development frameworks'. Viewed through these frameworks, issues that do not present themselves as a problem are deemed contextual, in a process that shapes development programmes by what they exclude. In other words, issues that cause human misery are only identified as issues to be addressed when they are seen as a problem within these frameworks.

While working to improve access to drinking water and sanitation services in towns around Lake Victoria (see Chapter 4), we came across repeated examples of onerous and difficult procurement bureaucracy practiced by the government and by a large international infrastructure investment programme. We heard stories of how this was preventing people from accessing basic services, was causing bankruptcy among local small businesses, and was incentivizing corruption by municipal leaders. This was consistently cited as one of the most severe development problems being experienced in these towns. They described predatory practices by municipal officials and project staff that were justified as being necessary in order to comply with procurement standards. When evidence of this was presented to project managers, they were obdurate. World Bank procurement standards that framed both municipal and project practice were sacrosanct. They resisted evidence, and could therefore never be part of the problem. Project leaders seemed blind to act.

Development problems are articulated as technical issues because the armoury of fixes used by the development industry is largely technical, and there are strong vested interests in keeping it that way. This process of 'technical rendering' (Murray Li, 2007) takes wider political issues and reframes them as technical problems. This effectively depoliticizes questions that are being asked and removes politics from the analysis. Where there are power imbalances, solutions offered tend to be aimed at helping people to adjust (e.g. focusing on technical inputs to improve capacity for the poor to adapt) rather than actions that would support activism to overturn inequity.

Problems are usually defined as being a 'lack of' something. This presupposes the solution. A lack of schools can only be fixed by building schools. If instead, the problem was framed as 'children are unable to go to school', then a range of other causes become possible. In Afghanistan in the 1990s, while school facilities were indeed sparse and inadequate for quality teaching, it was the policies that prohibited education which undermined primary education. As we shall show later, local action by parents became the basis for sustainable change. Problematization defines issues within frameworks, renders these technical, and offers pre-cooked technical solutions.

Development interventions are rooted in the principle of trusteeship that is based on the claim to know how others should live, to know what is best for them, and to know what they need (Murray Li, 2007). Programme designers determine the causalities that give rise to poverty and design interventions on this basis. The trusteeship principle separates those who need to be developed from those doing the developing. Tania Murray Li describes this as becoming over time a structure of 'permanent deferral' where subjects are 'destined to become rights bearing individuals, but (remain) always too immature to exercise those rights'.

A good example of how these frameworks shape intervention was revealed through the Institute of Development Studies' (IDS') recent work supporting the Participate Initiative. We carried out a review of 84 participatory research programmes, and supported 18 primary research projects with the poorest and most marginalized in order to generate messages to feed into the post-2015 debate (Leavy and Howard, 2013). The first substantive finding was that the poorest and most marginalized were more concerned with *how* development was delivered, than *what* development was delivered. They said that there were already schools, hospitals, justice services, loan schemes, and so on but they didn't get access to them because they faced social and institutional discrimination. The research revealed that the poorer people were, the more interconnected the issues became, and that one problem could not be solved without solving another. This required a different form of development. This conclusion was met by the UK Department of International Development (DFID), as if it was an interesting but marginal issue. But 'tell us what are the priorities of the poor and most marginalized', they said. 'Is it education or health or what? The Voices of the Poor research told us that security was important so what is this research telling us?' Because the whole framing of the post-2015 process was pre-constructed around sectoral goals, the only questions that could be asked related to which sector goals were more important and why. For the poorest people all of these issues were important and fundamentally interrelated. The problem articulated by the development industry was not the problem that they faced.

A brief review of development interventions

There are many critiques of international development. William Easterly in his provocatively titled book *The White Man's Burden* reviews case studies from the record of development assistance (Easterly, 2006). He notes parallels between the ways in which colonial powers operated and contemporary development assistance. Both claim their actions as being necessary to bring about beneficial order to less-developed peoples. Easterly points out that, in practice, they do nothing of the sort. He describes planners who design ambitious schemes such as structural adjustment programmes and good governance systems, and leverage national government counterparts to comply through conditional funding and expertise. He observes that they focus on top-down reform processes that are based on theoretical arguments that are not supported by evidence. Easterly concludes that development should be home-grown and that the West should assist this at the margins and disavow itself from its utopian beliefs that it can transform national systems.

In a similar vein, Dambisa Moyo in her book *Dead Aid* argues that development aid has created dependency and has enabled higher levels of corruption in ways that have harmed public accountability and sustained poverty (Moyo, 2009). She offers examples that show why local businesses are unable to be competitive and survive in the wake of vast donations that fill their markets with products that could have been locally made. She concludes that foreign aid perpetuates poverty. She cites literature that indicates a negative relationship between aid and savings, and a correlation between foreign aid and unproductive public consumption. Cooksey and Kikula (2005) observe that in Tanzania, district plans do not deliver outcomes. Traditional top-down planning approaches that lead to district plans 'have no relevance to the felt needs of the grass root communities. Instead such plans indicate what the district officers think the grass root communities need. As such there is poor ownership of not only the process but the outcome as well.' Claudia Williamson's wide-reaching review of literature on foreign aid concludes that foreign aid does not deliver intended results, and controversially suggests that 'it may be more beneficial to the development process if large-scale, top-down government-supported aid agencies are eliminated'. She notes how private actors spontaneously emerge, adapt to local conditions, tap into decentralized knowledge, and rely on feedback mechanisms for success. What these authors have in common is their depiction of top down aid failure. While we do not share all of their political positions or the solutions that they propose their critique of what is actually happening strongly resonates with our experience of aid programming.

Development interventions and the achievement of scale

Considerable attention has been paid to ensure that international development interventions achieve impact at scale. Jeffrey Sachs in his book *The End of Poverty* argues that extreme poverty can be globally eliminated through carefully planned development aid (Sachs, 2005). The desire for scale sees poverty as being a huge problem for which cost-effective solutions are required. It is rooted in a core assumption that with good planning and organization, success can be replicated and enlarged.

As noted earlier, over time various philosophies have guided the form and nature of development interventions. Despite changes, they have consistently adhered to intricate planning models. Post-World War II reconstruction plans inspired global development players to adopt successive multi-year national plans to implement structural readjustment. These were interventions targeted at the level of national policy that aimed to change the fundamentals of low-income economies, and achieve effect at scale. The planning models that accompanied these efforts have persisted in different forms. Poverty Reduction Strategic Plans, integrated development planning, and most recently Management for Results all subscribe to logical framework thinking.

Embedded in logical framework thinking is the belief that fundamental change happens because of carefully planned and coordinated action. Equipped with a comprehensive overview of the system that they wish to change, and sure in the knowledge that this remains predictable over time, planners pull levers on systems that they perceive to operate like a machine. This belief of the 'world as a machine' is prevalent across development programmes, and we see planning terminology including expressions of dashboards, inputs, outputs, re-engineering, levers, and so on. The shortcomings of mechanical models in business are well summarized by Peters and Waterman (1981) as being heartless and abstract, focusing on things rather than people, as devaluing experimentation and fostering a climate where mistakes are abhorred, and denigrating the importance of values. The mechanistic view of the world is the tip of the iceberg of a bigger assumption, namely that complex systems are predictable and static, if only sufficient analytical time and effort can be expended on studying them. The imperative of development planning has been to secure a sense of certainty in space and time in order to build long-term plans. It is attractive to donors and international organizations because it offers a sense of control and accountability. The value of financial control and contracting has de facto become a higher order value than the achievement of sustainable change. The requirement for accountability in delivery has incentivized the definition of outputs as opposed to more complex outcomes.

As Williamson (2009) notes above, managing development through highly detailed and rigid plans has not led to sustained alleviation or eradication of poverty in low-income countries, yet reports abound that suggest that progress is being made. These indicators of progress often relate to the logic that we define, and not to the reality of change. If we say that better farm income is contingent on increased fertilizer use, then increase fertilizer use can be reported as an indicator that increased farm income is on its way to happening. Reported success is being defined on the basis of what is being measured. John Hendra of UN Women notes that 'What matters gets measured, and what we measure is what ends up mattering' (Hendra, 2014). This is problematic because it is self-referential. The delivery of development goods does not lead to the results that are desired.

In Tanzania, the presence of water pumps in rural areas does not correlate with actual water supply. A mapping exercise by SNV in 2008 showed that only 57 per cent of all rural water points in Tanzania were working (SNV, 2010). Data collected showed that most of these installations had been designed and implemented in a top-down manner, with little or no involvement of water users. There was no sense of ownership amongst communities and water points did not reflect what people wanted or were willing to pay for. Ramalingam (2013: 103) reports that: 'In the opening pages of the 2012 report that announced the MDGs had been met, the qualification was made that some of these improved water sources may not be maintained and therefore may not in fact, provide safe water.'

He goes on to say:

> there is nothing said about water quality, available quantities, reliability, time spent on accessing and using water facilities, functionality of the water source and the cost or sustainability of the sources. One sobering finding is that much of Africa's water supply infrastructure is failing owing to a lack of maintenance; estimates are that some 50,000 water infrastructures across the continent are in a state of disrepair.

He makes similar points in relation to education:

> the education goal is very unlikely to be met by 2015. The World Bank's Global Monitoring Report states that, while primary school enrolment rates are up, completion rates, especially for girls, remain a major concern. UNESCO [United Nations Educational, Scientific and Cultural Organization] reports that, in one-third of countries with available data, less than two-thirds of children enrolling in primary education are reaching the final class let alone graduating... Social Watch, a think tank ... calculated that at present rates of progress universal primary education would be achieved by 2036 in the Middle East and North Africa and 2079 in Sub Saharan Africa. (Ramalingam 2013: 12)

> Take the example of India, where a 1996 Public Report on Basic Education identified that absentee rates amongst teachers in rural states was 48 per cent. This led to a nationwide programme to support improvements in the quality of education, which saw an increased budget for schools,

infrastructure, hiring, training and investments. This led to an increase in enrolment rates and other indicators. It has been claimed that MDG's made a contribution to this effort. However a revisited version of the Public Report in 2008 found that teacher absentee rates remained at 48%. Although the key target indicator of enrolment had improved, there was almost no improvement in basic literacy and mathematics. (Ramalingam, 2013: 58)

In both of these cases, outcomes are dependent upon the local and social and political realities on the ground. The presence of a technical solution doesn't mean that anyone can or wants to use it, or that it will be functional for more than a few months after it is implemented, or that its use will be beneficial. The stories that we tell in Chapter 6 show in much more detail how these complex realities play out.

In another recent publication, Allana (2015: 9) writes of some work undertaken by Mercy Corps in North Uganda and records that

while mapping out and investigating the existing trading relationships and food storage facilities in the region, the team found a number of high-quality grinding mills in some storage facilities, all of them in various states of disrepair. Many were built by NGOs [non-governmental organizations], and have succumbed to the tragedy of group ownership and dependency: no one has an incentive to maintain and use the infrastructure, and there is an ever-present expectation that another NGO will come and repair or replace the mills. Despite it not being a part of the commodity team's strategy, the team investigated further to find most mills were only in need of the most basic maintenance and repair, but there was a completely dysfunctional mechanic and spare part market.

This frequently happens on a much larger scale, and two examples illustrate this. A US$22 million Norwegian government investment in a fish processing plant on Lake Turkana in northern Kenya was launched in 1971 to provide jobs to the Turkana people through fishing and fish processing for export. The Turkana are nomads with no history of fishing or eating fish. Upon completion, the plant operated for a few days but was quickly shut down, because the cost of operating the freezers and the demand for clean water in this desert location were too high (Associated Press, 2007). In Lesotho, three development banks invested US$3.5 billion in 1986 on the Lesotho Highlands Water Project. This aimed to divert fresh water from Lesotho's mountains for sale to South Africa and also to generate electricity. However, the electricity proved too expensive, and the diversion of so much water caused environmental and economic havoc downstream. The development fund that had been raised from the sale of the water was shut down in 2003. Tens of thousands of people's lives were ruined by the diversion (Associated Press, 2007). In both cases, the projects were completed and outputs were delivered as intended but the outputs did not turn into positive outcomes.

A counter narrative to top down development rooted in the ideas of empowerment and citizen engagement has emerged over the past decades. The writings of the Brazilian educator Paolo Freire that articulated a philosophy of education as a 'practice of freedom' showed how people could critically engage with the world around them, and participate in its transformation (Freire, 1970). Social Scientists and development practitioners have created reflective practices that seek to build interventions from the perspective of those to whom intended change would apply. Participatory approaches to development described by Robert Chambers (1983) stimulated the adoption of the language of participation across many institutions. Andrea Cornwall notes that approaches such as participatory rural appraisal

> emphasize the importance of tuning into and building on people's own experiences, concepts and categories. Rather than importing concepts from elsewhere, they focus on enabling local people to articulate and analyse their own situations, in their own terms, and focus more on individual agency than structural analysis. This opens up the potential for a more nuanced and less essentialist approach to the issues of power and difference ... however PRA-based participatory practices appear to offer the facilitator little scope for challenging aspects of the status quo ... (Cornwall, 2003: 1328)

In his book *Development as Freedom*, Amartya Sen described an approach that would support the capabilities of people Sen, 2001. Some governments have invested in using Sen's capability model that regarded capacity as development.

Other approaches such as structured flexibility (Brinkerhoff and Ingle, 1989) aimed to secure the programmatic and financial accountability that donor bureaucracies require, yet enable adaptive management that can deal with changing context. But none of these processes have been able to make effective challenges to the dominant planning paradigm. Participation and learning based approaches have largely been incorporated into planning rather than offering an alternative to it, Donors driven by an evidence based philosophy only countenance 'capacity development' which delivers measurable short term results.

Thus development programmes continue to be built on the idea that change happens because we make it happen. This planned-interventionist stance builds on a positivist understanding of the world, where change processes are designed, based upon a comprehensive understanding that is certain and persistent over time. Here, it matters little where the imperative for action comes from, the important thing being that defined interventions happen in the way that they were designed to happen. Planned interventionism has manifested itself through a number of frameworks that are worth examining. In the following pages, we review large-scale integrated planning; technically driven development; governance and institutional development; and the rights-based approach.

Large-scale integrated planning – the big push

One dominant change theory used in large-scale development thinking is the 'big push'. Defined in the 1940s by Paul-Rosenstein Rodan, it describes 'a minimum level of resources that must be devoted to a development programme if it is to have any chance of success. Launching a country into self-sustaining growth is a little like getting an airplane off of the ground. There is a critical ground speed which must be passed before the craft can become airborne …' (Rosenstein-Rodan, 1957). Big push theorists argue that capital accumulation, economic growth, and rising household income will solve underdevelopment. Consequently, high levels of aid simultaneously applied across many sectors and bottlenecks will spur national development, both from the direct result of interventions and from the many positive interactions and externalities that come from multiple interventions. When this happens, a threshold effect occurs in which the capital stock becomes useful when it meets a minimum standard (Easterly, 2005). Foreign aid here aims to sufficiently increase capital stock to cross a threshold level through a big push: 'If the foreign assistance is substantial enough, and lasts long enough, the capital stock rises sufficiently to lift households above subsistence. Growth becomes self-sustaining through household savings and public investments supported by taxation of households' (Sachs, 2005). This last statement is the 'take-off' hypothesis. In the 1980s and 1990s, this approach was challenged on the grounds that it encouraged aid dependency and depended on macroeconomic stability to work (Kerlin and Kubal, 2002). More recently, big push has been challenged for its technocratic and prescriptive character that neglects the role of institutions and governance in sustaining economic development (Cabral et al., 2006).

A significant big push initiative in recent years has been the Millennium Promise. Structured around the MDGs, its flagship programme, the Millennium Villages Project (MVP), was designed as a 'bold, innovative model for helping rural African communities lift themselves out of extreme poverty' (The Earth Institute, 2014). This US$120 million experiment was launched in 2006 in 80 villages in 10 African countries. Tried and tested technologies were introduced to test the hypothesis that a critical platform of basic needs must be reached before economic development could take off. Pilot projects integrated packages of agriculture, environment, health, nutrition, infrastructure, energy, communication, education, and training. These experiments concentrated resources at the community level and prioritized them over rural–urban linkages and institutional reform. Projects aimed to demonstrate how to use community-based, low-cost interventions to reduce poverty and meet the MDGs, and identify mechanisms for scaling up the project. Although described as being community led and 'bottom up', the Millennium Villages were underpinned by a blueprinted campaign approach. Pedro Sanchez, director of MVP, described it as a new approach based upon an old paradigm (Cabral et al., 2006). It was essentially Integrated Rural Development applied at community level.

In 2008, the Millennium Villages programme was formatively reviewed by the Overseas Development Institute (ODI). Buse et al., (2008) declared only two years into the programme, that 'The Millennium Villages Project (MVP) has achieved remarkable results and has demonstrated the impact of greater investment in evidence-based, low-cost interventions at the village level to make progress on the Millennium Development Goals.' The report further exhorted 'countries to situate MVP scale-up in the context of a national development strategy. Donors should give special support to at least one country, which, having successfully implemented the MVP, now wants to take it to national scale.' Two years later Wanjala (2010) notes in a review on the Sauri Millennium Village in Kenya that although agricultural productivity had increased by about 70 per cent, overall household income effect was insignificant and negative. By 2012, prominent international development researchers and experts had taken issue with some of the MVP's claims of progress, specifically relating to stated declines in child mortality (*Nature*, 2012). Statements of declining child mortality occurring within Millennium Villages had been inflated through a questionable use of data. Reluctance by the programme to release data was further cited as making it impossible for independent verification of cost–benefit ratios, raising issues of trust (*Nature*, 2012). In a more recent review Munk noted that the lack of comparators makes it impossible to disentangle positive effects in the villages from broader recent progress across much of Africa (Munk, 2013). This is important because Africa contains 7 out of the 10 fastest growing economies in the world. Changes reported in Millennium Villages are not necessarily significant when compared with parallel changes in non-project sites. Moreover, Millennium Villages were affected by unanticipated external factors and unexpected consequences, including drought and political unrest.

The Millennium Villages programme was very powerfully driven from its inception. Initially funded by the Soros Institute, it attracted the attention of global development investors. Its designer and champion, Jeffrey Sachs, was persuasive and highly influential. He reduced huge and complex issues to simple actions such as eliminating malaria with the mass provision of insecticide-treated mosquito nets, or solving hunger with subsidized fertilizers and high-yield seeds. Despite the rhetoric, there is little transparent evidence to suggest that this approach has worked.

Technically driven development – the Green Revolution

Between the 1940s and the 1970s, research and development initiatives created a range of technical possibilities that had never before been seen in agriculture. New varieties of wheat, rice, and maize were deployed along with packages of chemical inputs and the promotion of irrigation to increase production where food security was fragile and famine loomed. Technology was regarded as a magic bullet that would increase agricultural production. The results were impressive. According to the Food and Agriculture Organization (2014), new rice variety IR8 more than doubled yields in the Philippines. In India, researchers published findings that indicated that, with fertilizer, this new variety could yield up to 10 times the levels of traditional varieties (De Datta et al., 1968). As production expanded, rice prices fell dramatically and both India and the Philippines became net exporters of rice. This was not to last in the Philippines.

As agriculture practice moved from traditional subsistence towards a commercial model, there was also a shift in local food security. Technology invested into rice and wheat improvement was not appropriate to resolve food security problems for communities that did not rely on these crops for their traditional diets. Ryan and Asokan 1977) note that 22 per cent of the expansion of wheat areas in six Indian states post-1965 came from a reduction in areas planted to pulse crops. Traditional subsistence production of pulses was replaced with commercial production of wheat and rice, much of which was sold on. This represented a significant shift in the way in which food was to be accessed by rural populations.

While there are fewer people now facing starvation in India, the quality of diet declined and, according to the Global Hunger Index (2011) report, the incidence of malnutrition grew from 1996 onwards. According to the United Nations Children's Fund (UNICEF), malnutrition in 2014 was more common in India than in Sub-Saharan Africa, with almost half of all Indian children under three either too small or underweight (United Nations Children's Fund, 2014). Szirmai (2005) documents some of the political and economic consequences of the Green Revolution. He notes that new agricultural practices stimulated profound changes that only became apparent as time passed. Credit facilities were developed in response to the need for farm inputs. These favoured larger farmers, but also created debt problems for people living in poverty who had never borrowed before. In some cases, they were compelled to sell land to pay these debts. Falling commodity prices that came about from increased supply hit the majority of rural economies hard, for small producers represented the majority of total farming capacity. The advent of agricultural mechanization reduced labour demand and rural employment fell. Within regions, class and wealth disparities widened as the poorest were disenfranchised. Between regions, differences in ability to exploit new technologies created new economic disparities. As food prices and rural opportunities fell, increased rural–urban migration contributed to new urban problems and human misery in unforeseen ways.

Environmental concerns became increasingly apparent in the intervening years. The Green Revolution had catalysed a shift from local varieties to those developed by professional breeders. This resulted in lower cultivation of traditional crops, dramatically reduced diversity within crops, and lowered wild biodiversity as traditional practices that had once maintained it were replaced. The loss of genetic diversity and ecosystem biodiversity resulted in increased susceptibility to pathogens, and created new reliance on chemical controls. New drought and salt-tolerant crop varieties created new possibilities for once marginal agricultural land, and agriculture expanded into new areas replacing natural habitats. Whether it is fair to attribute all of this to Green Revolution practice is a matter for debate. However, the threat of lost biodiversity from agriculture expansion globally has stimulated most nations to pledge action, as evidenced by the Rio Declaration of 1992 (United Nations, 1992) and the 2015 zero draft of the Sustainable Development Goals (United Nations Department of Economic and Social Affairs, 2015).

Worldwide, human health has also suffered from increased use of pesticides. In 1989, the World Health Organization (WHO) and the United Nations Environment Programme (UNEP) reported an annual case load of 1 million pesticide poisonings, of which 20,000 resulted in death (Pimental et al., 1993). These occurred mainly in low-income countries. Here, blame is alternatively laid on poor product labelling, and loose definition and enforcement of safety standards.

These criticisms contain some valuable insights into the nature of intervention. The technical interventionist approach of the Green Revolution did not consider power relationships or other political elements in society, including class structure and land ownership. It unwittingly created new levels of inequity and, for some, poverty. It has changed the way in which technology interacts with farming and has opened up a wide array of practices and protests. Criticisms relate both to the nature of the technology and to the way in which interventions happened. As a result, the Green Revolution has faced a backlash. Some have accused it of being part of an international conspiracy of capitalist agribusiness at the expense of human values and food requirements. Others have tried to reverse it. For example, the Indian state of Sikkim passed a state resolution to become a 'totally organic state' (Government of Sikkim, 2003), citing that the Green Revolution had gained little traction because of the area's rain-fed agriculture system they viewed chemical use as adding little to production and productivity, and sought 'sustainable and long lasting options more than quick result oriented options that have the deteriorating effect on ecology and environment' and to do away 'with the options which have more harms than benefit'.

Planners could not see these unintended consequences because, in a genuine attempt to provide a response to starvation, they looked only at the technical dimensions of food production. The agricultural research for development community has learned that science will never provide a silver bullet that will meet all agricultural needs. In the 2010 reform process of the Consortium of International Agricultural Research Centers (CGIAR), this has been explicitly recognized (Campbell, 2012).

Governance and institutional development

In the 1990s, a new development agenda took shape in the form of good governance and institutional development. During the preceding decade, World Bank structural readjustment programmes had been designed to transform low-income economies by tying government loans to the adoption of new policies. The World Bank and the International Monetary Fund (IMF) felt that management skills and organizational resources needed to implement these plans and policies were limited in many developing countries. Central bureaucracy performance was seen as particularly inadequate and this prompted a new emphasis on civil service reform. Institutional development thus became a priority within donor development policies in the 1990s as recognition grew that macroeconomic policy alone was not sufficient for growth and sustainable development. It was considered necessary to have good institutions to shape relationships between economic agents. As time passed, this evolved to also include political and social relationships. In the 1990s, development investors placed greater importance on institutional competence at policy level. However, unrealistic demands placed on weak public administrations eroded the capacity of national and local institutions to do other work.

Institutional development was mainstreamed as a tool to achieve donor programmes, and institutions were required to change so that structural readjustment could happen as planned. This was an effort to change the context within which development programmes happened. Institutions were de facto regarded as programme instruments as opposed to manifestations of political and social context. In the early days of institutional reform programming, 'good' institution function was determined economically with little consideration for political function. National ministries were assessed only for their technical capabilities, and developmental reforms proposed under the various schemes seemed unable to consider wider functions. Resistance to change was termed 'institutional stickiness' (Witt and Lewin, 2004). Measures to unstick institutions focused on ensuring compliance with externally defined development trajectories, rather than asking how development trajectories might interact with national contexts.

Governance programming took root as a development approach to foster improvements in the way in which public institutions conducted public affairs and managed public resources. From 1998, IMF loans required that borrowing countries undertook measures to improve governance as part of loan conditionality (IMF, 2005). The UN and World Bank adopted principles of good governance that matched with principles of liberal democracy. This conflation of institutional competence with democracy is important because it combined concerns about the effectiveness of government institutions with the legitimacy of the government. It opened the way for a new democracy-based development framework to shape the nature of development issues to be addressed. Duffield (2001) observes that economic liberalization was no longer sufficient; development malaise had to be tackled by supporting democratization, pluralistic institutions, and transforming societies and the indigenous values of members in the liberal image of the network of 'global governance'.

Accountability, transparency, participation, and inclusion have become almost universal principles underpinning governance initiatives within aid organizations and donors alike (Carothers, 2009). From the United States Agency for International Development (USAID), OECD, the Swedish International Development Cooperation Agency (SIDA), and the World Bank to NGOs, these dimensions run across political ideologies. But these terms can be interpreted in many ways. International financing institutions for example saw participation in Poverty Reduction Strategic Plans (PRSPs) as a route to national ownership, but national governments mostly regarded this as an external conditionality which they had to meet. In most cases, participation in PRSPs was superficial, limited to consultation and generally not inclusive (McGee et al., 2002). Ramalingam (2013) reports that 'The impacts of the PRSP experiment have been questionable. The World Bank evaluation of PRSPs in 2004 found that "The PRSP Initiative has not yet fulfilled its potential to enhance poverty reduction efforts in low income countries."'

Reviews of governance programmes have been unable to show their impact. Between 1995 and 2005, the Canadian International Development Agency (CIDA) invested more than Can$3.8 billion in governance in accordance with its 1996 policy for Human Rights, Democratisation and Good Governance (HRDGG) – a framework that was highly regarded. A review of this work declared their performance in management and delivery of governance programmes as ineffective (CIDA, 2008). While some of the reasons for this related to management, the review notes that 'governance is a complex, politically charged and inherently difficult field of development assistance, in which the context is continually shifting' and that 'CIDA did not adjust … to respond to existing requirements, let alone new challenges'. Similarly, a review of USAID Democracy and Governance Programmes 'found that many USAID staffers were frustrated by their inability to better answer the basic question: Are we having a positive impact?' (National Research Council Committee on Evaluation of USAID Democracy; Assistance Programs, 2008)

Nevertheless, international financing institutions have pushed institutional and policy changes in many countries through loan conditionality. Structural Adjustment Programmes and their successor Poverty Reduction Strategic Plans have propelled countries to adopt free-market approaches and agendas of privatization and deregulation. The rhetoric of free market liberalism is disguised in a language of technocratic expertise. Governance-based models of institutional development have models of institutional development have prioritized externally defined development agendas in ways that have subordinated local political processes, and local power dynamics. It is not clear whether this is deliberate in order to try to force change, or more simply a failure to recognize that local power dynamics are underpinned by deep-seated system patterns which are highly resistant to external change. Be that as it may, local power dynamics have been addressed as if they were technical issues fixable through technical solutions. When these do not change, this has been interpreted as obduracy and the response has been to exert more force through aid funding conditionality, and by questioning government legitimacy. Malcolm (1991) notes that any form of 'legal authority has to be validated by political authority', and that 'the basis for political authority is that is recognised ... or believed in by the people who are subject to it'. But the confluence of pressure on poor countries, and a new donor enthusiasm for political reform, has combined to propel economically less-developed countries towards practices that have no internal legitimacy. From the perspective of governance programming, it is not clear what positive results have been achieved. When analysed from a political perspective, the loss of political authority has far-reaching consequences.

The great irony is that from the perspective of the poorest and most marginalized, the issue of governance is paramount, but for completely different reasons to those articulated by institutions like the World Bank. The issue here is that services are available and policy and law are often adequate, but the reality on the ground means that people don't get access. That requires changes to the governance structures. Bales (2005: 16) recounts an instructive story in his book *Understanding Global Slavery*:

> In India, Vivek and Vidullata Pandit have been helping people gain their freedom from debt bondage for nearly thirty years. India has an excellent law on debt bondage, one that provides funds to all freed slaves to help them make a new start. Getting access to those funds should be as easy as presenting the freed person to a local official and documenting their bondage. To help protect newly freed slaves, the law mandates an immediate cash-in-hand payment to cover food and shelter. This is crucial since many slaves escape with just the shirts on their backs. In reality, obstacles are thrown up at every step, and even when a grant is approved for the person the money may never come. Corruption and government indifference is so deep that, Vivek told me, 'we just don't bother with government anymore; we know that it will take more effort than it is worth to get any help from the government for the people we help to freedom.'

Much of our own research comes to the same conclusion. As we described above the Participate Initiative research (Burns et al., 2013) showed that unlike the general population the reasons why the very poorest didn't get access to services mostly related to power, discrimination, corruption and failures of governance. People are deeply concerned about governance, but they need a quite different response to that which is being rolled out by the World Bank. Laying aside the issues of relevance and legitimacy for a moment, even in their own terms it is hard to see how these governance programmes can claim success.

Rights-based approaches

In the 1990s and 2000s, rights-based approaches (RBA) gained importance as a development framework. Following World War II, newly independent nations had brought a new type of discourse to international debates, based on their struggles for social, economic, cultural, civil, and political rights.

These rights and citizenship had not been bestowed, but had been fought for. However, with independence, this had been converted into a development discourse. Grass roots organizations that had emerged out of the struggle for rights in developing countries were demobilized. Manji (1998) notes that 'the concept of rights was codified and rarefied in laws and constitutions whose relevance or application was determined by the self-proclaimed, and increasingly unaccountable, guardians of the State'. Talk of rights became talk of development in a shift that depoliticized poverty and changed the structures that had organized around rights, into development organizations.

In 1986, the UN Declaration on the Right to Development was crafted at the initiative of radical third world states in a bid to create a New International Economic Order that was fair to poor countries. This emphasized the collective duty of all states to create a just and equitable environment and eliminate barriers to development. Laying much of the blame for global inequity on Western nations, and demanding accountability for this, created substantial opposition from the West. Cold war ideological differences further reinforced this with Western nations resisting the inclusion of development rights (water, shelter, food) as human rights. With the end of the Cold War, the nature of rights became less contested. The principle of indivisible, interdependent and non-hierarchical rights was finally accepted globally at the 1993 World Conference on Human Rights. It therefore became a modest step to frame development in these terms. However, the RBA that followed bore little resemblance to the UN Declaration on Human Rights, as there was no reference to global inequality, or to rights beyond one's own state.

Cornwall and Nyamu-Musembe (2004) define three reasons for incorporation of human rights into a new RBA development framework. They classified these as normative, pragmatic, and ethical. As a *normative* framework, RBA set out a vision of what 'ought' to be. It linked the more progressive approaches to development, such as participation, empowerment, and advocacy, to legislation. It changed the way the governments and development agencies regarded such practices. Critics, however, pointed to the fact that the poor have little access to institutions that might uphold their rights, and that finite resources demanded the establishment of priorities, which undermines the principle of indivisibility of rights and highlights the dilemma of dealing with competing rights (Farrington, 2001). Cornwall and Nyamu-Musembe (2004) observe that rights talk had different meanings depending on who spoke. Rights articulated by donor capitals meant different things to those articulated by the oppressed poor. It is the latter that has meaning, because movement away from oppression can only be sustainable when it comes from within society. They also observe that the RBA approach seemed to convey donor 'superiority' with respect to morals and 'with regards to insights into what would be in the best interests of the south'.

As a *pragmatic* framework, RBA provided new mechanisms for holding to account states that received aid. It increased the likelihood that policy measures would be implemented in practice. The UN agency, the Office of the High Commission for Human Rights (OHCHR), operates to a mandate to promote and protect all human rights, and notes in its guidelines that 'the human rights approach to poverty reduction emphasizes the accountability of policy makers and others whose actions have an impact on the rights of people. Rights imply duties, and duties demand accountability' (OHCHR, 2012). Under international law, the state is the principle duty bearer of human rights in any country. However, international organizations also were seen to have a responsibility to help realize universal human rights. RBA provided a framework for monitoring accountability over all global actors, both NGOs and transnational corporations. With a shift in aid delivery mechanisms from projects to budget support, RBA offered new ways for intrusive conditionality to be brought in.

As an *ethical* framework, Cornwall and Nyamu-Musembe (2004) note that RBA became a better way to define participation as a framework for a more genuinely inclusive process of popular involvement in decision-making over the resources and institutions that affect people's lives. The shift was to foster citizen claims to recognize and claim their rights, and for obligation holders to honour their responsibilities. They observed that RBA was articulated in four ways, namely as a set of normative principles to guide how development is done; as a set of instruments to develop assessments, checklists, and indicators against which interventions might be judged; as a component to be integrated into programming; and as the underlying justification for interventions aimed at strengthening institutions.

But has this approach changed anything? Vandenhole and Gready (2014) note that UNICEF was not transformed by the introduction of human rights-based approaches, and that the degree of organizational change brought about by the introduction of RBA into UN development analysis and programming had remained limited. A study on the impact of RBA on development showed that neither CARE, Oxfam nor Amnesty International were able to link development to human rights, and were not able to report impact in human rights terms (Bengtsson, 2007).

RBA means little if it is unable to transform power relations. In the context of bilateral development assistance, it is difficult to see how this could happen where there is no direct accountability to the communities who are the ultimate recipients. Without such accountability, rights cannot be claimed to be upheld through development programmes. The advent of RBA has been useful in debating the concept of rights, politics, and justice. Yet it has stopped short of assuring that development actors bear responsibility for the consequences of their actions. This has been less threatening to donor countries than the right to development, an approach that might have held donor governments responsible for negative human rights impacts that flow from projects they have funded. Courtland Robinson (2003) describes what these might be in documenting how millions of people have been forcibly displaced by development projects in ways that 'cost them their homes, their livelihoods, their health, and even their very lives'.

According to Uvin (2002), discourse changes can slowly reshape the margins of acceptable action, create opportunities for redefining reputations and naming and shaming, change incentive structures and the way in which interests and preferences are defined, and influence expectations. But this does not happen in a straightforward or linear way. While RBA made steps to incorporate some sadly missing political elements into the analysis of development, Uvin summed it up as 'the quest for moral high ground: draping oneself in the mantle of human rights to cover the fat belly of the development community while avoiding challenging the status quo too much, cross-examining oneself, or questioning the international system. One can see power at work here, which is to be expected' (Uvin, 2002).

A reflection on development frameworks and planning

The four development frameworks discussed cover much of development practice. While there are other frameworks they share similar characteristics. Large-scale integrated planning, technical-driven development, and governance approaches have been particularly linear in their cause and effect projection. Rights-based approaches while signalling some progress by embedding poverty, underdevelopment, and injustice within a wider system of power relations, also failed because it was externally driven. What is striking here is that there are strong reasons – from the perspectives of the poorest – for integrated local service delivery, bringing technologies to the service of the poorest, fixing the governance problems, and ensuring that people can claim rights. But a failure to understand the nature of change means that trying to implement such aspirations from the top down is destined to failure. Complexity per se is not a problem. For the most part complexity is what it is (Ramalingam, 2013). The problem is that solutions to problems within complex environments are constructed as if they weren't complex. We don't believe that the failure to demonstrate results is simply a measurement difficulty. We believe that it is a failure of approach. With a fundamental readjustment of the underlying principles of programmed improvement, development impact is not only possible but likely. This depends on understanding how change happens, and what sorts of interventions are congruent with that understanding.

References

Allana, A. (2015) *Navigating Complexity: Adaptive Management at the Northern Karamoja Growth, Health and Governance Program*, Toronto, Canada: Engineers Without Borders and Mercy Corps.

Associated Press (2007) 'Examples of failed aid-funded projects in Africa', 23 December. <http://www.nbcnews.com/id/22380448/ns/world_news-africa/t/examples-failed-aid-funded-projects-africa/#.VK5MByuUeSp> [accessed December 2014].

Bales, K. (2005) *Understanding Global Slavery: A Reader*, Berkeley, CA and Los Angeles, CA: University of California Press.

Bengtsson, L. (2007) 'The impact of rights based approaches to development – how can it be shown they make a difference', thesis, Malmö University, School of International Migration and Ethnic Relations, 61–8.

Brinkerhoff, D.W. and Ingle, M.D. (1989) 'Integrating blueprint and process: a structured flexibility approach to development management', *Journal of Public Administration and Development*, 9(5): 487–503.

Burns, D., Howard, J., Lopez-Franco, E., Shahrokh, T. and Wheeler, J. (2013) *Work with Us: How Communities and Organisations Can Catalyse Sustainable Change*, Brighton: IDS.

Burns, D., Aked, J., Hacker, E., Lewis, S. and Picken, A. (2015) *The Role of Volunteering in Sustainable Development*, Brighton: IDS/VSO.

Buse, K., Ludi, E. and Vigneri, M. (2008) 'Beyond the village: the transition from rural investments to national plans to reach the MDGs. Sustaining and upscaling the Millennium Villages', London: Overseas Development Institute.

Cabral, L., Farrington, J. and Ludi, E. (2006) 'The Millennium Villages Project – a new approach to ending rural poverty in Africa', ODI Natural Resource Perspectives, 101, August.

Campbell, B. (2012) 'RIO+20 and sustainable agriculture: how to feed the world without wrecking the planet?' *Huffington Post*. <http://www.huffingtonpost.com/bruce-campbell-phd/rio20-and-sustainable-agriculture_b_1581075.html> [accessed January 2015].

Canadian International Development Agency (CIDA) (2008). 'Review of governance programming in CIDA: synthesis report'. <http://www.acdi-cida.gc.ca/INET/IMAGES.NSF/vLUImages/Evaluations2/$file/Review_of_Governance_Programming_in_CIDA-EN.pdf> [accessed 7 July 2015].

Carothers, T. (2009) 'Democracy assistance: political vs developmental?' *Journal of Democracy*, 20(1): 5–19.

Chambers, R. (1983) *Rural Development: Putting the Last First*, Abingdon: Pearson Education Ltd.

Cooksey, B. and Kikula, I. (2005) 'When bottom-up meets top-down: the limits of local participation in local government planning in Tanzania', Research on Poverty Alleviation, Special Paper No. 17.

Cornwall, A. (2003) 'Whose voices? Whose choices? Reflections on gender and participatory development', *World Development* 31(8): 1325–42.

Cornwall, A. and Nyamu-Musembe, C. (2004) 'Putting the "rights based approach" to development into perspective', *Third World Quarterly* 25(8): 1415–37.

Courtland Robinson, W. (2003) 'Risks and rights: the causes, consequences and challenges of development-induced displacement', Occasional Paper, The Brookings Institute – SAIS Project on Internal Displacement.

De Datta, S.K., Tauro, A.C. and Balaoing, S.N. (1968) 'Effect of plant type and nitrogen level on growth characteristics and grain yield of indica rice in the tropics', *Agronomy Journal* 60(6): 643–7.

Duffield, M. (2001) *Global Governance and the New Wars*, London and New York, NY: Zed Books.

Easterly, W. (2005) 'Reliving the '50s: the big push, poverty traps, and takeoffs in economic development', Centre for Global Development, Working Paper No 65.

Easterly, W. (2006) *The White Man's Burden: Why the West's Efforts to Aid the Rest Have Done So Much Ill and So Little Good*, New York, NY: Penguin Press.

Farrington, J. (2001) 'Sustainable livelihoods, rights and the new architecture of aid', ODI Natural Resource Perspectives 69, June. <http://www.odi.org/sites/odi.org.uk/files/odi-assets/publications-opinion-files/2823.pdf> [accessed 7 July 2015].

Food and Agriculture Organization (FAO) (2014). 'Rice paddies', Fisheries and Aquaculture Department. <http://www.fao.org/fishery/topic/13472/en> [accessed 31 December 2014].

Freire, P. (1970) *Pedagogy of the Oppressed,* New York, NY: Herder and Herder.

Global Hunger Index (2011) 'The challenge of hunger: taming price spikes and excessive food price volatility', Welt Hunfer Hilfe, IFPRI, Concern Worldwide.

Government of Sikkim (2003). 'Sikkim Organic Mission: policy vision and mission'. <http://ofai.s3.amazonaws.com/Sikkim_Policy%20vision%20n%20mission.pdf> [accessed 31 December 2014].

Hendra, J. (2014) '"What matters gets measured, and what we measure is what ends up mattering" - Deputy Executive Director John Hendra', UN Women, 12 March. <http://www.unwomen.org/en/news/stories/2014/3/john-hendra-speech-on-indicators#sthash.8wWDBLtw.dpuf> [accessed December 2014].

International Monetary Fund (IMF) (2005) 'The IMF's approach to promoting good governance and combating corruption — a guide'. <http://www.imf.org/external/np/gov/guide/eng/index.htm#pt> [accessed 7 July 2015].

Kerlin, J.A. with Kubal, M.R. (2002) A Neoliberal Agenda for Decentralization in Transitioning Countries? A Comparative Study of Chile and Poland, paper prepared for the Georgia Political Science Association 2002 Annual Conference, Savannah, Georgia, 13 January – 2 February 2002. <http://www.researchgate.net/publication/228584737_A_Neoliberal_Agenda_for_Decentralization_in_Transitioning_Countries_A_Comparative_Study_of_Chile_and_Poland> [accessed 28 July 2015].

Leavy, J. and Howard, J. (2013) 'What matters most: evidence from 84 participatory studies with those living in extreme poverty and marginalisation', Brighton: IDS.

Malcolm, N. (1991) 'Sense on sovereignty', autumn address, London: Centre for Policy Studies.

Manji, F. (1998) 'The depoliticisation of poverty' in *Development and Rights, Selected Essays from Development in Practice,* Oxford: Oxfam GB.

McGee, R., Levine, J. and Hughes, A. (2002) 'Assessing participation in poverty reduction strategy papers: a desk-based synthesis of experience in Sub-Saharan Africa', Sussex, UK: Institute of Development Studies.

Moyo, D. (2009) *Dead Aid: Why Aid is Not Working and How There is Another Way for Africa,* New York, NY: Penguin Books.

Munk, N. (2013). *The Idealist: Jeffrey Sachs and the Quest to End Poverty,* New York, NY: Doubleday.

Murray Li, T. (2007) *The Will to Improve, Governmentality, Development and the Practice of Politics,* Durham, NC: Duke University Press.

National Research Council Committee on Evaluation of USAID Democracy; Assistance Programs (2008) *Improving Democracy Assistance: Building; Knowledge Through Evaluations and Research,* Washington, DC: National Academies Press; p. 196.

Nature (2012) 'With transparency comes trust', Editorial, Issue 485; 10 May. <http://www.nature.com/nature/journal/v485/n7397/pdf/485147a.pdf> [accessed 28 July 2015].

Office of the High Commission for Human Rights (OHCHR) (2012), 'Principles and guidelines for a human rights approach to poverty reduction strategies' para. 24. <http://www.ohchr.org/Documents/Publications/PovertyStrategiesen. pdf> [accessed 7 July 2015].

Organisation for Economic Co-operation and Development – Development Co-operation Directorate (OECD – DAC) (no date) Net official development assistance from DAC and other Donors in 2013. <www.oecd.org/dac/stats> [accessed 29 December 2014].

Peters, T. and Waterman, R. (1981) *In Search of Excellence*, New York, NY: Harper & Row.

Pimental, D., Acquay, H., Biltonen, M., Rice, P., Silva, M., Nelson, J., Lipner, V., Giordano, S., Horowitz, A. and D'Amore, M. (1993) 'Assessment of environmental and economic impacts of pesticide use' in D. Pimental and H. Lehman (ed.), *The Pesticide Question, Environment, Economics and Ethics*, London: Chapman and Hall.

Ramalingam, B. (2013) *Aid on the Edge of Chaos*, Oxford: Oxford University Press.

Rosenstein-Rodan, P. (1957) *Notes on the Theory of the 'Big Push*, Cambridge: Massachusetts MIT Center for International Studies, reprinted in Howard S. Ellis (ed.), *Economic Development for Latin America: Proceedings of a Conference Held by the International Economic Association*, London: Macmillan, 1961.

Ryan, J.G. and Asokan, M. (1977) 'Effect of Green Revolution in wheat on production of pulses and nutrients in India', *Indian Journal of Agricultural Economics* 32(3): 8–15.

Sachs, J. (2005) *The End of Poverty: Economic Possibilities for Our Time*, London: Penguin Press.

Sen, A. (2001) *Development as Freedom*, 2nd edn, Oxford and New York, NY: Oxford University Press.

SNV (2010) Water point mapping – the experience of SNV Tanzania. <http://www.snvworld.org/download/publications/water_point_mapping-_the_experience_of_snv_tanzania1.pdf> [accessed 7 July 2015].

Szirmai, A. (2005) *The Dynamics of Socio-Economic Development: An Introduction*, Cambridge: Cambridge University Press.

The Earth Institute (2014) 'Millennium Villages'. <http://www.earth.columbia. edu/articles/view/1799> [accessed December 2014)].

United Nations (UN) (1992) 'Rio Declaration on Environment and Development 1992'. <http://www.jus.uio.no/lm/environmental.development.rio.declaration. 1992/portrait.a4.pdf> [accessed 29 June 2015].

United Nations Children's Fund (UNICEF) (2014) 'The State of the World's Children 2014 in Numbers: Every Child Counts: Revealing Disparities, Advancing Children's Rights', New York, NY: UNICEF. <http://www.unicef. org/sowc2014/numbers/documents/english/SOWC2014_In%20Numbers_ 28%20Jan.pdf> [accessed 28 July 2015].

United Nations Department of Economic and Social Affairs (UN DESA) (2015) 'Transforming our world by 2030: a new agenda for global action; Zero draft of the outcome document for the UN Summit to adopt the Post 2015 Development Agenda (Goal 15)'. <https://sustainabledevelopment. un.org/content/documents/7261Post-2015%20Summit%20-%202%20 June%202015.pdf> [accessed 29 June 2015].

United Nations Millennium Campaign (2014) 'We the peoples: celebrating 7 million voices', December. <https://www.nelsonmandela.org/uploads/ files/wethepeoples-7million.pdf> [accessed June 2015].

Uvin, P. (2002) 'On high moral ground: the incorporation of human rights by the development enterprise', *PRAXIS: The Fletcher Journal of Development Studies* XVII.

Vandenhole, W. and Gready, P. (2014) 'Failures and successes of human rights-based approaches to development: towards a change perspective', *Nordic Journal of Human Rights* 32(4): 291–311.

Wanjala, B. (2010) 'The big push approach to rural development: the case of millennium villages in Kenya', Tilburg University: Development Research Institute (IVO).

Williamson, C.R. (2009) 'Exploring the failure of foreign aid: The role of incentives and information', *Rev Austrian Econ.* <http://dri.fas.nyu.edu/ docs/IO/12361/WilliamsonRAEAid.pdf> [accessed 7 July 2015].

Witt, M.A. and Lewin, A. (2004) 'Dynamics of institutional change: institutional stickiness and the logic of individual action', INSEAD; Working Paper Series. Euro Asia Centre.

CHAPTER 2
How change happens

This chapter argues that while most international development interventions are based on linear assumptions about how change happens, this is not in fact congruent with social reality. Not understanding that social systems are characterized by complexity and non-linearity has resulted in major development failures. The chapter shows how systems thinking and complexity theory can help us to develop a more meaningful understanding of how change happens and to underpin our intervention strategies.

Keywords: systems thinking; complexity; social change; theory of change; log frame

This chapter is about how and why change happens. Understanding change is crucial because international development practitioners frequently make changes that have no impact at all, or which have completely unpredictable impacts, or which make things much worse. Sometimes they make positive changes in one domain which have negative impacts in another. Sometimes they create changes which only last for as long as there is money for a project. It is only when we understand the nature of change that we can develop effective strategies to engage with it. Over recent years there has been a shift from development interventions which can show a logic which links inputs to outputs (and possibly outcomes), to a theory of change which has required assumptions to be tested and evidence to support theories of how change happens. But these processes are still fundamentally based on a view of logic that assumes linear relations between cause and effect and such assumptions are often not congruent with the world with which we are engaging.

The problem with both of these approaches is that intervention logic like 'the provision of toilets will lead to improvements in health outcomes' are based on assumptions that often don't hold up – for example toilets will be used (as toilets). Toilets don't get used because they are not culturally acceptable; or because there are too many risks for women in going to them if they are not easily accessible; or because the water table means that bacteria will flow into clean water sources; or because people think it is 'unclean' to have a toilet in their house; or because they don't have money to pay for them; or because the toilets are not 'owned' by anyone in the community and are therefore vandalized and materials sold for whatever small amount of money can be made from them; or because there aren't enough skilled technicians in the community to service and maintain them; or because they will displace the livelihoods of others in the community and so on. Usually

http://dx.doi.org/10.3362/9781780448510.002

it is a complex mix of factors. Simple intervention logics rarely work. In this chapter we explore in some detail the implications of systems thinking and complexity theory for generating meaningful change processes which move beyond simple logics. But we start with linear logic.

Logic models, predictability and planning

As we have seen in Chapter 1, the predominant development paradigm is rooted in planning. Plans tend to be based on macro strategies for change and linked to predictions about impact. Increasingly, emphasis has been on making planning logics explicit, and evaluating impact against those logics. This is typified by the almost universal introduction of the log frame. The logical framework, as it is formally known, was an attempt to get practitioners to articulate clearly the changes that they expected to result from their activities.

A logical framework asks people to look at activities, outputs, outcomes, and goals. It works roughly like this: if we carry out this activity – based on X assumptions – then we can deliver these outputs; if these outputs are delivered – based on Y assumptions – then we can deliver these outcomes; if these outcomes are delivered – based on Z assumptions – then we will meet our goals. The important link in this chain is the assumptions. Aside from being a highly bureaucratic process, it is mostly a theoretical and abstract construct (Vogel, 2012). The logic is articulated but it is often not grounded in evidence.

More recently there has been discussion about how organizations can develop 'theories of change'. This is a more flexible attempt to look at the nature of change, but the essential framing is still highly linear and quite reductionist. Quoting Ober (2011) Vogel says in relation to CARE International's work with peace-building initiatives: 'focusing on a single activity, programme staff were encouraged to express a statement about change as: "if we take x action, then y change will result, because ..." These statements were discussed within the programme, and subsequently evidence was sought to support them' (Vogel 2012: 15).

Theory of change thinking is also about making logical assumptions explicit (Vogel, 2012: 4) but with evidence to support those assumptions from a broader range of sources than would be usual for a log frame. Vogel articulates the theory of change as mapping out multiple possible pathways within a broader change process where a logic model maps out the intervention within that (Vogel, 2012: 16). She argues that complexity and systems thinking can be built into theories of change frameworks through good context analysis, critical challenge to assumptions, and so on, and asks for wider evidence of the hypotheses that are being put forward. But this remains deeply problematic because the system is still only seen as context. Those proposing a programme of work are somehow expected to know in advance what will happen when they implement, and to plan on that basis. To do this they need to carry out a detailed analysis of the context and then map out the many steps needed to get there. The more complicated the problem the more things that need to be taken into account in this planning process: 'Even well-funded initiatives can only take on part of bringing about a broad goal, and a key question to be decided is whether it is necessary to identify every precondition for a broad goal in order for an initiative to plan realistically and effectively. Unfortunately the answer is yes!' (ActKnowledge et al., 2003).

This is a response to a complicated landscape not a complex one. The Cynefin matrix developed by David Snowden (2010), and similar frameworks, helpfully distinguish between processes that are simple, complicated, complex, and chaotic. Simple usually refers to straightforward linear cause-and-effect relationships; complicated is characterized by very large numbers of interconnected cause and effect relationships – here despite the number of interlocking causal relationships outcomes can theoretically be predicted with enough computing power. Complex represents relationships which are not linear, and not predictable – where causality may only be discerned by looking back rather than looking forward. Chaotic is where there is no obvious relationship between cause and effect at a system level, no manageable constraints of any nature, and behaviour may well be random. Snowden additionally identifies a fifth domain of disorder which is the state of not knowing which type of system you are in. In fact social systems are made up of a mixture of all of these, but we frequently assume that they are either simple or complicated. Log frames and theories of change try to make simple and complicated analysis more and more sophisticated, but ultimately determining causality in this way is only likely to be possible in relation to very linear problems with clearly identifiable relationships between intervention and outcome. This doesn't apply to most of the issues that we would expect international development to be engaged with.

Complexity

So in controlled contexts where there are relatively constant factors, we can predict likely responses to relatively simple interventions. In social situations, the picture is much more complex. Stacey points out that 'There is as yet no single science of complexity, but rather a number of different strands comprising what might be called the complexity sciences. What they all have in common is concern with non-linear interactions' (Stacey, 2010). He goes on to say that 'linear models are models of certainty, while some non-linear ones are models of uncertainty'. Not only are they characterized by multiple interacting variables, but these are constantly changing as a result of their interaction with each other. So not only is each place and situation completely different from the next one, the same place is completely different from how it was before. And of course people are not entirely logical! As Stacey points out:

> human agents are conscious and self-conscious, they feel emotion and
> spontaneously improvise; they exercise imagination and spin fantasies;

they experience and act upon values and on societal norms, they conflict with each other and often seek to deceive and manipulate each other in the ordinary politics of daily life; they act out their neuroses and psychoses in leadership and other roles they take up and they are essentially interdependent. (Stacey, 2010: 73)

This makes prediction nearly impossible and it makes the idea of a counterfactual analysis of what would have happened if an intervention had not taken place a fairly naïve proposition, as no social situation is really similar let alone the same (Befani, 2012). Although, in a complex system we can anticipate and influence the dispositions of the system (Snowden, 2012).

Because we understand linear logical causality, we typically try to apply it even in the context of complex problems, which is like using a hammer to saw a piece of wood because we know how to use a hammer but we don't know how to use a saw, or we avoid these problems and focus on problems where we can identify simple linear change processes. This is important because most 'wicked' or intractable problems are characterized by complex processes of change. If we avoid them then international development becomes dominated by initiatives, which extend what we already know how to do, and we never construct solutions to the things that we don't have answers for. This coherently describes large swathes of international development and it is extremely worrying.

Throughout this book we offer many examples of non-linearity. This takes many forms, for example: where the interaction of things leads to unpredictable outcomes; where small changes create domino effects which result in big changes; where many small changes create system-level patterns, where nothing seems to be happening at all and suddenly everything changes; where change effects compound and amplify each other. If we do not understand the non-linear dynamics of change, it is hard to see how we can build effective interventions. In this next section we explore some of the key manifestations of complexity, which are relevant to intervention: emergence; attractors and tipping points; sensitivity to starting conditions and amplification.

Emergence

Emergence comes about when actions on the ground produce effects which are different to the sum of their parts. For example, a group of excellent individual football players of extraordinary skill may not be able to produce a team. A group of mediocre players may produce an extraordinary team where the interactions and pattern of play could not be determined by their individual level of skill. The team performance is the emergent outcome. Goldstein defines emergence as: 'the arising of novel and coherent structures, patterns and properties during the process of self-organization in complex systems' (Goldstein, 1999). Stacey (2010) offers a different interpretation. He says that while 'for some writers, emergence is the unpredictable arising of global, higher level properties from lower level self organization which is understood in terms of simple rules of agent behaviour', for him 'emergence refers to a pattern arising across a population that is not the realisation of a prior design or plan for that population-wide pattern but flows from many local interactions'. We have seen examples of both of these, but the focus on the way micro-level experience builds macro-level patterns which are often unpredictable resonates strongly with our experience.

A dependency culture is an example of an emergent pattern. Here a history of aid starts to lead to a situation where people won't function independently without external help. This is not the only emergent pattern that is possible. In other circumstances, the same intervention might lead to people feeling they now had strong basic foundations from which they could become entrepreneurs and build their own livelihoods. An example given in Burns (2007) related to the UK National Health Service. Here the radical extension of complaints procedures enhanced doctor accountability and enabled redress for patients who had suffered neglect or malpractice. However, this led to an increase in litigation, and this in turn led to a risk-averse culture preventing many practices which would otherwise have benefited patients. These emergent system patterns crystallize as norms that are hard to shift once they are established and this is why they are so critical for us to take into account.

Attractors, latent attractors and tipping points

Attractors are an important concept in complexity theory. They explain the ways in which social relationships shift from one equilibrium point to another. In complexity theory the social landscape is made up of ideas or positions or activities around which people and activity are centred. Coleman et al. (2011) describe these as a 'stable and coherent pattern(s) of thought and behaviour'. Stacey describes them as 'global patterns of behaviour displayed by a system' (Stacey, 2010). An attractor can be seen as an equilibrium of social relations which form a consistent pattern of system dynamics. Peter Coleman visualizes attractors as a dip in the landscape into which a ball may fall 'Metaphorically the attractor serves as a valley in the psychological landscape into which the psychological elements – thoughts, feelings and actions – begin to slide. Once trapped in such a valley, escape requires tremendous will and energy and may appear impossible' (Coleman et al., 2011; Figure 2.1). Attractors come in different forms; the metaphor of a landscape is sometimes known as a single point attractor.

We also have *strange attractors* which are more like tropes, or myths that govern behaviour in a sense of overall direction and pattern but not in a single stable location (Juarrero, 1999). Such attractors are difficult to detect externally but are understood locally: the way we do things around here that we all understand but we can't explain to any outsider.

With regard to the single point attractor, Coleman argues that many change initiatives could be represented by pushing the ball up the slope of the dip. Perhaps the ball is held on the slope while the 'initiative' is still funded

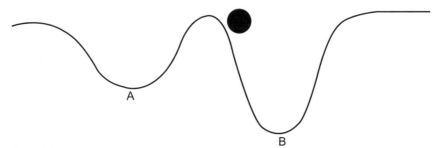

Figure 2.1 The metaphor of a ball moving across a landscape from one attractor to another
Source: Nowak et al. 2010

but then it falls back. There can be no sustainability of an initiative unless the ball is pushed over the lip of the dip, and pulled into another dip where it has stability. This requires both the creation or identification of another dip, and enough energy to pull people (the ball) towards that dip. A latent attractor is a set of ideas or positions or activities that people are starting to adopt, believe in, move towards, but aren't yet strongly manifest in social life. They need to reach a critical mass before they are strong enough to become visible. For example, attitudes toward women might gradually be changing but this is not yet manifest in social norms or institutions. At a certain point when there is a critical mass of changed attitudes, material change becomes possible. Suddenly, for example, it becomes possible to create schools for girls. Often this change is characterized by a tipping point. A tipping point is where all the pressure is building and suddenly change happens. Tipping points describe the straw that breaks the camel's back; the dam that bursts. If we were to look at the evidence we would observe that when we put a straw on the camel's back nothing happens. We continue to put straws on the camel's back and nothing happens. This evidence would suggest that it is possible put straws on camels' backs indefinitely with no impact. But later one straw changes everything. Change is not necessarily proportional to the extent of an intervention. Nothing may appear to happen at all – even for decades – and then everything seems to change all at once. This is a non-linear pattern of change. These types of tipping points draw on catastrophe theory; but in a complex system we can also get phase shifts, in which attractors shift, disappear or appear suddenly with no apparent trigger, even with the benefit of hindsight. This further illustrates the danger of any model, reference or measurement system based on assumptions of linear causality.

Underlying dynamics are as important to understand as what is on the surface. Change can be more easily catalysed if we understand that there are underlying shifts in attitudes and behaviours that are already happening. Stacey in a critique of Sanders (1998) articulates how that might happen:

> She proceeds to argue that despite an inability to make predictions of long-term states, it is possible to provide qualitative descriptions of whole system behaviour over time. This may be true, but only for the

attractor that the system is currently drawn to. It would not be possible to describe any new attractor that some system was capable of spontaneously jumping to, until the jump had occurred. Sanders tries to get around this by saying that it is possible to identify what she calls 'perking' information. This is the new initial conditions to which a system may be sensitive, that is changes or developments that are already taking place beneath the surface. It takes peripheral vision, or well developed foresight skills, to recognise a system's initial conditions as they are emerging. This enables one to see change coming and so influence it to one's advantage. Recognising these conditions before they emerge is the new leverage point. This attempt runs into the same problem as before. It is not possible to identify all of the initial conditions and measure all of them with infinite accuracy. So how can you have foresight if you cannot predict? (Stacey, 2010: 88)

Our thinking is quite similar to that of Sanders. We reject Stacey's critique here because the point is not to predict what will happen, but (a) to identify where they are already happening and (b) to identify points where things *might* happen.

Attractors help us to think about how shifts are made between one system dynamic and another – and by extension how shifts can be catalysed. A last thought from Stacey is worth reflecting on

For systems dynamics thinkers the aim is to identify leverage points for interventions that will enable them to identify where, when and how to initiate change and so stay in control. However the ability to do this in a system that is sensitive to tiny changes is called into question. That obviously has serious implications for the human ability to stay in control. (Stacey, 2010: 61)

The intellectual path that we are travelling on in this book lies between the soft system thinkers and complexity theorists who follow Stacey. We do believe that it is possible to intervene in an environment – to seed and to nurture – but we don't believe that it is possible to control. We do believe that it is possible to create conditions which shift the direction of travel of systems without being able to predict the detail of exactly what will happen and how it will happen. In this we are supported by many other thinkers and practitioners in complexity theory.

Sensitivity to starting conditions, small localized change and amplification

One of the common features of complexity theory is sensitivity to starting conditions. This means that once something happens – even something very small – it has a big influence on what happens next:

The specific behaviour displayed by the system within these limits is reasonably predictable over short ranges in space and short time periods, because it takes time for small changes to be escalated into completely different patterns. However over long ranges in space and long periods the specific behaviour of a system following a strange attractor cannot be predicted. This is due to the system's sensitivity to initial conditions, more popularly known as the butterfly effect which means that the long-term trajectory of the system is highly sensitive to its starting point. The usual example is that of a butterfly flapping its wings in Sao Paolo which alters the air pressure by a tiny amount that could be escalated into a tiny hurricane over Miami. Long-term predictability would then require the detection of every tiny change, and the measurement of each to an infinite degree of precision. Since this is a human impossibility, the specific long-term pathway is unpredictable for all practical purposes. The long-term behaviour of a system, therefore, is as much determined by small changes as it is by the deterministic laws governing it. (Stacey, 2010: 60)

What follows from this is that change is highly context specific and often emanates from tiny local interactions, thus small changes can have a huge impact over time because they shift the dynamics of the system. How a change is started will have a major impact on what happens next. So once a particular process gains traction it will frame the long-term trajectory of anything that follows, as we show in relation to evaluation in the next section (see example 5). Stacey makes some observations here, which are critical to our analysis. He argues that:

The possibility of the evolution of novelty depends critically on the presence of microscopic diversity. When individual entities are the same, that is, when they do not have any incentive to alter their strategies for interacting with each other, the model displays stability. When individual entities are different and thus do have incentives to change their strategies of interaction with each other, the model displays change of a genuinely novel kind. ... What emerges does so because of the transformative cause of the process of the micro interactions in which small differences are amplified into population-wide changes. (Stacey, 2010: 63)

Sustainable change does not then come from the transfer of something that is working in one place to another place; rather it lies in the amplification of micro-level interactions. To nurture these we need (a) to ensure that there is diversity at a local level and that any inquiry encompasses the diversity that exists within the system and (b) our focus needs to be on the most local level of interactions.

Amplification effects do not only happen on a global level. Amplification also describes the way in which when one thing happens, it can substantially amplify the effect of another. Climate change, for example, might impact on crops and reduce the level of production, but also have parallel effects. Because the rivers flood, roads are destroyed and this substantially amplifies the difficulties faced by local farmers. Not only are they producing less, now they can't get even these to market. An example that we observed relating to climate change in Ghana (Harvey et al., 2012) was the way in which it was taking men into the city in vast numbers, leaving women behind. Women's lack of land rights was always an equality issue, but it was amplified by this change in the system. If women have no formal access to land but are within a family economic unit, they have the means to subsist. If the men leave and they have no access to land, they cannot farm, so the effects of this discrimination are amplified.

In some of the individual stories that are told in Chapter 4, Seeing the system, we see the way in which different discriminations impact on each other. Here again we see how 'starting conditions' profoundly affect outcomes. So in the story of a disabled girl who was raped (Chapter 4), we can see that her vulnerability lay in the poverty of her parents who had to leave her alone in order to work. As above, unless we understand these amplifications we cannot understand the ways in which actions impact or fail to impact on people.

Systems and system dynamics

Systems describe a boundary within which complex relationships between people, processes, and their environment are held. We might see them as a set of boundaries within which complex change processes are enacted (Midgley, 2000). Systems should not be seen as real 'entities' but rather as perceived sets of relationships which have a coherence to those looking at them (Checkland and Scholes, 2004). Following a critical realist perspective (Bhaskar, 1978; Collier, 1994) we would argue that the dynamics that take place within systems are real, but they will be seen differently by each of the actors within them. Discerning what might be happening can only be achieved by overlaying the many different perceptions upon each other and looking at where there is convergence of understanding and analysis and where there is divergence. In what follows we want to focus on two key aspects of systems: interconnectedness and system dynamics.

Systems are important in conceptualizing change because they can be seen to exist at a level between structure and agency. One might consider the dynamics of global capitalism to be structural issues, as are deep-seated patterns of patriarchy, but these are created and sustained through the chystalisation of durable norms at a village, urban slum or district/regional level etc. By surfacing system dynamics, possibilities for transformative change can be identified, and transformative change at a system level can impact on long-term structural dynamics. In other words, local system dynamics can be seen as an intermediate level which is accessible to change either through intentional collective action or multiple undirected actions that open new pathways. Creating change at this level can in turn create the conditions for deeper structural change.

Interconnectedness within and beyond system boundaries

Every part of a system is interconnected. This means that changes in one part of a system can have a major impact on other parts. A lack of change in one part of a system can inhibit change in another. A common example can be seen in relation to primary education for girls. Here substantial investment has led to increases in enrolment of girls. This might be regarded as a success if we don't include in our assessment the number of girls who are forced to end their education because they are expected to get married within cultures where married women are not expected to be educated. Unless you change the wider system dynamics which are reinforcing early marriage it is not possible to shift deeper structural inequalities which relate to gender and education. This is not to say that we should not be bringing girls into school. Indeed we might regard this as intrinsically as a good thing, or believe that bringing girls into primary education will be a longer term factor in shifting the primary underlying system dynamic, but it does suggest that we need to widen the system boundaries in order to understand the impact of our interventions.

Even some straightforward linear change is subject to wider system dynamics. For example, polio in Pakistan was close to eradication, with a well-advanced vaccination programme delivered by community health workers from small clinics. The US government, in their bid to try and find Osama Bin Laden, used a Pakistani doctor to collect blood samples through a vaccination programme. The identification of the Bin Laden gene was used to identify the family which was in turn used to target Bin Laden. As a result of this the number of attacks on public health workers massively increased. So less people were prepared to be health workers and there was a resurgence of polio. The attack happened on 1 May 2011 and polio cases reportedly rose by 37 per cent in 2011 (Sinha, 2012) This might sound like an anomaly in a perfectly working system but actually these anomalies are common. Take for example the measles, mumps and rubella (MMR) vaccination programme in the UK. This was derailed by a single piece of research which claimed a link between the combined vaccine and autism. The research later turned out to be flawed. The response of the medical profession, which remained almost universally convinced by the effectiveness of the vaccine throughout the crisis, was to carry on providing the combined vaccine exactly as before augmented by a huge public information campaign, on the grounds that they were right. For them the context was not a relevant variable. As a result, vaccination take-up plummeted because they weren't trusted. If they had understood this and offered the single vaccine, despite the rightness of their argument, they would almost certainly have maintained the coverage that they desired. While more expensive than the combined vaccine, this strategy would probably have been far cheaper in the long run and would have delivered the public health outcome intended. The point we are making is that even relatively straightforward scientific interventions are intrinsically connected to the wider system within which they are located and can as a result produce unintended consequences and unpredicable results.

System dynamics

Sustainable change comes about by changing the dynamics of a system. By system dynamics, we mean dynamic patterns of relationships that structure pathways that enable or constrain people's agency, and incentivize them to use it in particular ways. Systems are characterized by complex feedback loops. A feedback loop describes a situation in which the outputs of a system are fed back as inputs. Success which breeds success is a form of feedback loop. A simple, less abstract, example is the relationship between homelessness and alcoholism (Figure 2.2). Alcoholism is a cause of homelessness, and homelessness is a cause of alcoholism. People who drink a lot use the money they need to pay the rent. When they get evicted, they have to live on the street. The street is cold and they get depressed so their level of drinking increases. This makes it more difficult for them to get a place to live and so on.

Figure 2.2 Homelessness and alcoholism: a simple feedback loop

A man contracts HIV. He is shunned by his community and becomes lonely. His need to form sexual relationships is amplified, and so the disease spreads further. These are described as reinforcing feedback loops. Their opposites are balancing feedback loops. The classic example of a balancing feedback loop is a radiator thermostat which reduces the heat input as the temperature rises in order to maintain equilibrium.

Feedback loops explain why it is crucial to look beyond simple causalities, and why (as in the relationship between alcoholism and homelessness) even the idea of finding 'root causes' can be problematic. These reinforcing cycles are what make up complex system dynamics. Sometimes there can be many different loops within a system dynamic, as we will see in Chapter 4. Reinforcing feedback loops often manifest in international development as spirals of decline. Thus it becomes more important to think of effective change as a process of breaking the cycles that describe the system dynamics rather than tackling root causes. The following are a range of very different examples which illustrate what we mean by system dynamics:

Example 1: HIV-AIDS in the Kalangala islands.[1] While Uganda by 2010 as a whole had made huge progress in reducing the incidence of HIV/AIDS to well under 10 per cent, in the Kalangala Islands prevalence was around 28 per cent. The Kalangala islands are politically and geographically isolated. There were already a number of interventions taking place on the island; many of these were education focused but it quickly became clear in a participatory workshop that Danny facilitated that even if girls were all educated and 'empowered' they still had to find a way to live within a system dynamic which incentivized multiple relationships and unprotected sex. The system dynamic was an economic one. In the Kalangala islands, the fish cluster and then move. When they move, the men move. When the men move they take new women. The women who are left behind have no livelihoods – traditionally they smoked the fish, but there are no significant other livelihoods – so the women have to take new men. This cycle continues with more and more sexual relationships fuelling a spiralling AIDS epidemic. However empowered and educated the girls are, they are sucked into the prevailing systemic norms because they have no alternative livelihoods. Changing this situation requires changes to the system dynamic. Without this, changes in education levels will be meaningless.

Example 2: counter-intuitive dynamics in peace processes. Rob Ricigliano and colleagues working in the Democratic Republic of Congo observed that the more the national level peace process got on track the more it threatened mineral exporters, who then manipulated armed groups through the provision of arms and logistical support, encouraging fighting, ceasefire violations, and mass rape on the peripheries in the east and north of the country. Ricigliano explained to Ben Ramalingam 'our effectiveness was undermining our effectiveness' (Ramalingam, 2013: 254). Ricigliano (2011) also cites the Israel–Palestine conflict in which 'observed over time the system does not seem to exist to perpetuate political settlement, but instead to perpetuate itself'. He suggests that from a systems perspective, the purpose of the peace processes is in fact the avoidance of reconciliation (Ramalingam, 2013).

Example 3: UK area-based regeneration programmes. There are many schemes in the UK where an investment is made in education and training in order to create local leaders and entrepreneurs in areas of 'deprivation'. The rationale for such initiatives is that they help to build local social capital and enable areas to develop and grow. However, a consistent pattern in all of these areas is that once trained, these people leave because they see better opportunities elsewhere. There are strong incentives for them to go and few incentives for them to stay. So however successful the training programmes are, if all of the people who are trained leave, then training is pointless if your aim is regeneration. You have to change the system dynamic to ensure a sustainable effect. If we are to change the system dynamic we need to ask a different question. Instead of, how do we educate our young people so that they can drive the future of our community?, we need to ask, how do we keep young people in the community? This might generate a quite different set of solutions.

Example 4: the Millennium Development Goals. The Millennium Development Goals (MDGs) were created as a framework for concerted action around a set of key goals that were framed as targets. The first MDG, to eradicate extreme poverty and hunger, was framed as a target to halve the proportion of people whose income is less than US$1 a day. One of the difficulties of a target-based framework is that it creates systemic incentives for programme managers to focus on the 'low hanging fruit'. The target is more likely to be met if people who have simpler, less complex problems are engaged with, and as a result the poorest of the poor are mostly untouched by these initiatives. The system dynamics shape a set of incentives which in turn direct behaviour.

Example 5: programming based on log frames. Large development donors from the Bill and Melinda Gates Foundation to DFID require logical frameworks to underpin all of their investments. As noted earlier, logical frameworks depict linear chains of causality that lead from a problem statement to suggested solutions and predicted outcomes. All programmes and their managers are assessed according to the extent to which programme outcomes correspond to the logics outlined in the log frame. This sets up a clear incentive for managers only to include in their programmes things that they know how to do, and about which they have a fair degree of certainty what the outcomes will be. This is a paradox, for the reason why so much fails in development is because we often 'don't know how to do things'. A programme manager whose job depends on showing defined outcomes is not going to risk innovation or departure from a path that was pre-planned. This is the system dynamic. We see some important principles at work here: the starting conditions determine the nature of the programmes which are likely to ensue; the evaluation process that theoretically happens after the intervention fundamentally affects what happens and how the intervention is constructed.

Example 6: Unintended consequences of collectivized agriculture. This example of Soviet agriculture cited in Eyben (2010) is instructive:

> The Soviet Union was able to report that collectivised agriculture was an effective means for sustaining agricultural productivity. In practice, the farm workers put their energies not in the collective farm but in their own small holding, and pilfered collective-farm resources to invest in them, and it was this that led to sufficient food being produced for the authorities to be able to demonstrate that the overall system was working. Without the farm workers realising it, their subversion was maintaining the very system they were resisting (Scott, 1988).

The implication of all of these, and a myriad of other examples, is that to create sustainable change you need to change the system dynamics. Otherwise, the dominant pattern will re-establish itself, and any initiatives outside the dominant dynamic will remain outliers. Because system dynamics are never linear, changing system dynamics requires an understanding of how change is happening in non-linear ways, and the means by which that non-linear change can be influenced. Let us restate this in a different way because it is important: a system is a pattern of constant changes either in disequilibrium or in equilibrium. It is not something static. It is not enough to shift from one activity pattern to another. To create sustainable change, you have to shift from one system dynamic to another When we talk about the ways in which norms shift from one attractor pattern to another, this is because a whole system dynamic has shifted, not just an attitude or a position or a law, and so on. If this does not happen, existing system dynamics will eventually exercise enough force to undermine the innovative activity or, as we will see in the following example, will introduce its own innovation to create new balancing feedback loops in order to maintain the status quo.

In December 2012 there was a mass killing of schoolchildren at Sandy Hook in the US. This is not an unusual occurrence in the US, but once again there was a national outcry. Popular support for tighter gun control increased and President Obama said that he would introduce gun control. Few people thought it would be possible and this turned out to be the case. Why was this? Explanations range from the historical association between gun ownership and freedom, and the political power of National Rifle Association (NRA). So what happened in this case?

After the incident the dominant political and media message was that guns need to be controlled to reduce school killings. President Obama made his position clear, but this only produced a counter-narrative from the NRA. They argued that if all teachers had guns then school killings would be reduced. This position was generated as a reaction to the public backlash against gun ownership. The shift in system equilibrium was countered by novel inputs to recalibrate it. Balancing feedback can take multiple forms – in this case introducing a new narrative into the system. Before these events the idea of arming teachers might have appeared absurd. But once they have happened it is possible to open up new pathways, and once introduced to the system (even in an embryonic form) they have the potential to take hold and escalate. Eight months later it was reported that

> 'a plan by a small Arkansas school district to arm 20 teachers and staff with 9 mm handguns has run aground after the state attorney says the program is not covered by state law...' David Hopkins, superintendent of schools in Clarksville, a community of 9,200 people about 100 miles northwest of Little Rock, says the move was in response to last year's tragedy at Sandy Hook Elementary School in Connecticut that left 20 students and six staff members dead. (Stanglin, 2013)

This attempt was not successful but in Dakota a bill was passed to allow the state's school districts to arm teachers and other personnel with guns. This opens up the real possibility (which wasn't there before) that a teacher will accidentally kill a child with a gun, and that in turn will set off another train of events.

What we have described is a system that is constantly in flux – constantly forging a new equilibrium. In the case above, the pattern which remains constant is the norm of gun ownership within the US. But the flow of power, politics, activities, discourses, structures, and so on is constantly changing. So if you only look at the pattern, all you see is a picture of continued gun ownership norms, you don't see the dynamic forces which are constantly recreating that pattern. Seeing these systems as dynamic is really important because if our core task is to shift from one system dynamic to another, it is crucial to realize that the system dynamic that we are trying to change is already constantly changing.

Approaches to change and intervention

In the next chapter we explore the elements that are necessary to create sustainable change and scale. Before moving to these, we highlight two strong conclusions for working with complex change.

Focus on system dynamics

Peter Coleman and his colleagues (2011) argue for a six-stage process in thinking about how to engage with complexity within contexts of intractable conflict. They argue that it is necessary to see the system; to map its dynamics; through the mapping to locate gateways and leverage points; to make sure that we understand how things are changing over time; to create conditions for positive, adaptive latent attractors to emerge and be sustained internally; and to try to undermine negative and destructive attractors. The stages they outline map very closely onto the practices that we have been developing over the past decade or so and which are articulated in this book.

Working with system dynamics is a way of cutting to the heart of the matter. It does not involve mapping every detail of every process so as to identify each piece that is wrong and change it (responses to complicatedness). It involves identifying key triggers and catalysts, small upstream changes, and so on, which will disturb the equilibrium of a system dynamic and make it more likely that the balance shifts to new attractors that we may also have been involved in creating. Time, as Coleman points out, is crucial because after each change in the system everything in the system changes. So any effective change process must be iterative.

Lewin's (1946) articulation of forcefield analysis, in which he proposes that multiple small forces acting across a system against a large force might be just as effective as a large countervailing force, is also relevant here. This is because when we attack a problem head-on we often just generate balancing feedback. We saw this in the gun control example, where the backlash in both political terms (NRA influence on political votes) and in terms of the discourse (arming the school teachers) is at least as strong as the force that the president is able to exert. Another example of this can be seen in attempts to control pests and diseases such as malaria. As a result of introducing antimalarials, malaria has evolved and developed resistance, requiring the generation of new control measures, which may in turn generate just as strong a reaction, radically escalating the problem. This suggests that a more distributed strategy to change the system dynamic is likely to be more successful than a head-on challenge.

Ensure all change processes are iterative

After every step that is taken in any change process, a different set of options or pathways are available than were there (or perceived to be there) before the action was taken. Similarly new constraints are constantly emerging. Navigating this change successfully requires a higher degree of flexibility than is typical in current programme designs. In dynamic contexts, programmes need to be reassessed and reoriented at regular intervals. Change processes must be iterative.

An example of this is provided in Figure 2.3. The programme objective may be to get from A to 1. The theory of change is that A will lead to B will lead to C will lead to 1. Unfortunately, the programme planners didn't know that there was a major barrier (dotted line) preventing movement between A and B.

So while many programme managers would feel tied to B (and keep looking for new ways to get over (or under) the barrier because they have to follow

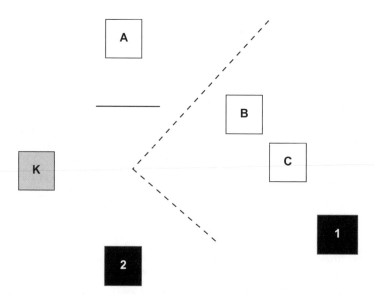

Figure 2.3 An iterative approach to decision-making
Source: Adapted from Burns, 2014

the theory of change that has been pre-constructed, a flexible programme manager might decide to go to K. She doesn't know the route from K to 1 but it looks more promising, so she heads toward K. When she gets to K she is able to see 2, which had previously been obscured (solid line). Now she has lots more options. If she still wants to go to 1 then K turns out to be a better route, but having moved past the wall (thick line) which obscured 2 she may discover that 2 is a better place to go.

What we have illustrated here is a model for integrating learning and action in development processes. It is how change happens in the real world, and it needs to underpin the way in which development interventions are conceptualized and designed.

The nature of the engagement in social systems that flows from complexity and systems thinking depends to some extent on the tradition within which you are working. Ramalingam's (2013) *Aid on the Edge of Chaos* deals with systems dynamics modelling, agent-based approaches, gaming approaches, and network analysis – and as such broadly follows and expands upon the more computational approach of the Santa Fe Institute. Although in his case studies he emphasizes the importance of social adaptations to these approaches. Using Net Map for collective decision-making for example, is articulated as a way of fusing computational methods with more participatory approaches. Others such as Snowden (2010) take a more constructivist approach which is closer to ours. Snowden argues for local engagement in multiple parallel *safe-to-fail* actions. These actions are generated from narratives gathered using a technique known as distributed ethnography, which reveals the potential that is in the system. Here the respondent tells a story and self-interprets it. Questions, such as 'what will I do to create more stories like these; fewer stories like those?', engage actors in locally contextual actions to influence the evolution of the system. Snowden's methods differ from ours because they focus on the positioning of whole stories in relation to a set of predefined criteria. Our work, which is rooted in the action research tradition allied to soft systems thinking (Checkland and Scholes, 2004), is built on a detailed analysis of the causalities and patterns within each story. In order to 'see the system' we collectively analyse detailed narratives to create a clear picture of the whole (see Chapter 4). We articulate two strategies for engagement with systems: a more structured and facilitated process – systemic action research – and a more organic process – nurtured emergent development (which we discuss in Chapters 5 and 6). Before we get to these we want to articulate a framework which illustrates what we think is required to enable interventions to go to scale and be sustainable.

Note

1. This example comes from a participatory inquiry facilitated by Danny in 2010 in the Kalangala Islands of Lake Victoria in Uganda. The inquiry involved working with people from across the islands to explore why they

thought the AIDS/HIV epidemic was so bad, and thinking through together what to do about it.

References

ActKnowledge and the Aspen Institute Roundtable on Comprehensive Community Initiatives (2003) 'How much should a good theory of change account for?' <http://www.theoryofchange.org/pdf/scope.pdf> [accessed 1 July 2015].

Befani, B. (2012) 'Models of causality and causal inference' in E. Stern, N. Stame, J. Mayne, K. Forss, R. Davies and B. Befani (eds), *Broadening the Range of Designs and Methods for Impact Evaluations*, DFID Working Paper 38, London: Department for International Development.

Bhaskar, R. (1978) *A Realist Theory of Science*, Brighton: Harvester Press.

Burns, D. (2007) *Systemic Action Research: A Strategy for Whole System Change*, Bristol: Policy Press.

Burns, D. (2014) 'Assessing impact in dynamic and complex environments: Systemic Action Research and Participatory Systemic Inquiry', CDI Practice Paper 8, Brighton: IDS

Checkland, P. and Scholes, J. (2004) *Soft Systems Methodology in Action*, Chichester: John Wiley.

Coleman, P.T. et al. (2011) 'Navigating the landscape of conflict: applications of dynamical systems theory to addressing protracted conflict' in D. Körppen, N. Ropers and H.J. Giessmann (eds.), *The Non-linearity of Peace Processes – Theory and Practice of Systemic Conflict Transformation*, Leverkusen: Barbara Budrich Publishers.

Collier, A. (1994) *Critical Realism: An Introduction to Roy Bhaskar's Philosophy*, London: Verso.

Eyben, R. (2010) 'Hiding relations: the irony of 'effective aid', *European Journal of Development Research* 22: 382–97.

Goldstein, J. (1999), 'Emergence as a construct: history and issues', *Emergence: Complexity and Organization* 1(1): 49–72.

Harvey, B., Burns, D. and Oswald, K. (2012) 'Linking community, radio, and action research on climate change: reflections on a systemic approach', *IDS Bulletin* 43(3): 101–17.

Juarrero, A. (1999) *Dynamics in Action: Intentional Behaviour as a Complex System*, Cambridge, MA: MIT Press.

Lewin, K. (1946) 'Action research and minority problems', *Journal of Social Issues* 2: 34–6.

Midgley, G. (2000) *Systemic Intervention: Philosophy, Methodology and Practice*, New York, NY: Kluwer Academic/Plenum Publishers.

Nowak, A., Bui-Wrzosinska, L., Coleman, P.T., Vallacher, R., Borkovsky, W. and Jochemczyk, L. (2010) Seeking sustainable solutions: Using an attractor simulation platform for teaching multi-stakeholder negotiation. *Negotiation Journal* 26(1), 49–68.

Ober, H. (2012) 'Peacebuilding with impact: defining theories of change', Research Report, CARE International UK <http://www.careinternational.org.uk/research-centre/conflict-and-peacebuilding/155-peacebuilding-with-impact-defining-theories-of-change> [accessed 28 July 2015].

Ramalingam, B. (2013) *Aid on the Edge of Chaos*, Oxford: Oxford University Press.

Ricigliano, R. (2011) 'A systems approach to peace building' <http://www.c-r.org/sites/default/files/Accord%2022_5A%20systems%20approach%20to%20peacebuilding_2011_ENG.pdf> [accessed 20 July 2015].

Sanders, T.I. (1998) *Strategic Thinking and the New Science: Planning in the Midst of Chaos, Complexity and Change*, New York, NY: The Free Press.

Sinha, K. (2012) WHO to declare polio global health emergency, *Times of India*, 15 May.

Snowden, D. (2010) 'Naturalizing sensemaking' in K.L. Mosier and U.M. Fischer (eds), *Informed by Knowledge: Expert Performance in Complex Situation*, pp. 223–34, New York, NY and Hove, UK: Psychology Press.

Snowden, D. (2012) 'Good fences make good neighbours', in W.B. Rouse, K.R. Boff and P. Sanderson (eds), *Complex Socio-Technical Systems: Understanding and Influencing Causality of Change*, Chapter 13), Amsterdam: IOS Press.

Stacey, R. (2010) *Complexity and Organisational Reality*, 2nd edn, London and New York, NY: Routledge.

Stanglin, D. (2013) 'Ark. School district's plan to arm teachers nixed by AG', *USA Today*, 2 August.

Vogel, I. (2012) 'Review of the use of "theory of change" in international development: Review report', London: UK Department of International Development.

CHAPTER 3
Catalysing large-scale and sustainable change

In this chapter we offer a framework which shows the elements that need to be in place to actively support system change, and we show the relationship between those elements. We argue that participation, learning, and network development provide the foundations for ownership and appropriate action, which in turn provide the foundations for scale and sustainability. Making sure that these are all present and deliberately acting to nurture the relationships between them is the key to sustainable large-scale change.

Keywords: participation; social innovation; scale; sustainability; system dynamics

A framework for catalysing systemic change

In this chapter we will explain what we see as prerequisites for catalysing and sustaining systemic change. We argue that participation, learning, and relationship and network building are the foundation stones upon which wider development aspirations must rest:

- *participation* in deliberation, decision-making processes and in action;
- *learning* to identify what change is needed and what change might be possible;
- *relationship* and *network building* to spread ideas and learning and to inspire new action.

The combination of these allows us to more clearly see the systems that we are engaging with, to understand the causalities that shape their dynamics (explored in detail in Chapter 4), and to learn what is necessary to engage with them (explored in detail in Chapters 5 and 6). We describe these as the critical process triangle. Through action, these processes generate:

- *appropriate interventions* that meet needs and that work; and
- *ownership* by stakeholders.

Appropriate interventions combined with strong networking leads to ownership, and ownership leads to:

- *sustainability* of outcomes;
- *scaling* of outcomes.

http://dx.doi.org/10.3362/9781780448510.003

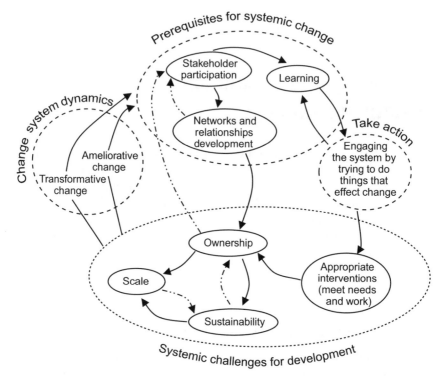

Figure 3.1 A framework for understanding how to achieve sustainable change at scale

We see these four as the key challenges for development, but they are inter-dependent and cannot be seen in isolation. We would argue that it is only when ownership is achieved that either scaling or sustainability will happen. The relationship between these elements is not linear (Figure 3.1). For example, it is only where there is appropriate action that there is ownership. Ownership feeds back into higher levels of participation, which in turn supports a learning process which reinforces appropriate action. This is in itself a depiction of a system with complex feedback loops.

Interventions that work well in a particular context cannot be achieved without processes of learning, underpinned by participation. Ownership is facilitated through networks, but can only come about if the interventions are appropriate. Where there is energy and enthusiasm (which comes from believing in the action that is taken) ownership will be generated and this in turn will ensure that activities are sustainable. Ideas and innovations only take off when there is a high level of ownership which is transmitted through networks – in the same way that a virus spreads through a population. Enthusiasm is built from a belief that something is important, and will actually make a difference; energy and momentum channelled through relationships.

Once this is established and there is a significant level of adoption, it is likely that participants will further evolve and adapt the innovation to meet the needs of its new context. Sustainability comes through a combination of ownership and appropriate interventions, and scale comes about through a combination of network development, ownership, and sustainability. It is only if the four challenges of ownership, appropriateness, sustainability, and scale are met that meaningful change which benefits the poorest and most marginalized is possible.

This change can take two forms or pathways. The first of these works to ameliorate the impacts of negative system dynamics, to create improvements for people's lives within unchanged power relationships. The second pathway works to transform system dynamics and power relationships. Palliative programming that addresses symptoms rather than causes can, in the short term, ameliorate the worst effects of damaging system dynamics. For example, people who are struggling to make a subsistence livelihood may be supported through some sort of social protection programme, but this does not mean that the system that produces the inequalities has changed in any way at all. Similarly, enabling girls to get education in countries where there are persistent gender inequalities is intrinsically a good thing, but it may have no direct effect on gender relations where, say, women are forced into a domestic life as soon as they marry. Instead of being transformative, these participatory processes are designed to accommodate system patterns that underpin systemic inequality. Here, projects and programmes seek to intervene in acceptance of system power imbalances and seek to relieve the burden that these entail. Njuki et al. 2013, p. 5) state that

> Gender accommodating projects accept existing gender relations while recognising that gender inequalities exist. Rather than address the root cause of gender inequalities and inequities, or interfere with existing gender power imbalances, the projects are designed to relieve the burden of the disadvantaged gender – e.g. providing a well to a village to reduce women's drudgery in water collection.

It has long been the rhetoric of good development work that interventions should aim to address the underlying causes of poverty. This would mean that system dynamics and patterns have been fundamentally changed. For example, were gender relationships to change such that women were able to work outside the home, where once they could not, a fundamental system dynamic would have changed. This does not mean that discrimination has gone away, for women may still have to do all of the domestic work as well as work outside the home. But it does mean that there has been a deeper change in the dynamics of the system. Transformative change is essentially change which shifts power relations – those which are directly coercive and those that are embedded in practices, discourses, and social norms which shape the pathways within which it is possible to enact agency. These can be seen as the dynamics of the system. Transformative change can only happen if it creates changes to the dynamics of a system.

These two types of change are not unconnected. Positive changes within the system can reinforce a dominant system of relations within which they sit.

Conversely they may have wider effects on the system which contribute indirectly to transformative change. Sustainable change is more likely to be change that fundamentally shifts the system dynamic. As we have articulated above, participation is critical to both of these pathways, but they have quite different political implications.

Pre-requisites for systemic change

In this section, we explore the three underpinning processes that are critical to system change: participation, learning, and relationship and network building.

Participation

We will discuss the nature of participation in more detail in Chapter 8. Here we want to show how an action-oriented framing of participation relates to learning and networks. There are profoundly functional reasons why participation is a prerequisite for change in complex social systems. People are the essential agents that make up complex social systems. Knowledge about social system dynamics is rooted in their experiences and is held by them. People's insight into what is needed and what will work can only be revealed when they are heard and able to engage. Participation from people who have a diversity of experiences fundamentally underpins the learning process which is crucial to developing effective action. But, also, people have a right to be heard and a right to engage in the issues that affect their lives; and when people feel that they have a personal investment in a process, this leads through networks of social relationships to strong community ownership. This, as we will articulate in more detail, leads to sustainability and scale. Participation can be seen as a foundation stone without which these are not possible in complex environments.

Typically in international development, participation takes place in a space constructed by governments, donors or NGOs within which people can discuss issues. Sometimes these are generated by the people themselves, but more often than not they are generated by those that set up the space (Gaventa, 2005). Within these spaces people are able to articulate their views, which may or may not be acted upon. Rarely is there an opportunity for people to analyse the data that they generate themselves or for them to act directly upon it. This is not the sort of participation we are talking about in this book.

We will describe two forms of participation, both of which are centred on action. The first is engagement in a more structured systemic action research process where the aim is to generate evidence in order to understand what action needs to take place and then to take action with others. The second is a more organic process where action is stimulated. It is observed and assessed and, if it successful, others begin to join in. Here we are drawing on the principles of action research, but we are constructing action research as a 'practice' rather than as a project or a programme. Yoland Wadsworth (2010) depicts this as the inherent practice of everyday life (see Chapter 6 for more details). At an individual level we are constantly alert. We are cycling and we go over a bump and the wheel turns and we automatically adjust it to compensate. Our challenge is to bring some sort of intentionality to that adjustment at the level of the system while knowing that we cannot control it. As processes move to scale, this form of action can be seen as more akin to building a social movement, and its mechanism is described well by the idea of shifting from one attractor to another.

When we talk about participation in this way we are describing a social process by which people take action and others either reject it or move towards it. If it is resonant enough – which means that it must be appropriate, work, and be meaningful to people's lives – then it will act as an attractor. As we discovered in the last chapter, in order to change the dynamics of system, it is necessary to create alternative attractors – deeper underlying shifts in perceptions, relationships, and attitudes, to provide foundations for new points of convergence to emerge. Once these reach a critical mass, tipping points occur which allow a shift in the pattern of social relationships to a new attractor. So participation in this context is either the enactment of innovative action or its adoption, followed by adaptation of action catalysed by others. Participation is not just about sitting in meetings; it is about acting directly to shift system patterns.

It is worth noting here that action can mean many things. Changing a discourse (Cornwall and Brock, 2005) is an action which in turn opens up space for different forms of action. Similarly, if someone sends a remittance back to their family when they are working as a Nepalese immigrant in Dubai, and others follow suit, then they are participating in building a system of remittances. If people build on this to create collectivized forms of giving or effective money transfer systems, they are participating in the adaptations that are transforming the social system. These are all forms of participatory action.

Learning

Participation is very limited without the capacity to learn. This is partly why the action research tradition is often linked to a Freirian notion of pedagogical empowerment, where learning is constructed around the development of critical consciousness of the world, exploring perceptions to and exposure of social and political contradictions (Freire, 1972). Rather than doing all learning before an initiative, we do it as we go along. This can be done in a structured way through systemic action research. When new knowledge and ideas are introduced into systems, it is important that there is a process to test these to see how helpful they are. Learning of this type requires the construction of a learning architecture comprised of learning processes across a system with strong connections, both horizontally and vertically.

In an action research process, participants analyse the situation, develop theories of change, plan action, take action, and then assess the impact of that action. After this cycle they analyse the situation again. It is at this point that they ask, firstly, given what we know are we still heading in the right direction and, secondly, if we are, is this still the best way to get there. This allows them to be flexible and to change course as they go. It means that they need to constantly generate and review theories of change in the light of new evidence. Effective learning involves hearing something new and then connecting it to what you already have, and doing something about it. It does not involve transplanting it uncritically into your circumstances. Action research cycles thus work to test innovations and where they need to change, to adapt these and test them again. This iterative process is an exercise in exploration that makes the important distinction between adoption and adaptation. Where adaptation does not happen, we often see the repetition of inappropriate interventions.

In the more organic processes of nurtured emergent development which we discuss in Chapter 6, there also have to be opportunities for people to learn about what others are doing, to take action, and to learn through experience and deliberation with their peers and others about what worked and what did not.

Relationship and network building

In complex social systems, knowledge, trust and enthusiasm flow through the relationships that connect people to one another. Naturally formed around dynamics of interest and power, social relationships describe the range of formal and informal arrangements through which people make sense and act and do things that matter to them.

Relationship and network building is crucial to the transfer of knowledge, but perhaps more importantly it is crucial to trust and social capital. Social capital is defined by the OECD as 'networks together with shared norms, values and understandings that facilitate co-operation within or among groups' (Keeley, 2007). Under this definition, we can think of networks as real-world links between groups or individuals – networks of friends, family networks, networks of former colleagues, and so on. Sociologists sometimes speak of norms as society's unspoken and largely unquestioned rules. Norms and understandings may not become apparent until they're broken. If adults attack children, for example, they breach the norms that protect children from harm. Values may be more open to question; indeed societies often debate whether their values are changing. And yet values – such as respect for people's safety and security – are an essential linchpin in every social group. Networks are the conduits through which norms are communicated and trust is established. These are key ingredients which people to work together (Keeley, 2007).

The distinction between strong ties and weak ties (Granovetter 1973) is a much-rehearsed theoretical framing, particularly in social capital literature.

Strong ties are based on community and kinship identities and affection. Weak ties are looser and more diverse connections. Strong ties lead to solidarity and mutual aid. Weak ties have a greater reach and can mobilize more people from diverse backgrounds in support of an endeavour. One of the more neglected aspects of the weak ties arguments is that a wider network of very different people allows people to 'see the system' more effectively from multiple perspectives. This in turn (as we discuss in detail in Chapters 5 and 6) allows them to navigate the system and work out where the leverage points within the systems are. They are able to see the fault lines and the flows of power, and the different interests and perspective in ways which people who don't have a range of weak ties cannot do. So a key task of the systemic facilitator must then be to develop ways of extending those networks, and reaching across these.

A central message from a range of our recent research projects is that relationships are as important as the activities themselves – because the activities flow from the relationships. This is an important point because there is a tendency to see relationships as forming pragmatically when the need arises for action, but in fact a lot of action arises because of the relationships. A key conclusion of an action research project on the impact of volunteering on poverty (Burns et al., 2015) was that where volunteers have made a difference, it is where they have spent time building relationships. When they live within communities and become embedded they gain access to local networks. Conversely, the communities that they are living with gain access to the volunteers' networks. This works best where there are long-term and sustained relationships with communities which do not break down when projects end. What is vital here is that networking is regarded as an intentional activity which is a prerequisite for sustainable change, not just as something that is there (to be harnessed) or not there. This was a central message of Alison Gilchrist's work on networks in community development. For her, the core practice of community development was the intentional building of relationships and supporting of network development (Gilchrist, 2004). Ramalingam (2013) similarly argues that 'the network is the development'. This is important because, if networks are limited, then the ability of processes to go to scale will be extremely limited.

Processes that foster participation, learning, and networks equip change agents with the means to generate critical knowledge about system dynamics, and to make informed choices about possible action.

Four systemic challenges for development

We argue that there are four systemic challenges for international development. Firstly, actions and interventions that are undertaken by and with people must be fit for purpose, and hence appropriate. This means that they work well for the people who are supposed to benefit from them. Secondly, people have to want the solutions and be enthused by them. This results in local commitment and ownership. Thirdly, results must be able to reach considerable scale. Finally, development actions need to be sustainable. This means that actions and their results need to persist over time – be sustainable as dynamics change and with increases in scale. Appropriateness, ownership, sustainability, and scale are not new ideas. Yet they have remained elusive to development actors. In this section, we explore these ideas and their interrelationship in more detail.

Appropriate actions and interventions

An appropriate action or intervention is one which people need and want, and one which works. In Chapter 1, we highlighted a range of large-scale development initiatives which simply didn't meet the needs of people. There are many reasons why the interventions of development actors are not fit for purpose. They are often answering a problem that is not a priority, or in some cases even an issue, for local people. The underlying rationale for initiatives may not actually be about people at all. Schraeder et al. (1998) concluded that trade remained an important determinant of northern aid policies, not altruism. There are many theories that correlate donor investments and political agendas and there is explicit evidence to link the two. For example, the business case for the DFID programme on Access to Finance for Development explicitly cites British commercial interests as a core goal: 'financial access which induces growth will play a major role in stability and promoting prosperity, and also create an environment for increasing UK commercial interests in Kenya in the long term' (DFID 2011).

Other programmes will have security interests as a central goal. Still others are based on trickle-down theories that deliver few positive benefits to the poorest and most marginalized, and often create serious damage (Burns et al., 2013). During Stuart's early professional years, he was assigned to work in the animal husbandry department of a provincial agricultural university in Irian Jaya (Western Papua), a remote province in Indonesia. This was a lower-tier faculty where even basic field trials had yet to start. A Japanese development investment initiative placed a new scanning electron microscope within a new laboratory constructed to house the microscope. The university had unreliable electricity supplies, could not afford the consumables required by the microscope, and had no research programme underway that could use it. Its functionality was its novelty and the status that the university could have because of its presence. In the simplest of terms, it did not fit within the prevailing research context of the university. It was part of a wider grand scheme to upgrade educational and research facilities across the country. It remained unused for the three years that he was there. As we have seen in Chapter 1, narratives of white elephant projects abound as testament to past development adventures. Robinson and Torvik (2004) argue that these projects are often built in the full knowledge that they are white elephants, because there are political drivers behind them.

We have already talked about the problems of rooting initiatives in predictive logics which generate flawed assumptions. There is also a deep problem with expert knowledge which is not generated by people who have a day-to-day understanding of the issues. The best technical solutions are not necessarily the best local ones:

> To support a better fit between programme and context, it may be that chosen interventions are not technically the most efficient or effective, but are justified as the most appropriate for influencing change within the social, political and environmental realities of their particular context. (Vogel 2012: 5)

The data upon which policies are based is often aggregated to give synthesized statements that indicate how many people are affected, but gives little sense of why these symptoms occur. In reporting findings of a case study, International Livestock Research Institute (ILRI) researcher Jo Cadilhon notes that 'Tables of numbers are not enough to take decisions; decision makers also need the stories related to the numbers' (Cadilhon, 2015). As we will see in the next section, local stories are crucial to understanding how and why things happen and to surfacing system dynamics.

Expert advice aims to forecast possible changes and offers interventions and policies to engage this. Yet, the complexity of social systems where such interventions take place compels experts to reduce the number of variables. The environmental scientist Wynne (1992) notes that 'These practices artificially reduce uncertainties and variations, for example by the ways in which averaging, standardization, and aggregation are performed.'

He goes on to observe:

> The conventional view is that scientific knowledge and method enthusiastically embrace uncertainties and exhaustively pursue them. This is seriously misleading. It is more accurate to say that scientific knowledge gives prominence to a restricted agenda of defined uncertainties – ones that are tractable – leaving invisible a range of other uncertainties, especially about the boundary conditions of applicability of the existing framework of knowledge to new situations.

Well-intentioned initiatives can generate unintended consequences which render them completely useless. One example is the Education for All initiative of the Kenyan government. Following the election of President Kibaki in 2002, the government embarked on an ambitious programme to ensure access to education for all, and mandated that all government schools should offer free education. While well intentioned, this resulted in public classrooms overflowing, with poorly paid teachers having to handle class sizes of 40 students or more. In many cases there were no desks and chairs, leaving children to sit on dirt floors. By 2012, Deutsche Welle reported that 'Many children drop out of the free, public elementary schools before reaching eighth grade because of unmet needs for school uniforms and shoes, books, pencils and notebooks. Many families cannot afford to provide their children with the necessities for school' (Verweyen, 2012). In Chapter 6 we explore a case in Afghanistan where parent-managed schools created bespoke opportunities that enabled girls and boys to access schools despite the prohibitions of government.

Some processes have been more adaptive: for example, the establishment of primary schools for children in transhumant pastoralist communities. School attendance means that children do not accompany the herds, and learn to read and write instead of how to herd cattle. This means that it becomes unattractive to a pastoralist family to send children to school for this compromises herd management and consequently household livelihood security. In Kenya some elements in government seem committed to finding alternative occupations for pastoral communities and seem unconcerned that that schooling compromises pastoralist food security, for they feel it incentivizes pastoralists to exit transhumant lifestyles, release land for settlement, and reduce land-based conflict. None of this is lost on the pastoralists who immediately equate basic education for children as being part of a wider mosaic of social engineering designed to undermine their cultural identity. Mobile schools have emerged as a way of enabling education to migrate with herds. Tested within pastoralist groups in North Kenya, they have had some success in making education acceptable to pastoralists (Seager, 2010). This process stands in stark contrast to that observed by Ramalingam (2013) in his discussion of rangelands. He observed:

> The lack of fit between the proposed solutions and the local context created numerous conflicts, which agency staff struggled to deal with. Modifications were made to deal with the lack of co-operation and compliance amongst target populations. But, interestingly, the most common response of the range managers was to suggest changes to the local context to make it suited to the imposed solutions. (Ramalingam 2013: 37)

Development interventions that do not deliberately and continuously take the wider system into account become futile. Providing education in a context where a high percentage of children are drug users or where children have to water the crops may be pretty futile unless the underlying issues are addressed. Appropriate action therefore requires a strongly participatory local process which supports local people to learn from their situation (and from others who may have something to offer to their situation) and to clearly articulate their needs. It is only then that scale and sustainability become possible.

Ownership, enthusiasm, and adoption

People adopt and organize around things that they have energy and enthusiasm for. These are things that they are motivated by, feel passionate about, and think will make a difference. This commitment comes about through direct experience or through trusted recommendation. When people have a real stake in something that they care about, they feel ownership. Ownership is different to 'participation' because it means that people legitimize it and take responsibility for it themselves. This means that they are not dependent, which is critical to sustainability and scale.

In general, spontaneous action follows enthusiasm. Hoggett and Bishop (1986) document the work of enthusiasts who indulge their passion collectively by participating in groups and observe the considerable organizational evolution that emanates from focus on such enthusiasm. They write of the way in which hundreds of people organized into hundreds of groups in a small part of London in the UK. The core argument was that things happen because people are enthusiastic about them. This could be gardening together, organizing a political rally or having discussions in tea shops. It is in these places that relationships are made, that discourse takes place, that ideas and knowledge are transferred, and that inspiration is sparked. In our view, it is from this inspiration and these connections that sustainable change is driven.

A simple example of community ownership comes from some work we were doing in Kisii in Kenya, where we were carrying out an inquiry into water and sanitation in the poorest Nubian part of the town. Some years ago a multimillion pound investment had been made in three combined toilet, clean water, and washing facilities. Within weeks of being finished they had been vandalized, and stripped down so that the parts could be sold. Very recently, in exactly the same place, UN-Habitat had installed a clean water tap. They gained the support of the local women's group who organized as a cooperative and sold the water at a very small profit. They also made enough to distribute some water free to some women who were very poor. This facility was never vandalized because it had support, engagement, and ownership by key members of the local community – in this case the women's group. There was much talk about building on this learning and renovating the two old blocks that were further down the hill. There were already discussions with the widows' group and the youth group – each of which wanted to run one of the toilet facilities.

Participation leads to ownership. Learning combined with participation leads to appropriateness. Together these lead to commitment to maintain a process, enthusiasm for a process, the attraction of energy to that process, the spread of the process, and the scale-up of the process.

Scale

There is a strong imperative to ensure that development actions that achieve good impact and address critical problems and issues encountered by the poorest go to scale. When we talk about scale, we refer to the size of the effect. We will argue that scale should not be articulated as 'extensive roll-out', rather as an increasingly accelerated 'take-up', and 'adaptation' of ideas that work.

Development scaling theorists Hartmann and Linn (2008) define scaling up as expanding, replicating, adapting, and sustaining successful policies, programmes, and projects in a geographic space, which over time reach a greater number of people. Their framework for scaling up places strong emphasis on pathways for scaling. Chandy and Linn (2011) define these as the 'Sequences of events that need to be taken in the innovation-learning-scaling up cycle to assure that a successful pilot or practice is taken from its experimental stage through subsequent stages to the scale ultimately judged to be appropriate for the intervention pursued'.

Hartmann and Linn (2008) describe models, vision, catalyst, and incentive as the principle drivers of scale, and define planning steps for scaling to happen. Others have differentiated between vertical and horizontal scaling. Menter et al. (2004) describe scaling up as leading to more quality benefits to more people over a wider geographic area more quickly, more equitably, and more lastingly. They add that this implies increasing the impact of an innovation or intervention. They go on to cite the CGIAR NGO committee definitions of vertical and horizontal scaling.

> Vertical scaling-up is moving higher up the ladder. It is institutional in nature and involves other sectors/stakeholder groups in the process of expansion – from the level of grassroots organizations to policy makers, donors, development institutions, and investors at international levels.

> Horizontal scaling up (or scaling out) is geographical spread to cover more people and communities through replication and adaptation, and involves expansion within the same sector or stakeholder group. Decision making is at the same social scale.

These approaches to scale focus on the extent to which development interventions themselves are able to expand. They focus on the institutions that intervene to find ways and means to enable them to manage ever-larger and more far-reaching processes. The assumption here is that interventions that work can be replicated across wider space.

Scaling up processes typically involve generating innovative ideas, piloting, redesigning programmes based on a pilot, funding large-scale production of process or product, and mass roll-out. To illustrate this, in 2013, Hartmann et al. (2013) reported four common approaches to scaling, by

- unbundling components of projects and scaling up successful parts;
- replicating and adapting area development projects that are focused on well identified, narrow poverty groups;
- scaling up comprehensive rural poverty programmes at national level;
- replicating (sub)sectoral interventions at national level.

The assumption is that once a 'best-practice' is discovered, it can be rolled out: thus we roll out things we know how to do; things that people in positions of power think are a good idea; and we expand innovations which appear to be effective on a small scale.

One of the problems with this approach is that even if the context is similar (which it often isn't), scale changes the dynamics of a system so that the environment that existed for the pilot is no longer the environment that the mass roll-out is going into. Moreover, pilots often attract greater levels of resources, closer attention from policymakers and so on. They often have innovative and strong managers with good facilitation skills. This is often not the case for programmes that are rolled out.

There are occasions where roll-out may work. Typically this would be in relatively controlled environments where the effect of the intervention is likely to be consistent across contexts and where there is a relatively uncontested view of the intervention itself. An example of this has been the mass manufacture and provision of mosquito nets as an anti-malaria strategy. But we would argue that an understanding of how change happens takes us in a different direction. It does not necessarily require large-scale intervention to achieve large-scale effect. The dominant narrative equates scale of intervention with the scale of outcome. This has meant that in the pursuit of big effects, big projects and programmes have been designed as a controlled 'big hit' on a big problem. Yet we also know that it is often small things placed carefully in the right place that achieve massive scale. Any demolition engineer will know that it is not the size of the charge that collapses a massive structure so much as the placing of the charge. The distinction to make here is that scale of intervention and scale of effect are very different.

Achieving scale of effect comes through catalysing emergent processes. Take-up is a better conceptual underpinning for scaling than roll-out. Take-up implies that there is a demand for change that takes hold and spreads in a manner akin to a movement – in a similar way that a virus spreads through a population. In the coming chapters, we will describe cases where small actions were able to achieve national scale in this way.

So far, we have argued that by using participatory practices, fostering a practice and culture of learning, and ensuring that this happens across relationship-based networks, we can stimulate both ownership of action and foster a process of innovation adaptation. The nexus of owned issues and appropriate solutions creates the space for a potential scale-up of effect as a result of take-up, and this leads to a phenomenon that is more akin to a social movement. There is one final facet that we must now explore, and it is that of sustainability. Scale will not persist (or even happen) unless the scaled form is sustainable.

Sustainability

In Chapter 2 we introduced the idea of attractors and described these as an equilibrium of social relations which form into a consistent pattern of system dynamics. Sustainability is enabled by shifting system dynamics toward new attractors. In any system, various norms of behaviour and activity predominate. Those norms are held in place by forces which we can call drivers. It is often difficult for dissident action to survive outside those norms because drivers pull them back into line. This means that it may be relatively easy to create a change but much more difficult to sustain it.

Let us give a local example that we have been directly engaged in from a UK context. This is the issue of open access to information. Open access is generally desirable for a lot of reasons. In a development context, this is particularly so as knowledge (research findings and other knowledge), which is often to be found in research journals, should be available to those who cannot afford it. Yet a very high proportion of that knowledge is published in journals owned by just three publishers. Few Southern institutions can afford the high prices. It would be possible for individuals and institutions to bypass these entirely and simply publish their work on the Internet. However, individual academics in universities have to submit articles for the Research Excellence Framework (REF). The REF is a process which takes place every five to seven years, and ranks universities based on the quality of their research. This quality is assessed on very traditional criteria. Articles in particularly well-ranked journals score highly, others less so. Publications published on the Internet largely count for nothing. This process is very important because the income that universities get relates to their ranking in the REF. So if you want a job in higher education, then you need to publish in the journals. If you decide to publish everything you do on the Internet, then you won't get promoted, so it is not in anyone's personal interest to do so. A department within a university could collectively decide to stand against this norm, but most would quickly be pulled back into the system dynamic. Thus the change would be unsustainable. This makes sustainable change problematic because to get a critical mass there has to be a deeper change in the nature of the conversations that people are having, and there has to be a new attractor that has a strong enough system dynamic to maintain its own integrity and not get pulled into the old dynamic. We will talk much more about all of this in the next chapter, but for now the crucial point is that sustainable change is not possible unless we change the system dynamics within which that change is taking place.

To reach the stage where we can change system dynamics, it is worth reflecting on a system familiar to all of us. Our bodies are complex systems within which equilibrium is maintained through changing environments. Our immune system plays an important role here. When a person experiences organ failure, medical science offers transplantation as an option. This would seem to be a straightforward process of simple replacement of a deficient part, yet things are not that straightforward. Although a new organ is apparently the right thing, the transplant needs to be carefully matched and must be accompanied by an elaborate cocktail of medication to prevent its rejection. Although apparently perfect, the replacement organ is not immediately fit for purpose. The body reacts to expel the foreign part despite the fact that its presence is objectively desirable. By contrast, one does not hear of organs being rejected by the bodies within which they were formed. This fact has heralded the advent of stem cell research as a means to generate replacement organs from within affected patients. The principle here is that elements that grow from within the system are not rejected by the system. They are intrinsic and this enables their function to persist. They are sustainable because they are owned.

Conclusion

Seeking system change has profound implications on the way in which we look to stimulate sustainable development. If we are able to nurture intrinsic processes, or change system dynamics in ways that would allow for intrinsic processes to emerge, we will revolutionize the way in which we achieve results. We will cease to seek to smash development rocks with ever bigger hammers and work towards a smarter form of development that engages complex systems. What we have presented in this chapter is an integrated model which shows the prerequisites of both sustainability and scale. Without understanding how these interrelate, large-scale interventions are unlikely to succeed.

References

Burns, D., Howard, J., Lopez-Franco, E., Shahrokh, T. and Wheeler, J. (2013) 'Work with us: how communities and organisations can catalyse sustainable change', Brighton: IDS.

Burns, D., Aked, J., Hacker, E., Lewis, S. and Picken, A. (2015) 'The role of volunteering in sustainable development', Brighton: Institute of Development Studies/VSO.

Cadilhon, J. (2015) 'Hard numbers and soft stories: Reaching policymakers and empowering women in Africa's agrifood value chains', 12 May <http://livelihoods-gender.ilri.org/2015/05/12/hard-numbers-and-soft-stories-reaching-policymakers-and-empowering-women-in-africas-agrifood-value-chains/> [accessed June 2015].

Chandy, L. and Linn, J.F. (2011) 'Taking development activities to scale in fragile and low capacity environments', Global Economy and Development Working Paper 45, September, Brookings Institute.

Cornwall, A. and Brock, K. (2005) 'What do buzzwords do for development policy? A critical look at "participation", "empowerment" and "poverty reduction"', *Third World Quarterly* 26(7): 1043–60.

Department for International Development (DFID) (2011) 'Intervention summary, Access to Finance for Development (AFFORD)' <http://iati.dfid.gov.uk/iati_documents/3717485.docx> [accessed June 2015].

Freire, P. (1972) *The Pedagogy of the Oppressed*, London: Penguin.

Gaventa, J. (2005) 'Reflections on the uses of the "power cube": approach for analysing the spaces, places and dynamics of civil society participation and engagement', Brighton: IDS.

Gilchrist, A. (2004) *The Well-Connected Community: A Networking Approach to Community Development*, Bristol: Policy Press.

Granovetter, M. (1973) 'The strength of weak ties', *American Journal of Sociology* 78(6): 1360–80.

Hartmann, A. and Linn, J. (2008) 'Scaling up: a framework and lessons for development effectiveness from literature and practice', Working Papers no. 5, Wolfensohn Center for Development, The Brookings Institution.

Hartmann, A., Kharas, H., Kohl, R., Linn, J., Massler, M. and Sourang, C. (2013) 'Scaling up programs for the rural poor: IFAD's experience, lessons and prospects (phase 2); global economy and development', Working Paper 54, January, Global Economy and Development at Brookings, p. 37.

Hoggett, P. and Bishop, J. (1986) *Organising around Enthusiasms: Patterns of Mutual Aid in Leisure*, London: Comedia.

Keeley, B. (2007) 'Human capital. How what you know shapes your life', OECD Insights. <http://www.oecd.org/insights/37966934.pdf> [accessed 8 July 2015].

Menter, H., Kaaria, S., Johnson, N. and Ashby, J. (2004) 'Scaling up, in D. Pachico and S. Fujisaka (eds), *Scaling Up and Out: Achieving Widespread Impact through Agricultural Research*, Chapter 1, Cali, Colombia: Centro Internacional de Agricultura Tropical (CIAT) 2004, Publication no 340, Economics and Impact Series 3.

Njuki, J., Waithanji, E., Bagalwa, N. and Kariuki, J. (2013) 'Guidelines on integrating gender in livestock projects and programs', International Livestock Research Institute (ILRI).

Ramalingam, B. (2013) *Aid on the Edge of Chaos*, Oxford: Oxford University Press.

Robinson, J.A. and Torvik, R. (2004) 'White elephants', *Journal of Public Economics* 89: 197–210.

Schraeder, P.J., Hook, S.W. and Taylor, B. (1998) 'Clarifying the foreign aid puzzle: a comparison of American, Japanese, French and Swedish aid flows', *World Politics* 50(2): 294–323.

Seager, A. (2010) 'Kenya's nomads welcome mobile schools', *The Guardian*. <http://www.theguardian.com/business/2010/jan/20/kenya-mobile-schools-initiative> [accessed 8 July 2015].

Verweyen, G. (2012) 'Kenya: unequal access to the school system', *Deutsch Welle*. http://www.dw.de/kenya-unequal-access-to-the-school-system/a-15880333 [accessed 8 July 2015].

Vogel, I. (2012) 'Review of the use of "theory of change" in international development: review report', London: Department of International Development.

Wadsworth, Y. (2010) *Building in Research and Evaluation: Human Inquiry for Living Systems*, Melbourne: Action Research Press and Allen & Unwin.

Wynne, B. (1992) 'Uncertainty and environmental learning', *Global Environmental Change* 2(2): 111–27.

CHAPTER 4

Seeing the system – participatory systemic inquiry

This chapter explores different ways of seeing the system. It focuses on two approaches both of which are underpinned by a narrative analysis. Systemic issue mapping enables the dynamics of complex systems to be seen. This in turn allows participants to identify leverage points within a system where action can be taken. System maps can be created from a variety of data including interview and focus transcripts, and life stories. Once these are collected, groups collectively analyse the stories and represent causalities and patterns on the large maps, enabling them to see the whole, and to see the relationships between the many factors depicted on the maps. Systemic story analysis allows us to see how system dynamics play out in the lives of individuals. This chapter shows how these processes work and illustrates with examples how system dynamics are revealed.

Keywords: system mapping; issue mapping; narrative analysis; life stories; participatory research

Approaches to seeing the system

Having laid out the reasons why we need to engage with complexity in international development and identified the key elements in that process, we now turn substantively to the question of how to do that. Chapters 4, 5 and 6 are a mixture of case studies and practical guidance on how to construct systemic change processes. In Chapter 2 we argued that in order to create deep and lasting change it is necessary to change the system dynamics that characterize the system that we are trying to engage with. In order to do this it is necessary to *see the system*. To be slightly more accurate we need to see the 'system(s)' because everyone concerned will see both the boundaries of a system and the interconnections within it differently. We can begin to understand how systems work through inquiry and through sense-making processes which surface the system dynamics. We call this participatory systemic inquiry (PSI).

PSI can be a stand-alone piece of work which informs programming and policy. It can feed into a systemic action research process, and it can directly stimulate action. These different trajectories are explored in the next chapter. PSI is a foundational inquiry which is able to provide a comprehensive starting point (first cut) on all of the critical issues that need to be resolved and the system dynamics which underpin them, and which can lay down a baseline depiction of those interrelationships that can be interrogated and adapted

http://dx.doi.org/10.3362/9781780448510.004

Table 4.1 Two types of PSI

Mapping-based PSI	Story-based PSI
Systemic issue and relationship maps leading to ...	Life stories leading to ...
distilled system dynamic maps	narratives of system dynamics as they impact on individuals
Case study 1: the Lake Victoria Water and Sanitation programme (p. 80)	Case study 1: the Bangladesh 'we can also make change' projects (p. 90)
	Case study 2: the Participate Initiative (p. 93)
Case study 2: the Ghana Community Radio Network Climate Change project (p. 87)	Case study 3: Systemic story analysis 3 – coda on the Ghana Community Radio Network Climate Change project (p. 97)

over time. This can then feed directly into programmes, into local action, or into an organized systemic action research process.

There are perhaps many ways to do this, but our work over the past seven or eight years has centred on two, shown in Table 4.1.

In the first column the inquiry process explores the interrelation of factors across a social system through a process of systemic mapping. Here we move from the creation of large-scale messy maps to the development of more distilled system dynamic maps. In the second column a story-based approach leads to the identification of systemic patterns through a collective analysis of change in individual lives. What is common to both of these processes is that they are rooted in the experiences of those people that will be the central beneficiaries of the inquiry (and any outcomes generated from it) and that the analysis is done by them and their peers. There is of course some overlap as mapping-based approaches may often draw on life stories (as well as the many other data sources) and story-based approaches create implicit, if not drawn, system maps.

Some key underpinnings for systemic inquiry work

In Chapter 2 we explored the way in which multiple factors across a system impacted upon each other. We showed how complex feedback loops can easily move beyond pre-constructed boundaries and have major impacts on wider system dynamics. We showed how small changes made at critical leverage points in the system could open up new pathways, and how concentrations of relationships and energy can create latent attractors which will lead to tipping points and beyond. So how do we need to design our inquiry process so that we can see these dynamics?

It is necessary to see systems from multiple perspectives

The system that everyone sees is different; the connections they see are different; the vision they have of different parts of the system is different; their interpretation of what is important is different. To understand how a social system works, it is important to see it from multiple perspectives and to juxtapose them in order to discern what people see in common and what they see differently. These differences can be debated in real time 'over the maps'. Maps can be compared and patterns identified. Seeing systems from multiple perspectives drives innovation and change so in a structured process of scaling, creating conditions under which diverse people and ideas can germinate innovation is absolutely crucial and in order to do this it is important to build a picture from very different parts of the system. Through his engagement with the UN post-2015 process, Danny compared the High Level Panel (HLP) with a series of Ground Level Panels (GLPs) of people from poor and marginalized backgrounds:

> One thing that struck me was the difference in composition of the HLP and the GLPs. The HLP was made up of people largely from an elite political class. There was the odd member of royalty and a few interesting academics thrown in, but by and large they were high ranking politicians. There was very little diversity in the group, and the interests were narrow. The GLPs on the other hand were highly diverse. Slum dwellers sitting side by side with pastoralists, transgender people, and people living in refugee camps … It is easy to stereotype people as 'poor' and see them as a huge sprawling undifferentiated 'category', but they bring far more diversity than people who hold power. (Burns, 2014)

It is very easy to create groups of 'people like us' and this has to be intentionally countered. When we do this we are able to bring into our frame of reference:

- dominant narratives;
- alternative and conflicted narratives; and
- hidden narratives.

The dominant narratives are the ones which reinforce the existing balance of power and which shape and maintain local social norms. Alternative narratives are counter-narratives which emerge from different locations within a system. These narratives are often, but not always, conflictual. For example, when we are looking at female genital mutilation, the narratives of the human rights NGOs are in conflict with those of the tribal leaders. An alternative narrative might come from women who are promoting a different way of creating initiation ceremonies for girls. Together these depict power relationships and schisms within local social relations. Hidden narratives are those that are not immediately visible. They are important because they can provide insight into ways of unlocking change within a system dynamic that are not always seen. A hidden narrative is not necessarily something that is deliberately kept secret. It may simply be one which is not visible to those external to the system, and to many within the system.

Here is a fragment of an inquiry that Danny was facilitating in 2013 with community representatives in Kachin state in Myanmar. The facilitation team suggested that, in addition to the people that they might normally want to meet with, they should also talk to people randomly – going into shops, tea shops, and so on. One of the groups went into a bookshop. They got into a long conversation about the difficulties of teaching children in Kachin when books could not be produced in Jinghpaw, the Kachin local language. This opened up a debate amongst the local community activists about the relationship between local language and education and how if they took action around this issue they might indirectly impact on the wider issue. It allowed them to think about a different place within the social system that they might act in order to support peace. In another quite different inquiry into homelessness in Milwaukee (Figure 4.1), participants constructed a large map of issues and the relationships between them. A range of dominant and repeated patterns appeared in the middle of the maps. These centred on the relationship between homelessness, drug use, and alcoholism. Right at the edge of the map a set of connections had been made to these, which related to cars. As participants focused attention to this area of the map they realized that this issue had been raised by more than one of the homeless people. They started to flesh out the map in more detail and articulated a pattern which centred on the way in which car ownership in Milwaukee was central to both day-to-day life, and to people's esteem. For various reasons this was leading to debt, which was in turn leading to homelessness which lead to alcoholism and drug use, which created a feedback loop which reinforced homelessness, and so on. So rather than focus on the issue of homelessness participants

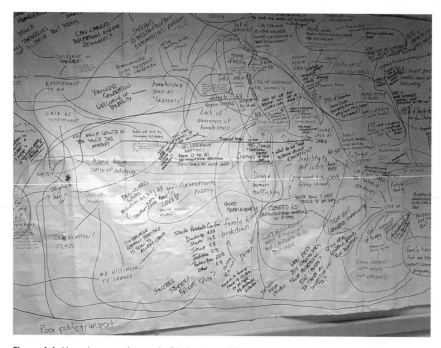

Figure 4.1 Homelessness issues in Sheboygan, US

explored the potential of alternatives to car ownership. Once again by seeing how issues connect to each other in complex non-linear patterns they can identify different places where action might be taken. To find these narratives we need to ensure that our inquiry is rooted across very different parts of the local system or we are unlikely to pick up the outlier stories at the edge of the map that lead to the centre.

It is necessary to capture the constant change in system dynamics

All systems are constantly changing. Every move within a system creates a change in that system. This might be a small localized change, or it might have a domino effect that ripples through the system. In some cases they will change the system dynamic itself. As multiple changes interact, the system changes in ever more unpredictable ways. The system we see today is different to the system that we will see tomorrow and quite different to that which we will see in three months' time. So to map a system is only the first step, and there also needs to be a process of identifying the dynamic change within a system. Change is happening in the system all of the time but this will not necessarily change the underlying system dynamics (as we illustrated in Chapter 2). The aim of systemic mapping is to understand the system dynamics in order to create sustainable change. It is always possible to create change within a system but it is not easy to create sustainable change. It may be helpful to create new maps which can look at changes over time. These also help us to see the dynamics.

The inquiry process itself may involve multiple methods

There are many different ways in which an inquiry process can unfold. Some have been particularly associated with participatory processes:

- transect walks, observation and explanation, photographs;
- participatory number generation – where statistics are generated through local participatory processes (Holland, 2013);
- connected real-time conversations – where one thing leads to another and people are connected in real time;
- peer research processes – where people open up dialogues and collect stories with and from their peers (Percy-Smith et al., 2003);
- dialogic spaces – where people talk about issues in groups (Burns, 2007);
- visual process – where people tell their stories through an act of creativity. this could be through drawing, song, story, and so on;
- interactive spaces where one inquiry becomes the foundation for another inquiry, for example a programme which is broadcast by a community radio station becomes the foundation for another round of inquiry (Burns et al., 2012);
- processes of immersions including the reality check methodologies.

But other more traditional methods of inquiry are also very useful:

- finding relevant information from secondary data sources;
- open and semi-structured interviews;
- surveys;
- network analysis.

The important thing to be clear about here is that it is not the data which makes the process participatory it is the question of who it is analysed by and how. In an action research process, at each meeting we have to ask the question anew. Do we have all of the information we need to understand what it is we are looking at? And if not, what methods do we need to get that information? These methods could be quite different every time. In the Bristol Children's Initiative project that was described by Burns (2007), the domestic violence action research group in Hartcliffe was finding it difficult to understand the full extent of the problem. They first sought statistics from the police and stories from women, and then after realizing this still didn't tell them all they needed to know, they agreed that professionals (community health workers and social workers) should keep a detailed record of each case for a month and then come together to review them. The methods they used varied according to their needs as did the data that they collected.

It is necessary to subject meaning making to collective scrutiny

In order to build a helpful picture of collective subjectivities it is important to ensure that there is some process of collective analysis from people across the system. In other words it is not enough to collect data from people in different parts of the system, it is also crucial that at each stage analysis is conducted by them. This is not only important for 'ownership' but also because it is only by understanding multiple interpretations of what is happening in a system that people can see how change might happen. Collective scrutiny can happen in lots of ways. For example, an inquiry team of community participants might analyse the data together or, when stories have been mapped, community representatives might be asked to engage in the refinement and analysis of that map.

Systemic issue mapping

This section is about systemic issue mapping. The process has evolved through a number of different projects. The first was the Lake Victoria Water and Sanitation programme (2009–10) which is described in this chapter. This was not a community-based programme but it modelled a way of doing participatory mapping that was later developed as a community-based process which we now call participatory systemic inquiry. The first attempt to do this was with the Ghana Community Radio Network in 2011 (Harvey et al., 2012). Since then the process has evolved in two ongoing projects: the first a community-based action research process on peace in Kachin, Myanmar, which has been underpinned by the mapping of life stories, and the second a much more extensive process working with eight local NGOs in India on slavery and bonded labour which has involved collecting, mapping, and then collectively analysing over 350 life stories. We start by exploring the reasons for mapping, we then look at the process of mapping, and finally we look at two case studies of systemic issue mapping.

The reason that we map is that mapping:

- allows the whole to be seen all in one place;
- allows the connections between things to be seen;
- encourages dialogue and analysis through the mapping process.

Wadsworth (2010: 7) says that: 'Instead of seeing one thing, person, event or activity as "the cause" of another problem, all "causes" are seen as simultaneously interdependent effects, and all "effects" are also "causes" in a larger frame of reference.'

It is very hard to see these complex interdependencies without mapping them. Also, the participatory creation of the map creates high levels of engagement and energy, which builds ownership for action.

The whole process involves four key elements which we will examine in turn:

- multi-stakeholder inquiry;
- construction and analysis of large messy maps showing issues and systemic relationships;
- construction and analysis of distilled system dynamic maps;
- validation and resonance processes.

Here we provide guidance on how to carry out each of these processes and how to connect them.

Stage 1: multi-stakeholder inquiry

Our approach to inquiry

The aim of the inquiry process is to build pictures of issues, actors (people and organizations) and the interrelationships between them. Here we seek to develop insight into problems, why they emerge, how they are maintained, and how they become entrenched. While we can never see the whole system we can usually reveal the most important relationships. Once we can see the ways in which different parts of the system influence each other it is easier to think about sustainable responses to those issues.

As we have described in Chapter 1, most development interventions are based on defining problems in terms of deficits, highlighting 'lack of skills, information, and understanding' or missing infrastructure. These so often lead to the implementation of white elephants because they presuppose solutions which are not appropriate, implementable or sustainable within the specific context. PSI methods do not rely on assumptions about 'what isn't' but rather try to establish 'what is' as a platform for generating solutions. They (a) engage people only on the real world issues that they experience by asking open questions which elicit what they think is important, (b) create pictures of the whole so that gaps and opportunities can be visually identified, (c) develop real-time theories of change, (d) work to foster action on these, (e) ask critical questions and challenge assumptions which restrict the possibilities for action, and (f) nurture many lines of response in a way that allows for complex dynamics to appear and inform solutions.

Who should be engaged in the inquiry process?

The purpose of the inquiry is to get a deep understanding of the key issues facing people in their localities and a picture of their dynamics. Our aim should be to identify issues and to find out everything we can about what is happening, how it is happening, why it is happening, where, and with whom. We do this through inquiry with stakeholders and other people who have power which can impact on the situation. Once we have started to engage stakeholders, issues emerge and these enable us to identify new stakeholders. Thus the process involves a constant interplay between the stakeholders and issues. For example, a discussion with a local doctor might identify the local health centre as a crucial location for inquiry. This might in turn identify a neighbourhood where there is a high concentration of illness resulting from poor sanitation, which we might want to inquire into further with residents. Alternatively it might takes us down a route of exploring why the health centre is unable to do any preventative public health work. It is also worth bearing in mind that there are knowledge holders who are not stakeholders, but who can be helpful. For example, a shopkeeper may notice a repeated pattern of behaviour or activity which no one else sees. It is also important to ensure that this knowledge is brought into the inquiry.

Frequently we discover important sites for inquiry simply by walking around (sometimes described as transect walks). We may discover unknown local community-based organizations (CBOs) from street signs; uncover domestic practices or paradoxical consumer behaviour; we may see how close toilets are to the washing-up of dishes and preparation of foodstuffs, and so on. The experience of almost all of the places that we have worked in is that we can organize all but a few meetings or group discussions at very short notice. This has a number of important advantages: firstly, it can limit the pre-prepared responses and the extent to which groups can be controlled by dominant voices; and, secondly, it allows us to respond rapidly to issues that have emerged perhaps hours or days before.

Inquiry teams (see following section) should be prepared to be flexible and opportunistic. This may mean splitting up into small groups as opportunities arise in the field, so some thought should be given to transport and translation options that allow for this. In our recent action research process in Myanmar we identified four types of people that the inquiry teams should explicitly reach out to. Each of the teams should aspire to engage a mix of people from these four:

- People in representative, leadership or authority positions. This might include tribal chiefs, religious leaders, NGO representatives, teachers or health professionals.
- People who we come across in the locality. Here we are deliberately trying to meet people from very different places. People might be met in tea shops, or collecting water from the water point, or working on the land, or buying or selling in the market. We might talk to different people in their homes. As long as the starting points are very different geographically, in terms of identity, and in terms of poverty and marginalization, then leads can be followed through snowballing approaches.
- People that are hidden. These could be disabled people, women, very income poor people, people living in informal settlements, and so on.
- Peers – community-based researchers can seek out people like themselves – here there is a high level of trust.

Engaging people from all of these categories ensures that a systemic picture will be built from diverse corners of any social and economic system. This, as we argued earlier, is very important from a systems perspective because to see as much of a system as is possible to see it must be seen from multiple perspectives and from multiple stances. Sometimes in our inquiry process we are looking at very specific issues, and it might appear obvious who should be involved in the inquiry. However, inquiry processes frequently reveal that the key issue in the inquiry is often not what was originally thought (see Box 4.1).

In the Kamukunji case described below, because the inquiry developed emergently, the people who needed to be involved in the process at the beginning were quite different to those who needed to be involved later on in the inquiry. In this case, the original proposal from SNV practitioners had been to bring together water actors to discuss the issue. But as soon as the inquiry team hit the ground they discovered that what appeared to

---

Box 4.1 Case study of water and sewage in Kamukunji, Eldoret

Kamukunji is a slum area located on the outskirts of Eldoret, Kenya's fifth largest town. An inquiry was made to explore why water and sanitation services were so poor. The Eldoret Municipal Council had invested in Kamukunji at a time when they directly oversaw water and sewerage services in the municipality. Since then water and sanitation services had been moved to a contracted water services provider, the Eldoret Water and Sanitation Company (ELDOWAS). In around 2002, the council installed a water-borne sewerage system and a house-to-house potable water supply system. At the time of inquiry in 2007, there were almost no active connections from the dwellings to either the water or sewerage systems. The smell of human waste was everywhere, and in all directions women could be seen carrying distinctive bright yellow jerry cans on their heads, the ubiquitous indicator in Kenya for carried water.

(Continued)

Box 4.1 (Continued)

The inquiry surfaced some tensions between landlords and tenants. When residents were asked their opinions about the state of water and sanitation services, they were vehement in their displeasure at the filth around them; and described how, when it rained, their pit latrines became engulfed and the resulting brown water flowed off in street-side ditches. The butcher at the end of one street became animated because his business would stop during rain. No one wants to buy their meat with shit floating under the sale platform.

Tenants could not connect their homes to the water and sewerage services. This was a matter for landlords. Any application to the council or to ELDOWAS was referred back if applied for by a tenant. Most landlords were absent, living in Eldoret, Kitale or Nairobi. They collected their rents via agents, who did not see their role as being anything more than rent collectors. They were, however, authorized to evict tenants and issue new leases. A tenant that bothered the agent with requests ran the risk of eviction. There was apparently high demand for low-rent accommodation. Some residents in the street cited examples where people had been evicted by agents to be replaced quickly with new tenants.

When the landlords were engaged directly by the inquiry team, another set of issues emerged. Firstly, there was the cost. To connect to the sewer system required a basic investment in a slab and a water closet. This required a standard of construction that did not fit with the existing wattle and daub mud constructions that mainly existed, and required new investment. Secondly, it would also require a connection to the water supply system. Third, this meant that monthly bills would need to be paid for the services and that would raise the rent. Any investment made in construction would have to be recouped by higher rent. Neither landlords nor tenants apparently wanted to increase the rent, but also no conversation about this had happened. Finally, and critically, it became clear that the council applied property taxes on all residences. Many homes existed 'off radar' because they were temporary and not documented as being in existence. Connection to sewerage services implied recognition of property existence. The council had adopted a policy of linking property tax to sewerage and water billing. They did this for reasons of expediency in tax collection, but that had the net effect that if a property was to remain 'off radar' it could not connect to any utilities. The bizarre manifestation of this, then, was a slum suburb that was home to a large-scale public investment that everyone really wanted and needed, but that was blocked from working.

Once these problems had been surfaced a customer satisfaction survey was facilitated with support from SNV, the results of which were used to table stakeholder issues. One key finding was that the community was never involved in the implementation of the investment. So ELDOWAS appointed a focal person to spearhead engagement with the poor in underserved areas. A youth group was engaged to conduct conversations around clean sanitation and was trained on water, sanitation and hygiene issues, connection procedures, and in handling grievances. ELDOWAS then embarked on a campaign to reach underserved residents with safe drinking water and basic sanitation. With support from SNV, and in collaboration with local stakeholders (municipal public health and education departments, owners associations, area development committees), trained youth groups spearheaded the campaign in two areas, one of which was Kamakunji.

Within three months, average monthly connection rate quadrupled from 10 to 40, resulting in 115 new connections. Stimulated by growing demands from prospective tenants, local 'champions' started converting traditional pit latrines to water-borne toilets at minimal cost. The team explored new ways to support plot owners and schools to connect and upgrade their toilets. The youth group was paid a commission and did well enough to secure a licence to collect garbage. Households began to pay monthly for this service.

The key challenge was to engage both landlords and tenants and devise solutions that were affordable, achieve the desired impact, and could be scaled-up in other neighbourhoods. Follow-up inquiry was needed to find out whether the new sewer connections forced tenants out due to higher rent; whether there was a growing demand for toilets; and whether pay-per-use public toilets could meet the demands of tenants unable to afford rents for connected houses.

be substantively a water issue, turned out to be an issue which related to landlord–tenant relations, which later became an issue about the unintended consequences of the way in which the local taxation system was constructed. What we learn from this is that we cannot pre-construct the participants in our inquiry process. If the inquiry had been constructed around the 'water actors', it would have quickly hit a dead end. The iterative learning process is as much about who should participate as it is about the next decisions to be made in relation to the inquiry.

Inquiry teams

The process of systemic inquiry usually involves a lot of people. We build inquiry teams of typically between 12 and 20 or so people. The Lake Victoria Water and Sanitation (LVWATSAN) programme that we describe below was facilitated by external researchers. In the Myanmar and Northern India projects the researchers have been community members or people from local community-based organizations. The LVWATSAN group involved about 20 people split across four towns. It may seem obvious to say it but it is important that there is a gender balance within the inquiry team group, and it is important that the people can speak local languages. This is not always straightforward even in a community-led inquiry. In one workshop that we supported in Myanmar nine languages were spoken across two clusters of villages less than five hours walk apart.

Inquiry facilitation and recording

Inquiry questioning and inquiry group facilitation is not like interview questioning or focus group facilitation. Typical interview or focus group questioning seeks responses to a framing that is already pre-constructed and based on researcher assumptions, whereas the priority for inquiry-based questioning is to start with very open prompts and enable people to tell the stories that they want to tell within the broad boundaries of the inquiry. Inquiries are not a space for people to go off on tangents which have no bearing on the issues; however, we frequently find that when people are allowed space to tell their stories, they reveal new and important issues, and ultimately they reveal what is most important to them. In discerning this we need to find out what people feel, what issues and analysis 'resonate' with them, and what they feel passionate about.

Detailed notes need to be taken of each meeting. It is very important to catch issues as far as possible in the words of those that say them. When summarizing a narrative it is too easy to inadvertently place a 'researcher' interpretation on it. We also frequently screen out the detail and are left with a headline issue without the detail to follow through later. We would expect a considerable quantity of notes at the end of a process. Typically a one and a half hour discussion might generate more than 10 pages of notes. A life story may be three or four pages of handwritten notes.

Having recorded a story or a discussion, facilitators should record their own reflections but keep these separate to the story. They might reflect on the following:

- What is the factual information that we need? This may for example be technical, legal, behavioural or financial information (we can find out where to get this after the story has been told).
- Have issues been mentioned which could be explored further? (Do this after they have told their story)
- What do we observe? What can we see in front of us that is significant?
- What conflicts or conflicts of interest are there?
- What differences in perception are there in relation to others we have inquired with?
- What underlying assumptions seem to be guiding the opinions, behaviours, and actions of the group? To what extent are they contestable?
- Were there possible opportunities emerging from the conversation which could be explored further?

Finally, in observing situations it is crucial to think about who and what is not present as well as what is present.

Stage 2: construction and analysis of 'messy' maps which show issues and systemic relationships

Analysing the stories

The next step is to turn multiple stories into a coherent picture of what is going on. We can do this by creating system maps. Whether the raw material for the maps is life stories or dialogue reports or interviews, the first stage in the process is to analyse them. In the India Slavery and Bonded Labour project local CBOs had collected 350 life stories. We divided people up into pairs and then divided the stories amongst them. We asked them simple questions. What is most important about this story and why is it important? We also asked them to think about the key causalities in the story – or, put another way, what were the causes and consequences of each of the factors they identified in the story. One way of doing this is to ask people to imagine that the story is a cartoon, and that there are only six picture boxes in which to tell it. What would be in each box to show how one thing has led to another?

Creating messy maps

Once all of the stories are analysed we ask people to map the factors that they have identified and the relationships between them. The aim of the maps is to understand the complex dynamics of the system. This is not a stakeholder mapping exercise. The primary focus of the maps should be issues, and what we are mapping are the different factors that the issues are comprised of. So participants mark the relationships with directional arrows showing causality. Formal system mapping (Ricigliano, 2012) involves marking each relationship with a + or a –. Using this method ++ means that an increase in one factor leads to an increase in the other; +– means that an increase in one factor leads to a decrease in the other; –+ means that a decrease in one factor leads to an increase in the other; and — means that a decrease in one factor leads to a decrease in the other. The example in Figure 4.2 is an illustration of this.

This helps us to see the effects of each relationship, but we have found it too complex to use in community situations – especially where people have had little formal education. So we have adopted a different protocol whereby arrows in red denote negative relationships and arrows in black denote positive relationships.

Doing it this way means that all of the key linkages from all of the stories can be depicted in one place in a very short space of time. We can also trace the positive trajectories just by following the colour on the map. The point of these maps is to take the knowledge from all of the different parts of the inquiry and depict it on a single canvas. Each pair or small group holds part of the picture and brings it together with the others to create the whole. Once their part is on the map it is subject to collective scrutiny so it is not only

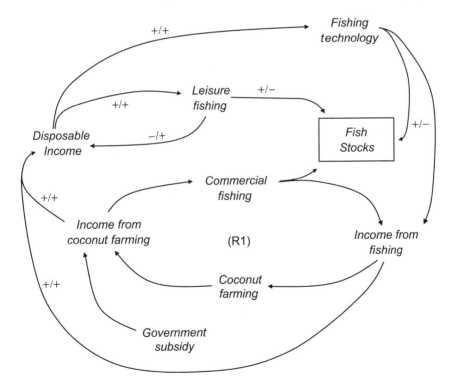

Figure 4.2 Declining fish stocks in Kiribati
Source: Adapted from Ricigliano, 2012

Figure 4.3 A large messy map: the dynamics of slavery and bonded labour in Bihar and Uttar Pradesh

their analysis applied to it. Later parts of the map can be taken out, distilled and neatened up, as we discuss in the next section. The map in Figure 4.3 is an example of a large map generated in Northern India by community-based NGOs working on slavery and bonded labour.

When the map is complete it is analysed by the whole group (see next section). An observation from Jody Aked from a mapping process in the Valuing Volunteering project (discussed in Chapter 5) reveals something about how the process works:

> The issues map was a hugely valuable tool. It was a complex map but explaining it told a story of the wider system which made visible connections, sticking points, as well as the internal and external drivers that structure action. While it does require a bit of preparation to think through how to explain all the arrows as well as delivery time to provide important context to the abstractions, it was one piece of paper that we could share with lots of different stakeholder groups. This made it easy to share insights between people, helping to surface multiple realities and perspectives. The other interesting finding that its use in Mangingisda illustrated was that once you have made visible the relationship between different issues, people can reach consensus on the need for action even if their starting points are completely different. The fishermen concerns

were about protecting their way of life. The women wanted to see progress and a role for themselves in it. The treasurer, who became a strong community advocate for this project for a time, was motivated by family breakdown. As a tool it was able to help turn differences into shared decisions. (Aked, 2014)

Turning for a moment to the practical side of map making, the first step is for participants to put up a canvas of white paper on a large wall (or sometimes a floor or large table). We usually do this by taping between 8 and 20 sheets of flip chart paper together. The largest maps may be 2 metres high and 8 metres long. Once the paper is up then everyone is encouraged to look at their notebooks and think about the interconnected chains of factors that emerged in their inquiries. They may want to start with a discussion or to get the knowledge that they are holding straight down onto the paper. One person will start to write and others will then either connect to what that person has written or start a new issue on a different part of the map. This should be seen as a participatory process and everyone is encouraged to join in. It doesn't matter if they get the distances wrong or make mistakes and change them, and so on. Linkages are made between the issues, and supportive evidence (e.g. quotes and facts) is also put on the map. If the map needs to be bigger more sheets can be added. Sometimes we will construct single maps. Sometimes it can be a really good device to construct multiple maps from, say, different locations and then compare the differences. In a learning exercise we sometimes ask different teams to produce maps so that we can learn from the different ways in which each team approached the exercise.

In constructing the maps we need a mixture of free creativity and discipline. The main discipline is ensuring that there is agreement on a set of colours and symbols. Different colours could denote very different things. Danny's mapping work has settled on four over the years for the very pragmatic reason that we mostly use marker pens to create the maps, and marker pens are almost universally sold in packs of four which are typically blue, black, green, and red. Examples in Table 4.2 are drawn from the LVWATSAN project and the bonded labour and slavery project.

After the first iteration of the map facilitators may wish to ask the participants if they want to make some of the lines thicker because these linkages appear in more of the accounts and stories that they have collected. In addition they may want to mark a relationship line with a * to denote points of conflict, major areas of disagreement or blockages in the system (resulting, for example, from vested interests). Similarly they might mark a relationship with a question mark to denote a possibility. The important point is that a key is agreed in advance and is consistent across the inquiries in different locations with different people.

Wherever possible photographs should be taken to illustrate the context and the issues, for example pictures of toilets/latrines, washing up, broken water pumps, queues, how things are located. These can be attached to the map to bring it alive.

Table 4.2 Examples of colour and symbol usage in system maps

Pens and sticky notes	What these are used for	Examples and notes
Red marker pen writing	Factors Factors are actions or conditions that cause things and are caused by things	Family needs to borrow money to pay for health care. They give their eldest son to the middle man in exchange for upfront cash. This leads to the boy working 16 hours a day. This leads to boy getting ill. Each of these is a factor linked by an arrow.
Blue marker pen writing	Places and people (stakeholders)	Mother, boys, middleman NGO, religious institution.
Green marker pen writing	Factual information or observations Sub-issues should not be listed as bullets below main issues. They should be depicted in causal relation to each other	Most boys in some villages have been taken to the city Parents received 2000 rupees for the child The money received by the vigilance committee is x There are 50 children at the orphanage Water costs 50,000 shillings to connect
Small pen writing	Quotes and short illustrative stories	'I went to the market and was approached by a man I didn't know. He offered me a mobile phone if I came to work for him'
Story codes (biro)	These are the number codes that relate to each of the stories. These can be added next to the factors in small pen	
Red arrow line	Negative pathway Link issues with a directional arrow	
Black arrow line	Positive pathway Link issues with a directional arrow	Whether to use a red or black arrow is a matter of judgement and what starts as positive could become negative
Blue sticky note	Anything that is your idea, thought, connection This is where you put anything that is not in the data that is being analysed	Nothing should go on the map in pen if it is not in the stories or other transcripts. These coloured sticky notes give you the chance to join the dots, ask questions, highlight gaps, propose possible solutions. What if …
Yellow sticky note	English translation	

It is crucial that we map what people say, not our own constructs or opinions. The only factors that should go onto the map should be those that are in the stories from the ground or the notebooks of the participatory researchers. A drainage engineer, for example, might be shocked at the state of the drains and map this as an issue but it may barely get a mention because people see other things as being more worthy of attention. Similarly an NGO worker might think that the big issue for someone who has been trafficked into a bangle factory is that he is working 16 hours a day without the right to go to the toilet, but for that person the real issue might be that they have been separated from their sibling. This does not stop us as researchers adding our own reflections as inquiry questions, but these should be clearly distinguished from inquiry data from the field. We do this by putting sticky notes onto the maps.

Supporting quotes and stories can be added in biro or fine pens by individuals. Similarly it should not be problematic for individuals to place factual and technical information (green) on the map once the core relationships have been laid down.

The following is a list of guidelines for mapping:

- You can put your material directly onto the map in pairs or small groups. You need not discuss each element as a whole group initially, or the process will take too long. You will want to discuss collectively once some of the key pathways start to go onto the map.

- You may want to practise the techniques of map drawing before you start working on the big map.

- Don't worry if the map is messy. The messy maps are just that. They may have lines criss-crossing them, depicting relationships. They will be written in multiple handwritings, some big and some small. Sometimes there will be more than one language. There will be mistakes covered up in masking tape and some elements may not end up where they logically belong. The idea is that everyone is involved. The map is as much a tool for discussion and analysis as a finished object.

- Make sure that factors are only put onto the map once. This means that you need to be aware of what else is on the map.

- Don't write too big, so there is enough space on the map. It may be clear right from the start that that there are big clusters of issues. You may want to very loosely plan where these might go on the map. For example, in our Myanmar work on the peace process in Kachin there was a part of the map which related to internally displaced people's (IDP) camp issues, another part which related to host community issues, and still other parts which related to other locations such as banana plantations. This was a more geographical division, but the map can also be cut by issues, or simply evolve organically.

- Try to be as specific as possible (observation in green should talk about actual amounts of money, actual ages of children etc., wherever possible)

Analysing the maps

Once the map is drawn the next step is to collectively analyse it. When analysing we are looking for a number of things:

- Issues: what seems to be happening?
- Connections: how are these things related?
- Cause–effect relationships, feedback loops, and so on.
- Patterns: are there patterns that can be discerned?
- Power relationships: individual, organizational and systemic.
- System dynamics and social norms: what are the factors that keep the system in balance (or not) within a particular pattern of attractors?
- Contradictions and paradoxes.
- Energy: where does the energy lie within the system?
- System change: what is changing within the system – how and why?
- Where do issues cross into what appear to be other systems?
- The unexpected: is there anything unusual or surprising, which might reveal new ways of seeing what is going on/challenge assumptions, and so on.
- Outliers and positive deviance activities that may be instructive.
- Potential solutions to problems that either lie within the map or are implicit.
- Opportunity points, entry points, leverage points where changes might nudge the system in the direction of solutions.

Examples of a simple cause effect relationship might, in the case of the water inquiry, be:

> Introduction of a water point leads to threat to the livelihood of water vendors which leads to vandalism.

In the case of the slavery and bonded labour inquiry it might be something like this:

> Family is in debt as a result of payments for medical treatment ➔ family offered money from middle man for boys over 12 ➔ boy taken to tea shop ➔ boy works 16 hours each day ➔ boy gets ill ➔ boy requires medical treatment ➔ new loan required ➔ another child has to be sent to the city to pay the debt.

Examples of patterns that we notice might be:

- There is a strong relationship between poor sanitary conditions and land issues across three towns.
- People are buying dirty water at a higher price than they could pay for clean water.
- It appears that girls between the ages of 12 and 15 are least likely to be attending school.
- Older boys are more likely to be sold into slavery.

Maps do not necessary provide conclusive evidence, but once we have noticed these patterns we are alerted to what we need to investigate further. All of the factors articulated above should be the subject of discussion and will help in the construction of the system dynamic maps, which are the next stage of the process.

Stage 3: construction of distilled system dynamic maps

The third stage of the process can be to create distilled system dynamic maps. This is not always necessary – sometimes the dynamics are really clear on a big map. A distilled system dynamic map, however, shows how things relate to each other, cause each other, trigger change, and so on. These can depict small aspects of the system that seem ripe for working on, or they can be simplified depictions of a larger process. The focus of these maps is explicitly as the title suggests: to identify system dynamics of the type that was discussed in Chapter 2.

Take the following example from an inquiry into homelessness in Brighton in the UK. One micro-level dynamic surfaced by the map started with a pattern observation that couples tended not to stay in hostels because hostels wouldn't allow couples to stay together. This had some potential effects that the inquiry team wanted to explore further – that people who were in couples were more likely to be on the street, and/or that there was an incentive for people not to be in relationships because if they were, they were less likely to get shelter. This in turn could lead to them having radically diminished emotional support which could in turn lead to alcoholism, and so on. All of this stemmed from the organizational imperatives of the hostels which segregated the sexes. Mapping this specific dynamic which was derived from the much bigger map helped us to see the different choices that were presented to homeless people and the different pathways and outcomes that emerged as a result of these. One of the important principles underpinning complexity theory is that the 'starting conditions' have a profound effect on the dynamics that flow from them. In this case, if the starting conditions are rooted in an assumption of single sex occupation, then a particular set of system dynamics will flow from that.

While the messy maps engage everyone in their creation in a fairly ad hoc way, and there is no requirement for agreement on what goes on the map, the distilled maps need to be agreed (Figure 4.4). A map scribe who has clear and neat handwriting should be identified at the beginning of each session. This is a role that could be rotated. Alternatively, cut-out arrows and sticky notes – each with an issue written on them – can be arranged on flip chart paper and moved around.

A group may choose to develop just one or perhaps even up to five different system dynamic maps from the bigger messy maps.

Figure 4.4a Creating a distilled system map

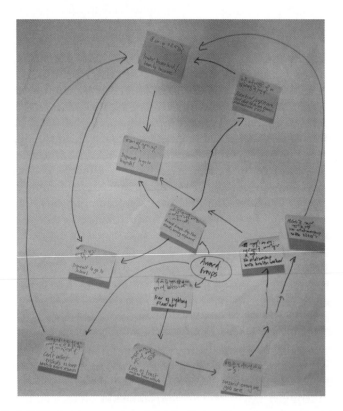

Figure 4.4b A distilled system map (created collectively with arrows and sticky notes)

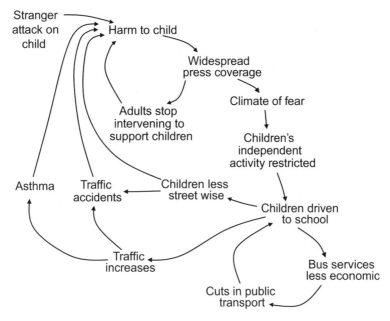

Figure 4.4c A distilled system map (neatly redrawn)
Source: Adapted from Burns 2015

Stage 4: validation and resonance testing of issues

Validation is a way of checking that the data is not just the view of only a few individuals. The messy maps and the distilled system dynamic maps can both be the subject of validation. People looking at the map should be able to say 'Yes, I recognize that pattern', 'Yes, that makes sense', 'Yes, but there is something fundamental mission' or 'No! ...' This can also be seen as a form of triangulation.

It is important to remember that we are not trying to validate a consensus position. Usually issues arise out of tensions characterized by differential power relationships so it is highly unlikely that people will have the same perspective. What can be done, though, is to get validation that the views expressed by different stakeholders are accurately represented, and the dynamics identified by those analysing the maps have credibility to some or all of the stakeholders. Very often it is possible for people to agree on what is happening even if they disagree on why it is happening or what it means. If the maps are substantively made and analysed by the stakeholders themselves, then the process of laying down the relationships and analysing is a validation in real time.

Another approach that we have used is to pre-organize a validation meeting during the week of an inquiry. Then when action researchers meet people, as they are gathering stories or other data (planned or otherwise), they can ask them to come to the meeting, and can give them concrete details of when and where it is. When they get to the meeting facilitators work through the maps with the new participants. Where it is not possible to pre-arrange meetings mobile numbers can be asked for to allow people to be invited to meetings.

In the Ghana Community Radio case study, which we discuss later in this chapter, the inquiry was taken into community forums for validation:

> After all the stations had completed their initial investigations, they held community forums – or *durbars* – to bring together community members, elders, chiefs and district representatives to re-listen to the broadcasts, discuss the findings and raise questions for leaders and duty bearers. These discussions were then broadcast out to the broader listening community, so as to ensure that those who were not present could also provide input. The *durbars* provide an important space where community members could articulate their concerns and get commitments from their representatives ... They represented the next step in moving from collective inquiry and dialogue toward action aimed at influencing local politics and power. (Harvey et al., 2012)

There are other forms of validation and resonance which can be part of a more formal iterative process. These might take the form of a large event where the evidence from one arena is analysed by people from another part of the system to see if there is resonance. In *Systemic Action Research* (Burns, 2007), Danny described such an event which brought together many strands of inquiry that had been generated across the British Red Cross. Here a large amount of the 'raw data' which had contributed to the individual local inquires was brought into a bigger collective space. This event, which comprised around 150 people, was about 50 per cent made up of people who had been directly involved in the original inquiries and 50 per cent new people from across the organization and beyond. This enabled horizontal validation – those from other inquiries could see where the resonance lay with their inquiries – and vertical validation – those at different levels in the organization and different parts of the organization could see if the issues resonated with their experience. These sorts of processes also enable us to see the dissonances between different levels.

Once they are validated, the maps provide the basis for action. This can either be fed into programmes and plans, generate action directly, or form the basis of new inquiry-based action research groups (see Chapter 5). We now offer two case studies to illustrate in a bit more detail the way in which mapping processes reveal issues that can then be acted on.

Systemic mapping case study 1: the Lake Victoria Water and Sanitation programme

The Lake Victoria Water and Sanitation inquiry is a strong example of systemic inquiry carried out across a large terrain. Here we developed the inquiry and mapping techniques that laid the foundations for more recent work which can be described as PSI. We use it as an example because it shows the ways in which system dynamics can be uncovered through a multi-stakeholder inquiry process. The focus of this case study is not so much on the mapping itself but on what it revealed.

The LVWATSAN was a UN-Habitat programme that was designed to bring clean water and good sanitation facilities to the small towns on the edge of Lake Victoria which had been neglected over the years. It was a cross-country programme for Tanzania, Uganda, and Kenya. The first phase involved work in 10 towns and the plan was to extend this to a further 30. This phase ran between 2009 and 2010. The programme was ostensibly an infrastructure project, but UN-Habitat was also required by its funders to build a capacity development programme into it. This was initially conceived as a fairly traditional training process, but they were persuaded to fund a more extensive inquiry-based programme which was systemic in two ways: firstly, because it was rooted in inquiry which sought to understand the system dynamics within the towns, and, secondly, because it saw capacity development as the capacity of actors within the system to change the dynamics of the system.

The aim of the programme then became threefold:

- To identify relatively straightforward areas for training.
- To identify infrastructure issues which needed changing, and to identify what sorts of infrastructure might be needed before it was designed.
- To identify key systemic issues which were likely to prevent sustainable outcomes and facilitate learning processes which might lead to their resolution.

The politics of what actually happened in the programme are complex and much of its potential was not realized, but for now we want to look at the sorts of issues that were uncovered and why it is necessary to adopt systemic approaches in order to engage with them. The purpose of looking in some detail at the LVWATSAN programme is because it demonstrates on a large scale just how critical is an understanding of power relationships and system dynamics. These dynamics were surfaced in all of our inquiries. Some of the system dynamics that were uncovered related to specific issues within the towns. Some were patterns that could be seen to be underpinning what was happening across towns. Each of the stories below is a fragment of the larger inquiry. Each depict a set of complex system dynamics explaining why simple solutions have failed and where leverage points for action can be identified and action might be possible.

Flying toilets in Nyendo

The team observed flying toilets in Nyendo town. They inquired into why this was happening. They discovered a fairly familiar pattern – when it rains, the water fills the pit latrines and shit flows across the area – but it is exacerbated by a set of complex system dynamics. There are drains running along the sides of the main roads to take this rain water, but these have been broken because people have extended their plots into the road. There is no tributary drainage system where people live. This situation is worsening because population growth is leading to higher prices and pressure on the land. This leads to people selling off parts of their plots, and the plot sizes getting smaller and smaller. This, in turn, is leading to the digging of more pit latrines which fill and overflow all the more easily with the rains. This leads the space available to be even more reduced and means that no one is prepared to give up any of their land for tributary drainage. Moreover, as the land gets more fragmented there are no straight routes for any pipes to be laid. So even if money can be found to lay pipes this is not a realistic possibility. There are laws about building, but there are no means to enforce them, nor do local officials have the power to take land for drainage. So as the pit latrines fill, a more satisfactory solution for people is to shit into a plastic bag, tie it, and throw it – flying toilets. As these bags are trodden on and begin to degrade, disease spreads. This complexity of multiple underlying dynamics makes it clear that no simple technical solution will ever be possible. It is, for example, going to be necessary to engage with the way in which population growth is leading to small land plots if the drainage issue is to be solved. Even this fragment of the analysis shows many different points in the chain of causalities where action could be taken.

Water prices in Kyotera

One very good example of a complex system dynamic is related to the use and price of water in Kyotera. One of the team's observations was that a 20-litre jerry can of clean water provided by a water operator from a tap cost 100 shillings compared to 200 shillings from a water vendor. Vendors carry dirty water up and down the hill, and potable water taps are at the top of the hill. It did not seem rational that people were paying double for dirty water. The system dynamics which supported this outcome included many other factors including solidarity with the bicycle water carriers, the taste of the water, low levels of trust in the new system, and so on, which may be emotional not rational. Nevertheless, they were coherent when viewed in relation to their whole lives. The simple technical solution was to provide cheaper water. The complex social dynamics clearly demonstrated that this could never be a solution without attention to many other factors in the system.

Toilet management in Nyendo Market

Nyendo Market is huge and sprawling, with thousands of traders and buyers gathered together in a bustle of human activity. With a history of seriously insanitary conditions, the market had been significantly improved with the introduction of drainage facilities, but there were still major problems relating to the public toilets. Toilet facilities had been built in each of the four corners of the market. We went to these toilets and talked to many people. One toilet operator had been badly beaten up. He showed us scars on his body. This happens regularly because many men are not prepared to pay to use the toilet. We witnessed women washing themselves outside one of the toilets because the women's facilities were broken and were not being repaired. In general, facilities for women were poor. We met officials from the town council who collected revenues that were necessary to keep the toilets running. One told us that the toilets were not paying for themselves because while the women paid for the toilets, the men often didn't. We talked to the lorry drivers and the fishermen. They had decided that they wanted to run their own toilets, but they couldn't agree a price that was viable for the council. As we talked to the lorry drivers and the fishermen an obvious question arose. If they could run their own toilets – why shouldn't the women? This possibility seemed to go against even the physical structure of the toilets, for each block was divided in half between men and women. But why not? As the inquiry progressed in the market, new questions were raised by the council official. If the women were the only ones who were paying and they ran their own toilets, would that make the other toilets financially unviable? A complex tangle of interrelationships was revealed and explored in real time. This example is interesting because it shows how inquiry reveals relationships and assumptions, and how challenging these can open up new possibilities, which in turn open up new challenges.

Leaking water systems in Bukoba

Bukoba is located in Tanzania on the western shores of Lake Victoria. Its population is approximately 85,000 people, and water is supplied to the town and surrounding areas by the Bukoba Water and Sewerage Supply Authority (BUWASA). Three quarters of the town's water supply is extracted from Lake Victoria, with the balance coming from the Kitela River and four springs. Analysis of the water system indicated that the 40-year-old main water intake in Lake Victoria was not submerged during periods of low lake water level, that the reticulation system leaked badly with approximately 59 per cent of pumped water unaccounted for, and that water quality was low with 29 per cent of samples falling outside bacterial contamination norms.

In 2008, UN-Habitat invested in upgrading the water intake and booster pump station and constructed a new facility one kilometre from its previous site. At the time of the inquiry process, this had been in operation for seven months. During the inquiry it became apparent that BUWASA wanted to expand the pipe network. However, the reticulation system had several critical design problems. The original pipe network from each sub-supply system (lake, river, borehole) had been joined together into a larger network. The designed pressure ratings for each system were different and, as a result, water distributed from the Kashura reservoir, into which the lake intake pumped water, was at pressures that caused pipe bursts. This also meant that the tank could not be filled to avoid such high pressure. At a meeting with the management of BUWASA, questions were asked as to how choices to invest in the intake were made. This conversation appeared uncomfortable to the management team who stated that this was a board decision, and invited us to talk with them. In the meantime, it became apparent that Agence Française de Dévelopment had recently committed some €5.8 million for the development of new intake, pumping station, and water treatment plant. This was surprising in the light of UN-Habitat's recent investment in the same. The conversation with the BUWASA board revealed a number of surprising opinions. Firstly, it was stated that the current new intake was poorly located and was extracting water from the harbour. Here, the board stated that ship oil and waste was being sucked into the town water supply. Secondly, they stated that the UN-Habitat investment was only an interim measure to address supply issues, but that a more robust supply and treatment solution was required. It was clear in the meeting that the chairman was the ultimate authority.

A chance meeting with the engineer employed to examine the French investment revealed a set of opinions that were serious enough to alarm. He stated that the UN-Habitat system was in good working order, that the new site proposed for the French intake was on the land of the BUWASA chairman who stood to gain long-term royalties, and that the waste outlet for the local coffee processing factory lay in the catchment of the new intake. In other words, the new investment also continues the pattern of investing in plans that stand no chance of delivering intended services, and seem subordinate to local political power plays.

A review of the UN-Habitat report on Bukoba focuses entirely on the technical challenges facing the town. The conversations during the participatory systems inquiry indicated that this had failed to capture political and power dynamics, let alone social and access issues. The investment choices made seem blind to emergent issues, with pre-constructed solutions. Bukoba was to be equipped with two intakes, two pumping stations, and a distribution system that bursts when loaded. It was unclear whether any clean water would reach citizens (for bursts have the unfortunate affect of sucking contaminants into the system). Consideration of the end users barely seems to enter the equation.

These are just a few of more than 30 major system dynamics that were uncovered in the towns in just one week of inquiry. The dynamics were mapped and analysed collectively. They illustrate how by revealing the system dynamics, we get a very clear picture of the different points at which action could take place to generate solutions to what are the actual problems. But as well as the intra-town dynamics, deeper patterns were uncovered across the towns, as well as systemic impacts resulting from the way in which UN-Habitat managed the programme (we discussed some of these briefly in the introduction to Chapter 1). Here we will describe just one – but very important – example.

Pro-poor policy across the towns

LVWATSAN was explicitly articulated as a pro-poor programme, but the evidence from the inquiry indicated that it was not pro-poor at all. In Kyotera, for example, a short walk to the outskirts of the town and beyond – where the poorest people live – revealed stories of people who did not and could not benefit from the UN-Habitat programme. The stories of just three households will serve to illustrate some of the problems.

A grandmother who is more than 80, maybe more than 90, looks after five children. The oldest is six years old. Their father (her youngest son) left and never came back. They live in a very small dwelling. The house is surrounded by bananas but they are impossible to keep up and the children are too small to cultivate the land. They live only on maize, posho, and beans, but the quality of the posho is very poor as none of children nor the grandmother have the strength to stir it. They can eat banana matoke when the bananas are ripe. They have water with a few leaves in it for breakfast. The children carry all of the water and they do all of the cooking. But there is no local water that is available for free and they have no source of income. They take jerry cans from the nearest water sources but they can only carry small cans so they have to make many trips. They have to drink it without boiling because the small amount of firewood that they are able to forage has to be used for cooking. Similarly they cannot use the little water they can get for washing. On the day that we visited they had no water at all, no food and no fuel. The only solution which doesn't involve paying for water is to build a rainwater harvesting tank if they can get the money for materials, but that will take 17 people five days to build.

A bit further up the road is a family with eight children. Six of them are very young, and two of them are teenage girls. Their guardian is their grandmother. The two older girls do most of the work for the family. They cultivate the land around the house. The grandmother's son constructed the house but then he died. The children's uncle lives in Kampala. He pays for their school fees (not always on time). The mother abandoned the children after a domestic quarrel. Food is not so much the problem. They can grow bananas, cassava, and sweet potatoes. They can get fuel from the ground – even burning the dried skin of the cassava. Water is the big problem. All of the children go to fetch water every day. They each go two times and it takes an hour for every trip. Sometimes it is two hours, because there is a very long line.

In the third household there is a grandmother and a young school-going girl of 10 who keeps her company. She has to go a long distance to collect the water. If the girl goes for water in the evening 'she can be defiled', so she can't collect it in the evening. This limits the amount of water the household can get.

The poorest people live on the outskirts of the town and have further to go to collect water. In the first story the children are too small to collect a lot of water even from the dirty water source and the grandmother is too frail. In the second story the two teenage girls, who are trying to study at school, are also cultivating for the whole family and they are the only ones who are physically able to carry water, which may take them each four hours a day. This has a major impact on their prospects for any education. In the last story we see that water cannot be collected at night because of the risks. So this young girl has to collect the water instead of going to school. The 'availability of water' in the centre of the town at a price is not the main issue and will not answer any of the questions posed by these families.

Moving now to Kisii in Northern Kenya. We walked into the offices of the private water company, passing posters which boldly advertised its pro-poor credentials. After some minutes of discussion it became clear that despite various applications to the Water Service Trust Fund (one of the main funding sources for the water company) there had been no application for Nubia – the poorest quarter of town – nor was one planned. It also became apparent that no one in the water company had ever been there (Kisii is not a big town). The company was focused on cost recovery: 'Most companies have been thinking about cost recovery. It's natural if I have not had enough food then I can't think of someone else.'

Its pro-poor work was articulated in terms of 'corporate responsibility' rather than as part of its core mandate, and this was clearly only something that they could engage in once they were making a profit. Most worrying was the ethos that came from the top which was captured so clearly by this statement: 'we are lucky everyone doesn't have rainwater collection, or we wouldn't be able to sell water'.

This is a deeply systemic problem because it is not in the interest of the water company to promote sources of water that are free. The provision of piped water for payment militates against the development of rainwater run-off systems which would undoubtedly benefit the poor.

In Bugembe this was made explicit by the multi-stakeholder forum (MSF) – which incidentally had no representatives of people living in poverty on it. Two comments from their meetings serve illustrate this: 'Urban planning is the focus, not necessarily that of the poor' and 'initiatives should target all, not just the poor. If you give to the rich the poor will get.'

At a later stage, we looked at the maps which had referred to micro-credit schemes that were being set up by the programme. In almost every town map there was a specific comment about the lack of access or relevance for the poorest. The Kyotera map recorded, 'micro credit not pro poor, strict conditions, no women participants'. The Nyendo map recorded, 'scheme is for those with jobs, not pro poor'. The Mutukulu map recorded, 'micro credit does not reach the poor'. The Bugembe map recorded, 'I wonder who will benefit from the micro credit. I am yet to understand the criteria to be used.' There was a clear pattern across the towns that was instantly discernable on the system maps. What was clear from these inquiries is that the LVWATSAN programme was essentially an exercise in urban infrastructure development not in access to water services for the poor, and this had profound implications for the type of capacity development that was proposed.

Reflections on the LVWATSAN process

As we have seen, the LVWATSAN inquiry process revealed many complex system dynamics at the level of local issues and across the towns. It makes clear how crucial it is to connect the infrastructure development to an understanding of the dynamics of local systems. We have offered real detail in this narrative because it is in the detail that we can see what works and what doesn't and why. For those 'looking down' from the UN-Habitat headquarters, all that can be seen is the budget and a set of delivered outputs.

There are two strong messages from these examples. Firstly technical solutions won't be effective if there is no understanding of the system dynamics within which they are situated. Secondly, individual and organizational capacity development to support solutions is not enough. In order to create change people have to be able to see where change is needed and where it is possible.

System mapping case study 2: the Climate Airwaves initiative – participatory systemic inquiry through Community Radio in Ghana

The techniques used by the Ghana Community Radio Climate Change project evolved from the LVWATSAN process, but here the process was facilitated by community organizations, and was a genuinely participatory process. Hence we see the methodological evolution from systemic inquiry to PSI.

In 2011, Danny worked with Blane Harvey and Katy Oswald to support an action research process on climate change in Ghana in partnership with the Ghana Community Radio Network (GCRN) (Harvey et al., 2012). GCRN is a network of 12 community radio stations which are staffed and run by local community volunteers who engage with issues of local importance to communities. They were at the start of a journey through which they would come to see inquiry-based processes as the means for generating interactive content for their programming and more widely opening up dialogues with the community. We created two community radio research teams. The first worked in Azizanya – a community whose residents had already had to move twice because of the encroachment of the sea. They looked at a set of interconnected issues around climate change, coastal erosion, land ownership, and tourism. The second went to the community of Afiedenyigba and looked at another set of interconnected issues relating to crop failures, loans, and access to markets. The community research teams talked to many people each day and came back together to construct system maps. Having created a series of messy maps Figure 4.5 was the group's first attempt to distil the system dynamics.

Figure 4.5 is an example of a macro-level analysis. The community research teams later zoomed in on some of the details to reveal some of the micro-level dynamics. What we can see in this map is the way in which the climate change issues resulted in unpredictability and crop failure, lower quality crops, and the loss of some varieties. It also resulted in a low fish catch. For some, these

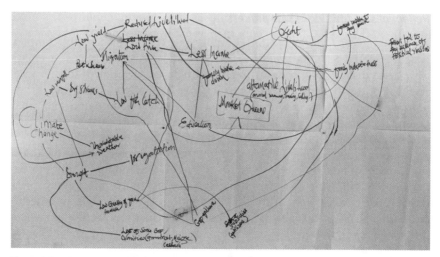

Figure 4.5a Macro level analysis of climate change dynamics in Afiedenyigba, Ghana original

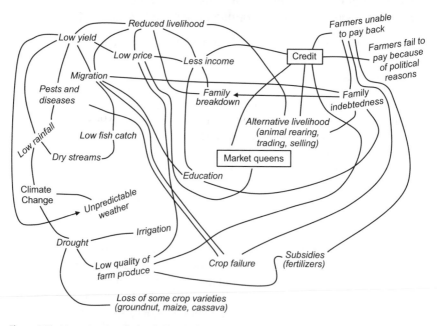

Figure 4.5b Macro level analysis of climate change dynamics in Afiedenyigba, Ghana – transcribed
Source: Adapted from Harvey et al. (2012)

led directly to migration as livelihoods disappeared, for others it led to debt to pay for fertilizers, or to bridge the gaps where no money was coming in, and so on. All of these led to high levels of debt. Migration directly contributed to family breakdown, and high levels of debt created greater pressures on families which increased the drive to family breakdown. Family breakdown further weakened the ability of families to generate income and amplified the need for debt. At the centre of the systems map were the market queens (*Magadzias*). These women were the primary buyers for crops, and also controlled the local money-lending system. In return for credit they controlled the crop prices, which in effect further lowered the income that the farmer could generate, which in turn led to further debt, and so the spiral continued. What the group was able to see through an analysis of these dynamics was that it was not solely the impact of climate change that was causing their poverty, but the way in which it was compounded and amplified through the relationship between migration, family breakdown, and the central position of the market queens. So if they were going to take action, then they needed to focus on the things that they had the potential to change. This allowed the group to ask 'how' questions such as, 'how might we reduce the power of market queens?', 'how can we improve the financial literacy of small scale farmers?', 'how might we strengthen families during these periods of financial uncertainty?'

Even in a relatively simple diagram with no directional arrows showing causality and no positive and negative signs, it is easy to see what the relationships are. One of the attractive features of these maps is that they are also easy to transfer and to explain to people who are not part of the inquiry. Just as in the Kamukunji example that we described earlier, direct positive outcomes emerged from the inquiry alone and how it was communicated by the radio station. This account describes the outcome:

> While the longer term impacts of this research are still emerging (the project concluded in August 2011) there are already concrete outcomes beginning to emerge from the process at the level of the communities themselves. Among the more marked outcomes to date has been the initiation of a new dialogue between community members of Azizanya and local and traditional authorities from the area. Azizanya as we mentioned above, is a community facing rapid coastal erosion and a tense related conflict over land tenure rights between fishing communities and local authorities looking to develop coastal land for tourism. Broadcasters report that the community durbar helped to renew an open (and broadened) dialogue on these issues, which have been the source of significant conflict and secrecy to date. Further, upon hearing the broadcast dialogues about these issues, neighbouring communities facing similar challenges approached the broadcasters requesting to be brought into the investigation as well. (Harvey et al., 2012: 111)

Systemic story analysis

So far we have shown how community-level maps can be built from stories of individuals and from stories about the community. From many micro stories we were able to get a picture of the macro patterns. But we can also look at this the other way around. From the individual stories we can start to understand how the macro patterns interact with individuals' lives – both creating spirals of decline and 'positive deviance' (Pascale et al., 2010) which enable people to create positive trajectories even where their peers are unable to.

Storytelling reveals system dynamics, which can be described in narrative form. It helps us to understand how change happens. As one explanation on the Wikipedia page on narrative inquiry nicely explains 'Story collecting as a form of narrative inquiry allows the research participants to put the data into their own words and reveal the latent 'why' behind their assertions' (Wikipedia, n.d.). Understanding why things happen is necessary in order to understand the relationship between things that happen (whether causal or not). In our narrative work we look at three types of stories:

- *Individual stories* that can tell us a lot about how and why things happen. For example, we may only have one story about how a disabled person moved from begging into employment, but it can tell us something about the factors which made that possible – which can then be researched more deeply.
- *Stories of individuals which tell stories of many people.* For example, the story of rape and sexual assault of disabled women in Bangladesh, which we discuss in the following pages, is a recurring pattern that describes the situation experienced by many women (even though details will be different in each case).
- *Stories which depict a collective experience.* For example, a community facing the flooding of its villages as a result of a dam or collectively experiencing conflict.

The stories can be told through a digital story-making process, or told as oral or written narratives. The point of these narratives is not to generate yet another set of sob stories about poverty that can motivate benevolent charity givers to send their money to save the poor. The point is to understand how local system dynamics impact on people and how they can be changed.

Story analysis case study 1: Bangladesh 'We can also make change' project

In 2013 Danny Burns and Katy Oswald facilitated an initiative that was coordinated through three international non-governmental organizations (INGOs) that worked on disability and older people's issues (HelpAge, ADD international, and Sightsavers). They wanted to support a grass-roots peer research process which used participatory methods, and which would reveal from the perspectives of people with disabilities what was important in their lives, and the dynamics of how those things happened. The work was started in Bangladesh. Together they designed a programme that centred around three inquiry groups. The first was of local people in the rural villages of Cox Bazaar, the second was of local people in the Bhashantek slum of Dhaka (one of the older informal settlements that had a basic level of infrastructure), and the third was a group of grass-roots community-based organizations which worked right across the country. Each of these groups was set up to undertake PSI through both peer networks and through inquiry with people in their neighbourhoods.

The make-up of the groups was important. Within the community-based research teams very few were literate. All of the members were either disabled or older people. Five of the group were either blind or partially sighted. Even in the CBO group only one had ever done any research before. These characteristics were important to the integrity of the research, but also to the way in which the research and the research teams were designed. Look through any manual of participatory research methods and you will see that it is filled with interesting visual methods from chapatti diagrams to complex system maps of the type described above. When you are working with blind and partially sighted people you have to completely rethink this approach. We decided to work with stories because within a strongly aural culture, people have the capacity to hold and memorize stories, and because stories do not have to be seen. When collecting stories we worked in teams.

We arranged for each inquiry team to have a volunteer alongside them to help to record the discussions that they had. The volunteer was instructed that they could write, but they must do nothing else. We went through a long process of constructing story prompts which began with things like 'tell me about a time when ...' This allowed people to generate very open narratives and to talk about the things that were most important to them. A prompt is not a question. It is more like a trigger which gives permission to people to tell the story that they want to tell. A story prompt that we have used in other situations is 'tell me a story of what you worry about just before you go to sleep at night'.

Over a period of thee months the teams gathered around 100 stories. Many of these had two or three sub-stories each relating to a different story prompt. We analysed most of these stories collectively in a week-long workshop. Participants were asked simple questions such as 'what is important in this story?', 'why is it important?', and 'what are the implications of what we have learned from this story?'. The researchers clustered the issues, developed their own analysis, and produced detailed recommendations.

The stories revealed a number of important things. Firstly, they identified patterns (stories-of-stories) and in doing so they also revealed the issues that people thought were most important. These were not necessarily the obvious ones. For example, in this inquiry process, perhaps the biggest issue was that of sexual violence faced by disabled girls, for this recurred repeatedly across the inquiry. Secondly, these stories showed the dynamics of change within individual lives. Different versions of the following story-of-stories were told across the inquiry:

> A disabled girl comes from a family that has a very low income and she is left at home alone. Her parents have to work and cannot afford for anyone to stay with her. Because she is left alone – and in a private space – she is raped. She is more vulnerable because of her disability. She may

not see her assailant because she is blind, or be able to escape because she is physically disabled, or be able to shout because she cannot speak, or understand what is happening to her because she is intellectually challenged. Once attacked, she may not be able to identify the assailant. If she is blind she may not have seen her attacker. If she is mute she may not be able to communicate who he is, and so on. Furthermore she may not be believed simply because she is disabled. In some of these stories – where the attacker was known – families tried to seek justice. But the perpetrator was a powerful local person and got the police to change the evidence. Once the justice system had rejected their attempts to get justice the perpetrators felt empowered to drive the family from the village.

In some of the stories these girls are now pregnant. In others the rapist was made to marry the girl, an outcome which was widely considered to represent 'justice' – although it is doubtful whether many of the girls would regard it this way. The story is filled with causes and consequences. This depiction of the flow of events helps us to understand the system dynamics. What we learn here is that her vulnerability as a woman to rape is radically amplified, first, by her parent's poverty, and, second, by her disability. If she seeks justice she is likely to become more at risk so there is a strong systemic incentive not to seek justice. We also learn that the impacts on disabled people frequently ripple out to their families (which in turn feed back to them). In the story above, the family is driven away from their community. In other stories, sisters could not get married because of the disability of their sibling, and so on. So it is not possible to meaningfully engage with these issues without understanding the wider relationship to family. In another story-of-stories we hear of disabled people who have managed to find an income. These stories were often characterized by extreme determination – such as a boy who gets a cart to sell from, despite his inability to walk easily. But when they do manage to get a job the stigma against them changes radically. Suddenly they are afforded respect and the abuse stops. Another pattern that we discerned from these stories is that most of the worst abuse came from the families themselves. In many cases any pension or allowance that the disabled person was entitled to – way too little to live on in any case – was taken by the families. The families always seemed to be in the way of disabled people leading autonomous lives.

Through these understandings we can begin to see where the critical points are in each of these lives that might break a negative pattern. We can begin to identify what is it that would break the dynamic that makes these girls particularly vulnerable to rape, and what is it that would break the dynamic that prevents redress and creates further harm. Solutions begin to emerge through new questions: What if we focused on securing the incomes of parents of disabled children? Are there ways in which we could ensure that disabled children are not left alone? How can local systems of justice be built that give meaningful redress to victims of rape? What needs to happen to support victims and their families when they are driven from their homes?

Story analysis case study 2: the Participate Initiative

The Participate Initiative was a programme of participatory research carried out by 18 participatory research organizations across the world, and supported by IDS and the Beyond 2015 campaign of civil society organizations (CSOs). The aim of this work was, through research, to bring the voices of the very poorest and most marginalized into the global process to decide what would replace the MDGs. The research employed a wide variety of participatory methods, but what was common to many of them was the collection and analysis of stories. These stories are able to reveal a great deal about the system dynamics that people have to navigate. Here, with reference to some of the stories, we show some of the different ways in which that can be done.

Stories that depict compounded discriminations which lead to spirals of decline. Through the collection and analysis of stories in the Participate Initiative we learned about the dynamics that draw people further and further into poverty. Here is a transcript of a story created as a digital story by the Sustainable Livelihoods Foundation in South Africa. It is the story of Cebisa:

> This is my community. I was born and raised in this community.
>
> A place called Langa. A very small, but very busy community.
>
> You can see people rushing to taxis on their way to work;
>
> children on their way to school;
>
> self employed people.
>
> Across the street from my home there is a shack 113
>
> Where a family used to live.
>
> But now a young boy age 12 lives there alone
>
> First his uncle and his grandmother died
>
> Then another uncle was sentenced to 18 years in prison
>
> A year later his mother died from HIV and AIDS
>
> This young boy was born HIV positive
>
> I watched this boy going to the clinic on his own to fetch his medication
>
> I was told he was dropped out from school because his peers teased him
>
> I watch him being abused by the community members

Each and every day I observe this young boy becoming more angry and more aggressive

Last Sunday evening it was something to 9

I hear the gun shots, dogs barking, police van

I was inside the house. After a moment I looked at the window

I see this boy sitting alone, barefoot, head in hands

Staring ahead, not moving, barely dressed

I could see the tears on his eyes. I asked myself 'what is this boy thinking'.

What's going on in his head

Slowly I approach him and I ask him 'boy, what is wrong?'

And the boy cried, and he told me he is hungry.

And at the clinic he was told to bring an adult to take his medication.

And he told me he don't know who to ask.

I just feel his pain. I hug him. I told him that 'you have me'. (Cibesa's story, n.d.)

As with the story of disability and rape that was discussed above, these are not voyeuristic stories of poverty designed to evoke sympathy. They are stories which describe in detail the dynamics of the system within which these people live and make choices. They are critical to understanding change. They enable us to understand the relationships between things that happen in a way that statistics on orphan children with HIV will never be able to do. In Cebisa's story we can see both the system and the dynamics that affect the boy. Because of the nature of his circumstances a lot of people around him have died. As a result he has a lack of support from close family. The derision expressed by his community is what is stopping him from going to school. This is important because here we begin to understand that it is not the lack of school provision that is restricting his access. Similarly, his interaction with the health services are characterized by a lack of understanding and a system which is not designed for people like him. His lack of access has nothing to do with a lack of availability. In both cases it is institutional discrimination and discriminatory local social norms combined with poverty and isolation that are limiting his possibilities to escape from his desperate life. We also see how one thing leads to another. The taunts from the community make him more and more angry. This is likely to lead him into conflict which could bring him in to further danger. What we see here is the way one inequality compounds and or amplifies the next. It is a dynamic not a static system.

Box 4.2 is another story from the Participate initiative from slum dwellers in the Philippines.

Box 4.2 Sara Mendoza, born in Santa Ana, Manila

In 1993, I moved to live under a bridge on a rented house when I got married; four of my six children were all born here.

... we lived a quite peaceful life here. But when the demolitions started in 2005, our life changed drastically. We were moved to PNR nearby (Philippine National Railways); we stayed there for a year. Then another demolition started in early 2006 and in July that same year we were moved to Cabuyao, Laguna Province (50 km away from Manila). It was done during a typhoon signal number 2. Our things and us were transported with a truck with no roof and so we and our stuffs were all soaking wet.

When we arrived there, there was no house. It was just a piece of land that we have to clean and remove all the weeds and to build a house ... When we were relocated, we were given 1,000 pesos (about USD $25) by the government. Once we got to the area, an amount of 25,000 pesos were given to start building the house ... We had to wait 2 weeks before we had the money to build our house. In the end, we were not able to spend the money on making the floor of the house, but on food because my husband could not work there, we were living already there and we have to eat to continue to live. During rainy season our area gets flooded and the houses are surrounded by rice fields. The soil of our house erodes during rainy season.

At the beginning my husband continued his work in Manila and rented a small place to live. He is blind, and is a masseur. In Manila he had regular customers for massage. I was staying in the relocation site and I would come from time to time to Manila. We talked if we would send the children to school in the province with me living there with the youngest children, while my husband would be living in Manila with one of our eldest who wanted to continue school there. But it was taking double expenses; with our budget of 200 pesos a day it is not enough. Sending money to the province was also not possible. To send 100 pesos there, the fee is 60 pesos.

So my husband decided to live altogether in the province and our daughter studying in Manila lived with a relative to continue school. But it was impossible for the kind of livelihood my husband has. We tried there but we couldn't get customers, we had no other source of income and no savings. So we tried to find other ways to earn a living. We tried to sell stuffs, we tried scavenging. We tried to import stuffs from there to sell in Manila and earned money through commission. We asked for alms, as we do sometimes here in Manila when needed, but there, there is no highway, no traffic.

Our weekly budget was really not enough with 5 children to feed and pay for all the other expenses like kerosene for light, water and wood for cooking. Electricity there was installed only after 1 year. For the first time in my life, we starved; there was no food for my children. But we tried living there despite of hunger. We tried but we really couldn't survive living there.

I would like to say something on the schooling of my children (except for one) ... my other children really had to stop school for a whole year. I was not able to transfer them to a school in the province, because if we did so, the scholarship they received from Manila would be stopped permanently. We first tried for a year to see if it was possible for us to live in the province. When we came back to Manila, my children were all ashamed to go back to school. They ... were afraid to get teased or bullied because they were a year behind from them (so) I had to work hard to motivate them and to explain them how important education to get a better job when they grow up.

After a year, in 2008 we moved back to the bridge ... our houses were gone. We were not allowed to build a house to live in. We rented instead something near the bridge, but the rent was 750 pesos a month and we couldn't continue. For example, with our income, we were setting aside 20 or 30 pesos everyday to pay the rent at the end of the month. Children needed 20 pesos each to go to school and they are 6 children!

(Continued)

Box 4.2 (Continued)

> As we are thinking of the future, we did not sell the house from the relocation site. ... For me I want to keep the house. It's like an investment for my family. For us it is a once in a lifetime opportunity to own a piece of land ... my neighbour is living there taking care of the house because stealing stuff there is recurrent when no one lives in it ... there are many conditions and restrictions for this house we are paying. For example, if the house remains empty with no one living there or you are not able to pay for a certain number of months, they will take it back even if you already got the electricity and water installed.
>
> In my opinion, the people who can stay there (in the relocation site) have a permanent job or have a member of the family working abroad. Some have capital to build a small store or a place in a nearby market. In short, there is constant income for the family. Unlike us, our income is very unstable. For them transferring their children from schools in Manila to the province is not a problem. They can continue sending their children to school because they have a stable financial situation. (ATD Fourth World, in Burns et al., 2013: 19)

This story clearly explains the interlinkage between different issues of education and livelihoods and the fact that even when people are relocated with 'property' it doesn't work for them because they cannot earn a living and they cannot go to school. It is only through the detail of this story that we understand why. The next story is comes from an informal settlement of Nairobi.

> Many people in Mathare are scared to go outside at night because of some threats such as mugging and rape. Women are scared to use the toilets in the night, that is why they use flying toilets, and this can lead to health problems, while older men are even scared to go out during the day time. We decided to tackle the issue by trying to map all of the places that it took place. We discovered that the hotspot of violence were in the areas of no lights. We were pleased to see that security lights had been erected, small business have been set up, the security that was created is leading to benefits. Small change can lead to improvements, but a few days later vandals came and destroyed the light. We were very disappointed and the mugging continued. You find that the security lights which are here, people tamper with them and they end up having light during day time, it is now day time and the light is on. Most of the people who spoil the lights, maybe, they are the ones that commit the crimes around here. (Spatial Collective, in Burns et al., 2013: 18)

This is a story of issues faced by a community. In this story it is clear that while work was done to understand the problem, it cannot be resolved unless attention is paid to the wider system dynamic. Muggings take place where there are no lights, so we ensure that there are lights. This assumes somehow that the perpetrators are passive, and that once the lights are there they will stop mugging. But the situation is dynamic and each action creates a reaction.

What is clear from the stories that we have recounted above is that single interventions which do not take into account the whole life of a person will fail to benefit the very poorest. In the case of the disabled woman who is raped, part of the solution lies in addressing the poverty of her parents, part in her isolation, part in the discriminatory social norms of the community, part in local corruption, and so on. If an intervention were to offer her 'work' or 'education' or any other pre-packaged intervention, it would completely miss the point. Cibesa's story depicts a catalogue of interrelated factors that amplify the negative position that the boy finds himself in. In the story of the bridge, the presumed solution of the authorities – relocating people to new properties – fails completely because they have no idea of the realities that these people face. In the example of the lights the solution fails because there is no understanding of the wider system. Each one of these stories helps us to understand the system dynamics.

The story that is told is not just a story. It is a part of a dynamic process. The story is told and it invites us to ask questions – like how could the attitudes of the local community toward children like this be changed? These questions then become a platform for an interactive dialogue about what is happening. This is similar to the process that happened with the GCRN where the broadcast becomes the basis for the next iteration of an inquiry, allowing us to test the resonance, draw in new evidence, challenge the pattern, and so on.

Story analysis case study 3: a coda on the Ghana community radio inquiries

In the section above we showed how the mapping process enabled a systemic analysis to be constructed. But in the context of radio, these were recast as stories that were broadcast. Radio as a medium for story-based inquiry offers interesting possibilities, illustrated by the following extract from a write-up of that project (Harvey et al., 2012):

> Broadcasts cannot only be seen as an output, but also as an essential ingredient of future inquiry. A piece might be broadcast and stimulate a phone-in response from listeners which might develop some themes and amplify others. The phone-in might also articulate further questions or areas for inquiry and investigation. This could lead to further programming and so on. The product is therefore a catalyst for sense making, and the sense making underpins further inquiry which in turn leads to further broadcasts.
>
> Another aspect of radio as a vehicle for action-oriented inquiry relates to the different kinds of knowing as articulated by Heron and Reason (2008). Meaning is not just conveyed through the text of the words or other visual representations, but also in the texture of what is said – the emotion, the energy, the pace, the pauses, the use of Language. Radio can have the effect of distilling the emotion through voices, much as a black and white photograph can distil the meaning in a photograph (when colour photography often cannot). Emotion is not just an expression of individual feeling; it is also a vehicle for connection and resonance ...

Radio programmes create new stories that are built from the original stories. Like we described above they are stories-of-stories. It then has the ability to use those stories to add new layers to the inquiry. In this way the broadcast is simultaneously an output and an input to the next phase of inquiry.

Conclusion

System maps and narrative analysis which reveal system patterns are important because they allow us to see the whole; to see the system dynamics; and to identify, in the midst of complexity, what is happening, what needs to happen, and how change might happen. They help us to see the key driving forces and where the leverage points for change might be. The processes that we have described enable us to see how system dynamics impact on individual lives by holding a mirror up to the system dynamics that people live amid. Developing interventions with this in mind enables them to be appropriate to the needs of the individual and means that change is more likely to impact on the poorest and most marginalized. From this foundation we now turn to questions of how to engage with the system. We identify three pathways to engagement:

- *PSI as a planning tool* is the weakest of the three options because while it offers a deeper and more systemic baseline analysis of the issues than would typically be the case for development interventions, the process stops there. It doesn't offer the prospects of action generated from real-time iterative learning. We won't elaborate further as the LVWATSAN process described above can be seen as an example of this approach.
- *Systemic action research* is a structured process that integrates learning and action. Here an understanding of complex system dynamics leads to the creation of deliberately focused action research inquiries.
- *Nurtured emergent development* is a more organic process where actions have a cascading dynamic, and scale is built through attractor dynamics.

They are not mutually exclusive. Elements of each can be infused into the other to create hybrid models. We explore these in the next two chapters.

References

Aked, J. (2014) 'Riding the waves of change: the challenges of volunteering in highly complex poverty contexts. Reporting on action research among volunteers in Mangingisda, Palawan', Institute of Development Studies and VSO.

Burns, D. (2007) *Systemic Action Research: A Strategy for Whole System Change*, Bristol: Policy Press.

Burns, D. (2014) 'Seeing the world through a different lens', Field Reports and Reflections, Participatory Methodologies, Participation, Power and Social Change, An Institute of Development Studies blog. <https://participationpower. wordpress.com/2014/08/14/seeing-the-world-through-a-different-lens/> [accessed 1 July 2015].

Burns, D., Harvey, B. and Ortiz Aragon, A. (2012) 'Action research for development and social change', *IDS Bulletin* 43(3).

Burns, D., Howard, J., Lopez-Franco, E., Shahrokh, T. and Wheeler, J. (2013) 'Work with us: how communities and organisations can catalyse sustainable change', Brighton: Institute of Development Studies.

Fubesi, Cebisa. (2013) *Ndenzi – What have I done?* [online] Sustainable Livelihood Foundation/Participate Initiative, Brighton: Institute of Development Studies <http://www.workwithus2015.org/projects/slfdst.html [accessed 8 July 2015]

Harvey, B., Burns, D. and Oswald, K. (2012) 'Linking community, radio, and action research on climate change: reflections on a systemic approach', *IDS Bulletin* 43(3): 101–17.

Heron, J. and Reason, P. (2008) 'Extending epistemology within a co-operative inquiry' in P. Reason and H. Bradbury (eds) *Handbook of Action Research: Participative Inquiry and Practice*, 2nd edn, London: Sage Publications.

Holland, J. (2013) *Who Counts? The Power of Participatory Statistics*. Rugby: Practical Action Publishing.

Pascale, R., Sternin, J. and Sternin, M. (2010) *The Power of Positive Deviance: How Unlikely Innovators Solve the World's Toughest Problems*. Boston, MA: Harvard Business Review Press.

Percy-Smith, B., Burns, D., Walsh, D. and Weil, S. (2003) Mind the gap: Healthy futures for young people in Hounslow. Discussion Paper. University of the West of England.

Ricigliano, R. (2012) M*aking Peace Last: A Toolbox for Sustainable Peace Building*, Boulder, CO: Paradigm.

Wadsworth, Y. (2010) *Building in Research and Evaluation: Human Inquiry for Living Systems*, Melbourne: Action Research Press and Allen & Unwin.

Wikipedia (no date) 'narrative inquiry'. <https://en.wikipedia.org/wiki/Narrative_inquiry> [accessed 29 June 2015].

CHAPTER 5
Systemic action research

Systemic action research (SAR) is a structured learning and research process which allows participants to engage with complex systems. SAR brings multiple actors together to intervene in causal chains that lead to downward spirals and negative outcomes for people and communities and to sow seeds that might lead to upward spirals. Theories of change are generated and tested in the field. This creates a highly adaptive iterative learning process.

Keywords: action research; participatory action research; systemic action research; volunteering; systemic conflict transformation

The action research process

We have discussed action research and systemic action research (SAR) processes extensively in other publications (Burns, 2007, 2014, 2015), but it will be helpful to situate the practices described here in some of that thinking. We will then explore two cases of how SAR has been built into international development processes.

Action research is an iterative learning process which combines reflection and analysis with action. It is rooted in an assumption that we learn as much from action as we do from deliberation. It is a process where participants work through repeated cycles of assessment, action planning, action, and evaluation (Reason and Bradbury, 2008; Coghlan and Brydon-Miller, 2014). This is typically articulated as a four-stage cycle. The Kolb cycle is most commonly quoted (Kolb, 1984) but there are many versions. When the cycle is completed it starts again the new situation is analysed; hypotheses are generated, refined or reformulated; new action is planned, and so on. Burns (2014) has found it helpful to explicitly articulate a fifth stage in the cycle specifying the generation of contextually situated theories of change (see Figure 5.1). In action research processes, dynamic theories of change are generated with each iteration of the process. Different theories of change may be articulated by people with different positions in any complex social system and it is important that there is a space for these to be contested.

Cycles of this type are now in fairly common use. What makes action research different is the frequency of the cycles – typically no more than two months apart. This allows for a rapid iterative and real-time learning process where action is informed by analysis and analysis is informed by action.

The PSI processes identified in Chapter 4 provide an evidential and analytical foundation for the action research which then follows. A key role for the systemic inquiry is to enable the right questions to be asked. This

http://dx.doi.org/10.3362/9781780448510.005

Figure 5.1 Building theories of change into the action research cycle
Source: Adapted from Burns (2014)

is a vital first step to generating appropriate action. A great deal of policy and research goes wrong because it asks and answers the wrong questions. By making visible how things are related to each other and how they impact on each other, this becomes possible.

As we have seen, PSI has to start from multiple places within the system and include stakeholders from across the system. The same principle applies to systemic action research (Burns, 2007). Action research groups should involve a wide range of different actors. Diverse stakeholders will create challenges to the interpretations of others and subject their thinking to critical scrutiny. Some actors within the system will see and be able to act upon leverage points that other actors will not have access to.

Inquiries involving diverse stakeholders will often need to be held in parallel because of the reality of power and conflict and vested interests. This is self-evidently crucial in situations of conflict or war, but also important in everyday situations. For example, in processes looking at whether markets benefit the rural poor it might be helpful to work separately with private sector actors and smallholder farmers. By creating multiple inquiries and bringing them together later, people are likely to be more honest; and much more of the whole can be seen because divergences and points of contestation are surfaced. Where there are consistent patterns across multiple groups, and where resonance reverberates through these groups, then greater weight can be accorded to the analysis – which in turn provides a strong foundation for action. To some extent this approach is a challenge to a common assumption of participatory research: that collective sense making and dialogue will lead to consensus. Often this is not possible, and what is needed are shifts across the system which open up new pathways that were not possible before (Burns, 2014).

Because possible pathways for action quickly become crystallized through social norms and so on into systemic patterns and system dynamics, the focus of an action research process then needs to be on changing the system dynamic, not on small changes *within* the system dynamic. The participatory systemic inquiries enable us to see the system dynamics, and from there it is possible to see leverage points in the system and the different points in the dynamic where change might be affected.

One starting point for identifying where to take action is to look at the chains of causalities and feedback loops to see where potential for action lies. Another is to explicitly locate alternative attractors within the system. These are likely to be points where there are counter-narratives to the dominant narratives – which appear to have some traction even on a very small scale. Participants will also need to look for where the strong energy seems to be in the system – narratives which excite or anger people and so on. The potential for change in a system often exists in the domains where there is a visible emotional response to issues. Another angle is to look for positive deviance (Pascale et al., 2010) where people on the ground are already identifying different ways of doing things or have planted seeds for doing things differently which seem to have potential. Action can take place in any part of the system and does not have to focus directly on the issue at hand.

Once a PSI has been carried out (as illustrated in Chapter 4) groups will be able to identify the key questions that they want to explore. Often these emerge from a cluster of issues which are represented in the distilled system maps, or a set of interlinked issues in a causal chain which have emerged through stories. A core question underpins each action research strand or stream. There may be three or four action research strands in an action research process each looking at different issues and involving different people. Action research strands are typically between one and two years long, with core group members meeting every four to six weeks to deliberate.

Action research processes are characterized by regular meetings that focus on the key issues, problems, and dilemmas. These are interspersed by actions, activities, and interventions. At each of the meetings, people deliberate and discuss what they believe is happening and describe their theories of change, and then they propose action. In every meeting of a systemic action research process, the groups consciously challenge their own assumptions about where they need to go, why, how, and who with. They will ask question such as:

- Are we still confident that we are going in the right direction?
- Are our success criteria the same as they were (last time we met)?
- Do the theories of change that informed our last actions still hold?
- Do we need to change our intervention?
- Do we still have the right people in our inquiry?
- Do we have all of the information that we need?

- What new actions do we need to take?
- What practices and methods do we need to use at this stage?
- Do we need to produce any outputs or feedback from our work at this stage?

(adapted from Burns, 2007)

In the meetings, analysis is subject to scrutiny, decisions on action are justified, and methodological shifts are documented. Every meeting is recorded which means that there is a clear decision trail and a record of real-time meaning making. This means that when new directions are taken, people are aware of what the situation was when they started which allows dynamic baselines to be constructed. This helps later down the line when participants want to assess the impact of their work. In between the meetings, action is taken, and that action is assessed and new actions discussed during the meetings. Typically, in the first meetings, the conversation will be more general and attention will be paid to whether the right people are there, and whether the groups have the information that they need. As the process evolves, questions become more focused and action becomes more central. A critical feature of an action research process is that ideas are tested in action, and if they don't work, they are refined or abandoned and new ones tried. This means that meaning making is not just an intellectual analysis. It is tested in real time and this makes it very robust. Testing through action is what builds ownership, because people often don't 'trust' external analysis. They trust what they can see is working.

The purpose of an action research group is to generate new and creative solutions to problems and then to test them through action. In other words, they are not there to plan things that people know how to do already – for example set up a training programme. Action research facilitators need to encourage people to think through creative solutions to problems. Generating creative solutions requires us to see issues through a different lens to the one we normally see things through (see Box 5.1). Seeing issues from multiple perspectives opens up conversational pathways that point toward solutions that had not previously been perceived. This in turn is made much easier when there is a diversity of people engaged in the meaning-making process.

Most activities will not cost significant amounts of money to implement and are more dependent on community people organizing them for themselves. Some activities may cost more. For example, groups might want to invest in a collective form of transport, or decide to repair a bridge collectively (for which you need materials), or experiment with new seeds, or ask for advice from some experts, or produce materials, and so on.

Local action may only be one element of the action research process. A learning architecture needs to be built to link the different learning strands to each other. It will link the learning to formal programme structures. It also creates spaces for deliberation and sense making up the hierarchy and into policymaking arenas. In the Myanmar example that follows, the aim is

---

Box 5.1 Conceptualizing creative solutions to problems

In a training exercise that Danny used to carry out with tenants in Scotland in the 1990s, he would draw a picture of a person standing behind a high wall that seemed to stretch into infinity and asked how they might get to the other side. The answers were highly diverse.

- Take some bricks out to make a hole.
- Smash a hole in the wall.
- Acid to burn the cement.
- Grow a tree up the wall so that its tentacles start to break up the bricks.
- Dig a tunnel under it.
- Dig a hole which collapses its foundations.
- Take a ladder over it.
- Pull it down with a rope.
- Build a mound of earth up to the top of it.
- Walk along the wall until it ends.
- Find an alternative to getting over the wall.
- Invite the people on the other side to your side.
- Invite them to throw you over some ropes and pull you over.
- Take a hot air balloon over it.

The point of this is to show that seeing the wall from multiple perspectives enables people to see many more possibilities for action. How you see fundamentally changes the potential for solutions. For example if you are focused on today, then the solutions that are possible are quite different to those if you are focused on 20 years. If you plant a tree it will grow into the wall and crack open the bricks, or will grow so tall that it can be climbed to enable you to get over the wall. This is why these inquiry processes are so important. They allow people to see from multiple perspectives and then come together to explore the potentials that they have revealed.

---

to integrate the action research into the formal peace process. In the VSO example, it is integrated into global organizational structure.

In the following pages we describe these two action research case studies. The first was a multi-level programme on volunteering which took place under the auspices of VSO. Here, action research took place at a local level with communities, and at national and global levels with the organization. The second is ongoing work in Myanmar which is ground-level community-driven research designed to produce answers to questions raised by intractable conflict, and to articulate issues that need to be fed into the peace process. The focus here is on the design, illustrating how the action research is able to engage with complexity.

Understanding how volunteering impacts on poverty – a systemic action research programme with VSO

VSO is a UK-based INGO which was formerly known as Voluntary Services Overseas. Traditionally it supported UK volunteers to work and experience life abroad. In recent years it has substantively broadened the base of its work, and it now supports and works with a wide range of volunteers including local community volunteers, national volunteer programmes, corporate volunteers, and new short-term volunteering programmes such as the UK government's international Citizen Service Scheme. VSO has also changed its focus away from an organization that promoted and supported 'volunteering' to become an international development organization whose aim is to achieve impact through volunteering. While there is copious literature on the impact of volunteering on volunteers, we discovered that there is very little literature indeed on the impact of volunteering on poverty, marginalization, and inequality.

To address this, an initiative known as Valuing Volunteering (Burns et al., 2015) was conceived to research how volunteering affected and impacted on poverty and social inequity. It was stimulated by a desire to learn within VSO, but also by an imperative to respond to demands from its core long-term donor, DFID, to show how it was impacting on development. In 2010, VSO approached IDS with a view to developing a multi-country action research programme in Nepal, Philippines, Mozambique, and Kenya. All countries had VSO-led programmes in-country. However, in addition to exploring examples of VSO-led volunteering, researchers were to investigate broader volunteerism including examples of other organization-led and community-led volunteering.

In each country, research was led by an international VSO volunteer, recruited for their research experience. These worked with international and local volunteering organizations, NGOs, government institutions, corporates, and community organizations interested in volunteering, and with individual international and local volunteers. Each lead researcher focused their action research studies around two thematic areas that had been identified and agreed with their communities of practice. Across the four countries these encompassed VSO's key thematic areas, namely education, livelihoods, health and HIV/AIDS, participation and governance, and the cross-cutting themes of gender and youth volunteering. The volunteers were all 'placed' within different organizations. For example the Kenyan researcher was hosted by a local community organization, whereas the Philippines volunteer researcher was placed with a prominent university. Each also had to build a relationship with the local VSO offices.

IDS designed a training programme for the volunteers where they practised PSI and learned how to do action research. Once they were in-country, they spent the first part of their time building relationships. IDS supported them with regionally based research accompaniments, one for each country. In these sessions we explored the emerging issues together, discussed how to develop methodologies and gradually built up the analytical categories through which the research would be brought together. Towards the end of the first year we held a write shop for the whole team where together we built a conceptual framework for the project. At the end of the second year we held a workshop where we critiqued case studies from each of the countries and refined our analytical categories. All of this fed into the final write-up. Each researcher wrote up their participatory inquiries and their action research studies. The published write-up comprised 12 case studies. In addition, most researchers also carried out national-level inquiries within VSO and with the wider volunteering sector in their countries. Some carried out interviews and discussion groups with volunteers and these were written up as separate pieces. The last stage in the process was a major analysis workshop which drew together people from the ground, the researchers, VSO staff, and people from across the volunteering sector. Their analysis provided another layer of research for the global synthesis report.

The aim of the programme was not to provide quantitative data on actual impacts of volunteers, but rather to understand through evidence how and why volunteering impacts, and what (if any) is the unique contribution of volunteering to development outcomes. The research programme worked with over 3,500 people across the four countries – giving credibility to the patterns that were identified. It worked at multiple levels. Community-level inquiries directly related to volunteers and community members. National-level inquiries fed into learning for VSO at country level. The global learning architecture enabled cross-country learning, learning into the VSO system, and learning into other global volunteering organizations such as Peace Corps, the British Red Cross, and United Nations Volunteers (UNV).

The researchers worked in their country for a period of two years, to properly understand their context and to collect detailed evidence. There was an anthropological and experiential element to their work in that they were immersed in the situation for long enough to fully understand it. One of the researcher inquiries was a self-reflective piece on their own role as volunteers and on their own effectiveness with regards to impacting on poverty.

Researchers used a mixture of methods to generate different sorts of data including exit interviews, dialogue groups with leaving volunteers, open dialogues, peer research, systemic mapping with multiple stakeholders, and action research processes. This enabled them to see issues through multiple lenses. The inquiries also used a wide range of different methods. These included peer research, interviews, digital stories, participatory mapping, and action research dialogues. This allowed patterns emerging from very different processes in different places to be triangulated.

One of the SAR inquiry case studies in Korogocho, Kenya, adopted a particularly open approach. This started with what was in the community, mapping where volunteering was happening and then generating action on the ground and knowledge for local organizations.

> With the help of a local counterpart, who had in-depth experience of the Korogocho context, a volunteer team of representatives from a range of local CBOs and volunteer groups was recruited. Members were given training on a range of participatory techniques including systems mapping and given the freedom to steer the research process. This gave them ownership whilst the training in systems and critical thinking enabled them to deconstruct and better understand the complex factors that caused poverty in Korogocho; ultimately they were then better positioned to take positive action to address the causes of that poverty.

> Over the course of nearly two years of research, the majority of team members remained engaged. And even after the fieldwork officially concluded, members carried out radio-shows on local stations to discuss findings from their work. (Burns et al., 2015)

Other SAR inquiries focused on specific programmes. For example the Nepal work focused on education, and surfaced critical patterns about the one-way transfer of knowledge from the volunteer to local teachers. It also revealed how volunteers were failing to effectively engage with deeper systemic questions of why children from the poorest backgrounds were not able to attend school. Through the inquiry, different versions of this pattern became visible across the countries. In a similar way, deep inadequacies in the ways in which volunteers were prepared to engage with complex local politics were surfaced – particularly in Mozambique. Having identified these sorts of patterns, researchers were able to explore potential solutions with participants, and over time these were fed into a global learning process. On a more positive note the inquiries showed how volunteers generated results through relationship building and helping communities to innovate by connecting external ideas to internal practices. This ground-level learning has fed into organizational learning processes that are subjecting the whole of the way in which VSO does its work to scrutiny. The research has opened up the possibility of setting up practical task groups to deal with relatively straightforward issues such as language training; pilots to model bottom-up programming processes in a country; and action research processes to explore how VSO could be more intentional about issues such as merging outsider and insider knowledge and modelling social norms.

Community engagement for sustainable peace – a SAR programme in Kachin, Myanmar

In this section we outline the shape of an action research programme that is currently underway in Myanmar. Its roots lay in a meeting of peace practitioners and systems thinkers called by the Berghoff Foundation in 2007 to explore the theory, practice, and potential for systemic conflict transformation. The central notion in systemic conflict transformation is that it is not enough to focus solely on the core protagonists within a conflict. This is because what they do is shaped by the system dynamics around them, and it is critical to change these in order to sustainably change the conflict. The workshop led to the publication of an edited collection, *The Non-linearity of Peace Processes: Theory and Practice of Systemic Conflict Transformation* (Körppen et al., 2011). It also led to the development of a close relationship between Danny and Peter Coleman at the Centre for Cooperation and Conflict Resolution at Columbia University, New York. Peter was working on the 'dynamic' character of systems, and introduced Danny to Stephen Gray and Josefine Roos who were working on a range of peace initiatives in Myanmar. They were grappling with the questions of how to meaningfully engage communities in determining their own peace agenda, and how to do so in a way which had systemic impacts. This connection led to the development of the community engagement for sustainable peace project in Kachin State Myanmar – a Systemic Action Research project, initially funded by the United States Institute for Peace (USIP) in October 2013.

Project and context

Myanmar is a country characterized by intractable conflict (Coleman, 2011). These are conflicts which appear to be resistant to resolution. Since 1948 conflict has raged between the many ethnic minorities and the military government which is dominated by the Bamar majority. There are more than 15 independent ethnic armies who have at various times been in conflict with the military government. Many tens of thousands of people have been displaced. In recent years Myanmar has suffered one of the highest levels of landmine casualties. It is also the second largest producer of opium after Afghanistan, and in some states – notably Kachin – drugs are a major factor in people's narratives about the conflict. Myanmar is a largely rural economy and is very poor, ranked 150 out of 187 countries on the Human Development Index. In 2010, after close to 50 years of military control, a quasi-civilian government took power. It is still dominated by the military but it is hoped that the 2015 elections will be free and fair. This has opened up possibilities for peace, but while there is a peace process on the table it is extremely fragile and the prospects for sustainable peace appear slim to many people.

Most peace processes are what is known as 'track one' or 'track one and a half' processes by which it is meant that they centre on heads of state and military leaders. Track three processes, which involve dialogue at community level, are much talked about but almost non-existent in practice. The assumption underpinning our engagement has been that ceasefire and peace agreements notoriously break down when underlying economic and social issues are unresolved, which was why it was so important for this programme to be community based. In each township, the SAR process engaged local civil society networks of groups such as farmers' unions, religious organizations, women's unions, and so on.

The design of the programme

This action research process undertook the following steps:

- training workshops in participatory processes and open story collection;
- collection of stories from peers and community members;
- collective analysis workshop;
- analysis workshop generating critical issues for exploration in action research groups;
- set-up of action research groups;

- a more focused story collection process which enabled the dynamics of the specific issue of inquiry to be uncovered;
- opportunities for action were identified and the action research began.

Stories were collected across the three towns of Hpakant, Laschio, and Laiza. They were collectively analysed in a large workshop. This analysis will underpin the work that they do in the future. The Laiza group which has organized the most quickly, has secured further funding, and has now begun the action research process. We hope that the others will follow suit shortly. The mapping process identified some interesting system dynamics and helped the groups to think about what was important to focus on in the action research.

They noticed for example that there were a large number of arrows going into a section of their map at the intersection between internally displaced people (IDP) issues and host community issues. The convergence point was around cutting down timber. The group discovered that a lack of cash in IDP camps was prompting IDPs to cut down trees for timber. The trees that were available were those on the land of the host communities. This created significant conflict between the two communities. Participants also noticed on the map that the host community had major livelihood problems and had been selling land to banana plantations and loggers. Both of these were cutting down large swathes of trees. This was creating a scarcity of wood and was in turn fuelling the conflict between IDP camp residents and local communities.

This analysis allowed people to think about where along these chains of interconnected issues they might intervene. They might try to find other ways for people to get cash, or create interventions to mediate the conflicts, or try to stop the land sales to banana companies, or try to get trees planted or ... here are always many possibilities, and these become the substance that the action research groups will work with. As a result of identifying this dynamic and others that related to host/IDP relations, the group decided that this was one of the key focus areas that it wanted to prioritize for the action research groups. They selected:

- IDP return to villages;
- conflict between IDPs and host communities;
- the impact of drugs on the conflict.

For each of the three issues the group carried out a new PSI. They collected 40 stories or so for each, and then produced new system maps to identify the causes, consequences, and other interlinkages between issues. Another workshop was held to analyse these. In the last two days of the workshop we called three half-day meetings which involved a wider range of stakeholders. These were the first meetings of the action research groups. The groups each comprised 15–20 members of which no more than 4 were from the Laiza core group. Others came from a wide variety of backgrounds. These included drug users, ex-drug users, pastors, soldiers, and so on. After the first meeting the groups had already identified a few actions that they wanted to take.

For example the group working on the relationship between host communities and IDP camps are organizing a youth forum and recreation space on the IDP camp to stop bored youth drifting into the town and causing trouble. So we can see that even right at the beginning activity contributing to the peace process was starting to be generated.

As the research groups evolve they will also feed their findings into a number of forums at state, national, and civil society levels over the coming year and beyond. Those trained and being drawn into this work will gather evidence, conduct analysis, prepare briefings and presentations, and implement communication and advocacy strategies that bring local perspectives and evidence to bear on the policy and decision-making processes of Myanmar's peace process. These linkages are supported by the core project team's vertical links between these communities and national and sub-national dialogue forums. At the end of the process there will be a final week-long workshop for all of the townships, ideally with participation from civil society and other peace process actors. The aim of the workshop will be to share what has been learned about the issues, to share some of the solutions to problems that have been generated, and to share insights about the process itself. Decision makers will be invited to learn from the work that has been carried out.

Organization

Having described the design and the process, it is worth reflecting on some of the organizational issues. There was a layered structure to support the process. Danny was the methodological advisor to the process and facilitated training workshops with the groups. A team based in Yangon facilitated the early training workshops, liaised with local groups, and organized the logistics. The real work on the ground was done by local networks of CSOs. These included women's unions, farmers unions, church organizations, and many others. In the first phase, the budget was managed by the team in Yangon. In the second phase the budget was decentralized to the civil society networks and was used to fund core support posts, meetings and meeting logistics, and activities generated from the action research groups. Ownership and decision-making over the process happened at the township level. In Kachin there is a powerful tradition of collective decision-making so all of the groups were involved in almost all decisions. All of the early workshops were carried out in English and then translated into Burmese and Jinghpaw (the main local language in Kachin). Stories were collected in local languages and kept as a resource in local languages. They have been translated to enable us to facilitate. When we have generated large system maps they have been written in Burmese or Jinghpaw, with yellow sticky notes with English translations to allow us to follow and facilitate. The second phase of story collection and mapping was entirely in Jinghpaw and the groups will work in their own language. This allows them to take complete ownership of the process. It was difficult to build real ownership until we had secured money for the groups to work with. This has taken some time as donors have been reluctant to fund activities before they know what they are – a problem that is faced time and time again by processes that work with emergence. But the Laiza group is now funded and working autonomously.

Conclusion

SAR is a structured process for bringing different stakeholders together to explore and try out action around a set of issues. It is a research process that examines the complex dynamics of change exemplified in this chapter in relation to poverty and conflict. By working to understand system patterns using PSI, SAR takes a deliberate course of action that starts with participant-identified and owned issues, and tests actions that participants in the process feel might work. By tracking the results of action, local participants become researchers in observing and recording changes that happen as a result of their interventions. They report these changes and their analysis through a framework of meetings. They discuss their evidence and analysis in their groups, with other action research groups, and beyond. This allows their findings to be triangulated and sense making to take place in relation to a wider group of stakeholders. This in turn seeds new rounds of inquiry that use this evidence, analysis, and resonance testing to adjust action. This work not only impacts on ground-level process but can also inform policy and organizational change. It is an effective process for those that seek whole-system change, and sustainability at scale, and provides strong formal accountability.

References

Burns, D. (2007) *Systemic Action Research: A Strategy for Whole System Change*, Bristol: Policy Press.

Burns, D. (2014) 'Systemic action research: changing system dynamics to support sustainable change', *Action Research Journal* 12: 3–18.

Burns, D. (2015) 'How change happens: the implications for action research', in H. Bradbury (ed.), *Handbook of Action Research*, 3rd edn, London: Sage.

Burns, D., Aked, J., Hacker, E., Lewis, S. and Picken, A. (2015) 'Volunteering in the new ecosystem of international development: How volunteering can impact on poverty and the environment?' Brighton: IDS/ VSO.

Coghlan, D. and Brydon-Miller, M. (eds) (2014) The Sage Encyclopedia of Action Research, London Sage.

Coleman, P.T. (2011) *The Five Percent: Finding Solutions to (Seemingly) Impossible Conflicts*, New York, NY: Public Affairs.

Kolb, D.A. (1984) *Experiential Learning: Experience as the Source of Learning and Development*, Englewood Cliffs, NJ: Prentice Hall.

Körppen, D., Ropers, N. and Geissmann, H.J. (eds) (2011) *The Non-linearity of Peace Processes: Theory and Practice of Systemic Conflict Transformation*, Leverkusen: Barbara Budrich Publishers.

Pascale, R., Sternin, J. and Sternin, M. (2010) *The Power of Positive Deviance: How Unlikely Innovators Solve the World's Toughest Problems*. Boston, MA: Harvard Business Press.

Reason, P. and Bradbury, H. (2008) *Handbook of Action Research*, London: Sage.

CHAPTER 6
Nurtured emergent development

In this chapter we challenge the idea that scaling comes about through innovation, piloting, and roll-out. We argue that scaling can be seen as closer in form to the building of a social movement where many ideas are seeded, take hold, and draw people to them, building ownership by channelling enthusiasm through networks. Maintaining that energy requires constant adaption to local circumstances to ensure that the form that each new manifestation of the process takes is appropriate to where it is located. We describe some of the different ways of supporting and facilitating this sort of process as nurtured emergent development.

Keywords: participation; iterative learning; networks; social innovation; scale

In this chapter, we explore five short cases of what we call nurtured emergent development (NED) processes. While these also develop iteratively through learning, they are different to SAR because they are not mediated through structured spaces for dialogue but through real-time learning. While more organic in nature, these processes do not emerge spontaneously. Actions need to be taken to enable all of the critical factors that we outlined in Chapter 3 to be in place. We might describe this as tending to the system and perhaps draw an analogy with the way a seed grows into a plant. The soil is prepared and needs to be fertile, the seed is planted and needs to be of good quality, the plant is fed with water and nutrients (compost), it needs to interact with its environment – bees need to be encouraged to pollinate it and birds need to be encouraged to eat slugs, and so on. Sometimes the seedlings need to be protected and invisible until they are strong enough to survive on their own. Once established they grow and quickly spread. These are all interventions.

To situate what follows, we would like to introduce the work of Yoland Wadsworth (2010). Yoland is a pioneer of SAR and has been very influential to our thinking. Her latest thinking has followed a similar trajectory to our practice and has helped us to conceptualize it. Yoland highlights the similarities between inquiry-based research and 'everyday life'(Wadsworth 2010: 20). In essence she argues that everything we do is a form of iterative inquiry. She draws a comparison to riding a bike describing a bike rider as 'a more or less successful little action-and-researching living system'.

Our bike rider is more or less:

Constantly closely observing complex aspects of self in relation to a complex environment

http://dx.doi.org/10.3362/9781780448510.006

Constantly making sense of and responding to what is observed in multiple simultaneous and interacting ways – slowing down when there is uncertainty, speeding up when it's familiar and predicable and the same course of action seems to be working.

Experimenting with new tricks just for the joy and novelty of it when all seems to be going well!

Keeping a grip on reality and everything staying connected and purposeful

Enjoying the satisfaction of numerous small achievements, the pleasure of successful skill and anticipated environments, celebrating desired destinations reached, and unexpected happenings yielding unexpected benefits and surprises

Challenges met. Observations overcome. Mourning those that couldn't be. Learning from the new experience

Repeating what works. Searching for the new where it's not ... then interpreting, evaluating, analysing and forming conclusions about new valued states to add to or revise the old ones

Continuing to stay in balance

Staying balanced by keeping moving forward

Keeping moving forward by staying balanced

Looking every now and then to audit progress against intentions, plans and expectations

Pausing every now and then to take in inputs of fuel and resources (and deposit outputs ☺)

Energies expended, outputs and outcomes identifiable

Bike and rider in subtle communication: each subtly constructing and being constructed by each other.

In more or less productive micro-sequences of doing and being.

In other words an organised bike-riding 'processual system': achieving dynamic stability (or dynamically balancing) in constantly re-assessed relationship to regularly changing contexts, propelled by intentional purposes, sufficiently fuelled energised and resourced.

What Wadsworth is saying is that even things that we do everyday, that we ostensibly know how to do, require this constant micro-cycling through assessing, planning, acting, evaluating. When we cross a road we look and check out the situation, we decide when and where we will cross, we act, and second by second we evaluate. Is that car speeding up? Do I need to speed up?

Then having reached the other side of the road we reassess our situation and so the cycles keep repeating. With every step the situation has changed and opens up completely new pathways and opportunities for action. One thing leads to another. Thus the process of living is a process of interconnected inquiry and action.

Wadsworth draws an analogy with parenting that explains what we describe as nurtured emergent development. None of us really know how to parent until we are actually parents. Very few people have plans of how they are going to parent and, if they do, they very quickly change when reality bites. The child is constantly changing, the environment it is in is constantly changing, and the parents are constantly changing. While there is a body of expert knowledge on parenting, nobody that we know has read much of it directly. Occasionally we read an article in a magazine or on the Internet. Some of us occasionally read a book. But mostly we watch what our friends do, and learn by observing our child, seeing what is going right and what is going wrong. What is actually happening is that in micro moments when we are lying in bed with our partner or walking through the park or ... we assess the 'whole' well-being of our child, we look at what is working well and what is not working well. We generate ideas about what to do – theories of change if you like. We plan action, we take action, we assess what impact that action had, and then we reassess the overall well-being of the child. When we are developing our own theories of change we actively try to find out what the people that we know and trust (and the people that they know and trust) are doing right, and we learn from it – perhaps try it – perhaps adapt it and try it, and so on.

Perhaps the critical point in these micro-level examples and social change process is that, whether conscious or unconscious, if we stop going through this cycle of inquiry and action then we quickly hit dysfunction. If we stop micro-analysing every movement we make on the bike and the environment around us, we will very quickly end up in a ditch or a traffic accident. If we don't think about what is happening to our child and parent according to a prescription, our child will quickly become a casualty of bad parenting. It is critical that we build these processes into our everyday practice, and it is this which enables 'appropriate action' leading to 'sustainable action' at a personal level and 'scale' at a social level.

Over the next pages we explore a number of cases which demonstrate how these processes can work in practice – each emphasizing different aspects of the seven elements that we outlined in Chapter 3. The first case is about the spread of schooling for girls within local communities in the face of Taliban prohibition in Afghanistan. The second story is about the growth of a social movement – the anti-poll tax campaign in the UK. The third tells of how local livestock farmers in Kenya created a completely new market structure that met their needs and spread across the country. The fourth is an account of farmer participatory extension and research in Egypt where small farmers were assisted to adapt to a new reality. The last is a description of the growth and development of Community-Led Total Sanitation (CLTS) as a response to open defecation.

In these examples we (or in the case of CLTS, close colleagues) have had a facilitative and sometimes catalytic role, working on the issue. We recall key moments where we were told by senior colleagues or officials that we were wasting our time and that what we were doing would never be taken seriously enough or grow big enough to have a significant impact.

Girls' education, Afghanistan

In this story we see the way in which a latent attractor within society is nurtured and nourished to build countervailing power to the dominant political power.

In the 1920s, King Amanullah of Afghanistan introduced secular education for girls and boys as a central feature in his plans to reform and modernize Afghanistan. He wanted to transform the country in the same way that Kamal Attaturk had done for Turkey, and his reforms were radical. These heady days of modernization were not to last, and Amanullah was overthrown in a process that found its political roots in strong clerical and military resistance to his reforms. In the minds of many Afghans, this early history linked policies of child education with a neo-liberal political movement that opposed clerical rule.

In the years that followed, children's access to primary education continued to improve under successive kings who enabled half of the population to access primary schools. When Afghanistan became a socialist republic, education for all was reformed and consolidated. This raised women into the public sphere and by the late 1980s, women played significant roles in academia and public services in mainly urban areas.

In 1978, Afghanistan formally became a communist country in a move that split the country in civil war. The government called in Russia to bolster position in a move that heralded bloody conflict that has continued ever since. Resistance came from various Islamic-based Mujahidin groups who appeared as popular heroes in an epic confrontation, both by most Afghans and by the West who had their own reasons to back anti-Soviet resistance. The Mujahidin's rejection of communism encompassed a wide rejection of several modern reforms. One of these was the promotion of a secular education programme aimed at men and women. The secular programme was tailored for a socialist state, and this met with a unified backlash in the countryside, and precipitated a call for Jihad (Nolan, 2006). With the advent of the Taliban regime from 1996 onwards, this became consolidated into policy and secular, government-run primary education was replaced with Madrasa-based Qur'anic instruction, which focused exclusively on religious education. This particularly affected girls who were latterly forbidden from attending school after the age of eight.

Taliban edicts did not lie easily with many Afghans. Women in particular felt that this denied the chance for their own daughters to be part of a better future. Physicians for Human Rights (1998) reported that, in 1998, almost all interviewed women felt that women should have equal rights to education. Many men felt this as well.

During the 1980s and 1990s, a number of NGOs provided primary education services, mainly in rural areas and in refugee camps. The biggest of these was the Swedish Committee for Afghanistan, in 1999, providing schooling for 160,000 children, 19 per cent of whom were girls. In 1994, the development agency, CARE International, conducted an analysis of how it might help provide primary education in the district of Khost in eastern Afghanistan. Through a series of conversations, communities described how in some villages, parents had organized themselves to run impromptu schools. These were being convened in mosques and community rooms where the children were being taught religion, maths, and literacy. Literacy skills were highly prized since many village men were then working in the Gulf States to support their families at home. Letters had become a critical form of communication yet literacy levels were very low, especially among women. Enabling children to read and write family letters had immediate and profound utility, and elicited strong support from parents and community elders alike.

These mosque and home schools were self-managed and seemed to require little external support. Presumptive teachers were often community prayer leaders or retired village elders who received a teaching stipend from parents. This self-organization provided an immediate basis for CARE to engage. To support this community initiative, a programme was launched and named the Home Schools Project. In 1994, prior to the Taliban takeover of the area, CARE piloted this in 10 villages of Khost province. Interventions covered technical and organizational support to village education committee groups, basic training of teachers, and the provision of teaching and learning materials.

During the first year, a number of influential former communist party members in Khost raised objections. They rejected the idea on the grounds that the constitution of Afghanistan declared education to be free, and they believed that CARE was trying to bring in Western cultural values to change the education system to a Western one. CARE Afghan staff initiated a series of community meetings to explore these fears. These conversations galvanized community action to resist what they saw as ideological propaganda from party members and to continue to form and run home schools.

In 1995, as national resistance politics played out across the country, Khost was taken over by the Taliban. With their arrival a new set of objections to the education initiative became apparent. Taliban policies precluded any secular education or any form of education for girls who were over eight years old. To preempt a shutdown of the programme, the CARE provincial administrator visited the new Taliban governor of Khost and the Southern Zone to explain the programme. Here he described the schools as being community initiatives run by parents and village committees.

Despite Taliban policies, communities wanted to school their boys and girls and to determine how their school was managed and what was taught. The Home Schools Project supported this intention by helping communities to manage and organize, building teacher skills and providing basic learning materials. For the two years of this pilot initiative, 52 schools provided education for 694 girls and boys to reach grade 2. Here, all costs involved in running these schools were born by parents, save for the support of the project. Hassan (2006) notes that in remote areas, away from Taliban attention, parents organized schools in the traditional way, in the mosque, in the *hujira* (guest room of a house), in a public building, or in the open air under a tree.

Most rural communities in Afghanistan are blood related, and it is perhaps more accurate to refer to many village communities as extended family clans. Public leadership within such a clan resides within an elder committee or *shura*. Decisions relating to village and family affairs are made here, many of which relate to private family matters. In the matter of running schools, village education committees were authorized by *shuras* to identify teachers who could be trusted with the care of the extended family children and, as a consequence, those selected were by and large known and trusted family members. Selected teachers had a basic education and were then trained to teach.

Taliban officials who challenged these schools encountered resistance from a culture which prioritizes family over tribal or national imperative. In other words, national perspectives on the appropriateness of secular education (particularly for girls) came up against family and clan assertions of autonomous private right. This gave community-managed schools considerable resilience because they were owned by communities, framed in ways that made their services appropriate and adaptable, and were manifestations of local intention.

At that time, the Taliban governor noted that CARE was providing a wide range of services and gave explicit assurances that all of these could continue in safety. The Home Schools Project continued for another two years. Based on the experiences of this pilot, CARE launched a larger initiative in late 1997. The first Community Organised Primary Education (COPE) project worked to provide community-based education (CBE) in 258 classes for 8,570 children. In 1998, as programme director for CARE in Afghanistan, Stuart was summoned to the Taliban Ministry of Education and challenged as to why CARE was providing schooling for girls when national law forbade this. He was instructed to close them. Stuart replied that CARE was not running schools but was responding to requests that were coming from local indigenous schools. These were the initiatives of local communities who were educating their own children. It was beyond CARE's mandate as a foreign group to instruct local people. CARE had neither the power nor the right to do this.

It became apparent that the Taliban were confronting a social force that had political implications. Despite their substantial national control, the Taliban struggled to secure local support. While many of their policies resonated well with local traditions, some such as these relating to child rearing and home-based education didn't. While placing pressure on a foreign service agency was politically tenable, closing local home-based schools was not a decision that they were willing to take. As a result, home schools flourished and became more and more popular, with single-class schools expanding to several classes and grades. By the time the Taliban lost national control, CBE had taken hold in Afghanistan, and appeared resilient to government pressure.

Following the departure of the Taliban and the advent of the Karzai administration, substantial Western investment increased the scale of CBE. CARE was awarded leadership of a large programme entitled Partnership for Advocating Community Education in Afghanistan (PACE-A). With three other NGOs, PACE-A worked to offer education services to rural populations, especially girls, until these services could be incorporated into the national Ministry of Education primary school system. This programme targeted 106,500 children in 3,973 classes in 19 provinces between 2006 and 2011. At the conclusion of the project, more than 2,500 CBE classes were handed over to the Ministry of Education. These classes were categorized into three clusters, namely:

1. CBE class clusters that would serve as the nucleus of new Ministry of Education primary schools;
2. CBE clusters that could be transferred to existing nearby Ministry of Education schools;
3. CBE clusters that would continue as outreach classes, linked to Ministry of Education schools.

In a subsequent review of these transferred classes, many category 1 schools were discontinued, and pupils were transferred to the local Ministry of Education. Here there was a drop in attendance of approximately 20 per cent, most of whom were girls. Also, daily attendance rates fell. One reason given for this was that the distance that pupils now had to walk to reach school had increased. However, with the category 3 schools most continued as before. Where this was not the case, the main reason cited was that community appointed teachers had been replaced with Ministry of Education appointed teachers. Many girls were not allowed by their families to continue attending school when locally trusted male and female teachers were replaced by an unknown male Ministry of Education appointed teacher (PACE-A, 2011).

The project final report further reflected that community mobilization processes and school management committee training would be a challenge for the Ministry of Education as it asserted more control over CBE. The evidence on continued community engagement with education after handover of CBE classes to the Ministry of Education was mixed. Community ownership of education tended to falter when the government controlled the situation. The report felt that there was compelling reason to continue supporting CBE, even as the Ministry of Education took more control, if access for girls was to be assured.

Reflections

Participation. In response to the war-time collapse in schooling, parents of young children had mobilized within extended family clan structures to form their own schools. Without any form of external support, some parents had arranged for a teacher, a place, a payment system, and basic materials. When CARE surveyed the area staff observed this self-organizing behaviour (that we would now suggest indicated a latent system attractor), and recognized this as something with which they could engage. Parent action provided a strong basis for careful support. Already established home schools were offered and accepted support of school materials, teacher training, and management support. New schools were created by linking these experiences with other interested parent groups who were inspired by the news of what was happening. Throughout the story, parent control over schools directly correlated with attendance and performance. When a new dominant attractor compelled parents to release control over their schools, girls' attendance dropped dramatically.

Learning. Community schools were a new idea for many parents at that time in Afghanistan. Parents and communities had never substantively engaged in forming or managing schools for their children, and they had to learn, by trial and error, how to do so. The initial schools were single class arrangements that only taught at one level. As children progressed, as schools became established, and as political context changed, so too did the schools have to adapt. The level of organization required had to evolve to more elaborate means to ensure that children were being well taught, that teachers were being paid, and that the space around them enabled continuation. CARE supported communities to form education committees to oversee the management of these schools and their external relations. They provided support to form organizational arrangements, and to experiment with ways to handle new challenges. An example of this was the home-grown method of teacher payment using wheat instead of cash, and organizing means of providing adequate support to retain teachers. The challenge to the schools from district officials was handled by education committees who resisted efforts to shut them down. CARE fostered this process by supporting education committees with organizational skills that enabled them to adapt to change. Other changes handled by these groups included the expansion of schools to become multi-class and multi-grade; to enable girls to remain in school after puberty and withstand traditional prohibitions; and to hire and retain teachers over time. None of these committees had ever managed a school before, and had to develop the skills to do so in this context, simply by doing it, and learning as they went.

Networks. The use and development of networked relationships can be seen in two areas. At community level, a range of different players were engaged. The collective of parents and family elders used their individual influences to draw in the required resources to run a school. The clerics that ran the mosque were co-opted to make the guest room available for a school. This had a double function of providing necessary space for the schools, but also for adding a sense of legitimacy to the schools. One could hardly call a mosque-based school un-Islamic, a dangerous pejorative in those times. Familial networks were used to identify candidates who could become teachers. Coming from within these networks meant that teachers were known and trusted. The network provided a social capital-based safety mechanism to ensure that children were safeguarded from abuse.

CARE worked to foster intra-community networks by connecting education committees with one another, so that they might exchange experiences and learn from one another. This had the effect of nurturing a new set of relationships that extended to other school service providers. As time passed, other educational support services were linked in, including UNICEF with their school kits, University of Nebraska and the German Technical Cooperation Agency (GTZ) and their respective primary school curriculums, and later to government education systems.

Appropriate action. Home schools started through parent action, and quickly evolved with support to become better fit for purpose. At the beginning, home schools had little or no choice as to the curriculum they had available. Available textbooks portrayed images of war and contained propaganda that parents did not like. The advent of the new curriculum came about through the engagement of refugee schools in Pakistan with curriculum developers such as GTZ Basic Education for Afghan Refugees (BEFARe). This curriculum, designed for use in non-formal settings, was introduced into schools, but it was the choice of the education committees to use it. Schools quickly took this on board and results quickly improved. Teachers had to be paid, and cash was in short supply. To address this, committees came up with alternative payment forms such as payment in wheat. Many schools commenced their existence outdoors and were ill-equipped. With time, committees would negotiate ways to construct schools through mobilization of village labour. Teachers became innovative in their practice. Some would engage local farmers to assist in basic science lessons. One teacher was observed to paste his classroom walls with word cards to enhance literacy teaching. Each school began to develop its own style that fitted with the conditions.

Ownership. When the Taliban arrived in Khost, they objected to the presence of schools, especially those for girls, and tried to close them. In one instance, community members went to the local Taliban leadership and said 'we're paying the salaries and we want this to continue' (Griffin, 1997). The resolve of parents in running these schools was persistent over time, and propelled them to take risks to defend the school and to invest. When the Taliban demanded that CARE close the schools, there was not even the possibility that they could do this, for schools ran of their own volition. Later on, with the arrival of the new national Ministry of Education, the much larger administration of the new government had more power than the Taliban and were able to take over schools in an agreement with the expanded project. Although well intended, this elimination of community basing effectively removed ownership and attendance fell. Schools that were not subsumed in the national structure retained their performance.

Scale. The schools spread in the early years through a process that was facilitated by CARE, but that had the hallmarks of movement. While CARE nurtured processes and offered support, it was the self-organizing basis of movement that CARE sought to spread through connecting communities that had schools with those that did not. The project offered some useful technical support that tipped the balance towards action for those communities that did not initially have the confidence to create schools. This was measured and commensurate with demand. For example, the programme only offered assistance to help in school construction when a school had been in existence for a year or more. Moreover, the assistance offered was only roofing timbers, doors, and windows, which would only be provided when the school had completed the walls. As the project expanded, this principle was retained meaning that the schools could only develop at their sites, or expand to new sites on the basis of intrinsic will. Under PACE-A, the programme took on the form of a mega-project across multiple areas. Clearly the experience of designers was captured by this expansive potential. While CBE remained central to the philosophy of the project, the end position was not as we might have expected, for the migration to the Ministry of Education seems to have achieved the reverse effect of scaling, and caused shrinkage through loss of ownership.

Sustainability. The formation of each school in Khost and in the early COPE project was an intrinsic process. Parents wanted it, and made it happen. Interventions that engaged this became increasingly fit for purpose, and the movement began to grow. There was an air in those days that these schools represented an action of self-determination by parents raising their families in the middle of some quite autocratic diktats. This quiet resistance juxtaposed a latent system attractor against a dominant political equilibrium, and slowly built a practice that increasingly resonated with society on an increasing scale. Schools were resilient to pressure and could not be shut down. They persisted and grew to provide education services for many years.

During the early days of home schools many criticisms were levelled at it. One of these was that the programme was not sustainable because the normal place for a school was within the domain of the national Ministry of Education. Community-run schooling was accepted as a stop-gap measure until such time as the government could regain its competence to resume its normal role. But in this case it was the imposition of government control that compromised sustainability.

Anti-poll tax campaign, UK

This is a story about how innovative political action was stimulated, which created an alternative attractor that was so strong by the time it impacted that it was impossible to stop. It is about how a movement was built and spread.

This story of the growth of a political movement took place in the UK in the late 1980s (Burns, 1992). Margaret Thatcher, the then UK prime minister, announced that local taxes, which had previously been calculated on property values, would now be charged at a flat rate for everyone. In other words a millionaire and a cleaner would pay exactly the same. This was viewed both as unjust and also unmanageable for many people living in poverty who could not afford to pay.

While the trade unions and the other political parties denounced the tax they stopped short of organizing any action to resist it. Within local communities, however, pockets of resistance started to open up. Groups were set up called anti-poll tax unions (APTUs). They provided information about what was going on and called for people to refuse to register for the tax and to resist the bailiffs. Bailiffs are people who take your household goods when you haven't paid a debt. Over the next years hundreds of groups set up across the UK. In Avon County where Danny lived there were more than 50. Some had more than 500 members.

The groups spread like wildfire. People from neighbourhoods which didn't have an APTU would be invited to meetings by their friends in areas which did. They would find out what was going on, and would go away inspired to set up their own group. They would call their own local meeting and invite people from other groups to help them to set it up. From week to week, the size of the groups grew as more people heard about them. People were drawn to them because they could get good information there, because they experienced a powerful sense of solidarity, and because they didn't feel helpless because the groups were designed to take action. People stayed in the groups because they were not told what actions to take. They were encouraged to take the actions that they believed were right or felt comfortable with. So for some it was very uncontroversial action like writing to local or national politicians or liaising with lawyers to organize resistance to the court process; for others it was blockading bailiffs, and so on. People were starting to organize a mass non-payment campaign. Many were involved in organizing local demonstrations, and these local demonstrations created the foundation for a national demonstration of nearly 500,000 people. The strategies evolved over time, they weren't planned or pre-constructed. Over time there was a convergence on non-payment as the strategy that most people thought would be successful and were prepared to engage in, but the growth of non-payment was also fuelled by the atmosphere of tension within the country which helped to contextualize it as part of something that was manifestly bigger.[1]

So what were some of the key factors? A *network* structure was created that allowed information to transfer from group to group so that people could learn from each other about what was happening, and what was working and what wasn't. The *ownership which led to scale* did not happen totally organically, it happened because the conditions for trust were created. For example the Easton (a neighbourhood in Bristol) APTU organized a street representative for every street in the locality. That person went to every household, door to door, and talked with the people who lived there about the issues. They carried out a survey which asked 'if more than 75% of people in your street refuse to pay the tax, will you also not pay the tax?' People were given the results of the survey and invited to a meeting. This meant that people felt confident that they weren't alone and it helped pull them towards a course of action that was personally risky. The non-payment campaign formed an alternative attractor which was coherent and therefore drew people away from the traditional social norms of compliance with the law. It drew more and more support because people could see that it was working as information transferred very quickly, and because trust was built amongst those that were engaging. The networked information structure allowed the disinformation that was put out by both the Conservative Party (and the other opposition parties) to be countered by real stories of what was happening which people knew to be true because they trusted the people that were telling them.

The whole structure was *participatory*. Everyone in the groups had a role. Decision-making was made democratically in weekly or two-weekly meetings.

People remained engaged because there wasn't any prescribed activity. They did what they thought was the most appropriate thing to do and were supported in that whatever it was. They spread the word because it was their movement and they felt *ownership*. In some areas which were controlled by small leftist parties, people didn't feel ownership of the APTUs, and these groups remained small. Where political parties and the unions were urging protest, people knew that this would make no difference. Instead, they designed action that would make the difference that was needed in their lives. The *action was appropriate* to their needs primarily because it was their action and they designed it. One of the reasons for the scaling was that so many people were involved, so that even before they had converged around non-payment, they were collectively organizing within the movement around the things they thought were important. All of these things were critical to the movement's scaling and sustainability. Many movements fall apart after a mass demonstration. This one grew until there were 10 million people who refused to pay the tax. Thatcher resigned and the tax was abolished.

Lolkuniani Market in Samburu, Kenya

This is a story of how powerful local participation led to social innovation, with new possibilities becoming visible at each step. This was an emergent process which went to scale because of the networked learning that evolved.

In 2006, a new market was born in a dry and remote corner of Samburu District in Northern Kenya. Once a small settlement in the vast northern plains, Lolkuniani is now a vibrant weekly livestock market. Every Thursday, hundreds of men and women trade cattle, sheep, goats, camels, hides, and skins. Around the market are scores of small enterprises selling food, supplies, and veterinary products. Lorries from far away Nairobi, Marsabit, and Mombasa bring local women with goods for sale at the market, and leave with livestock to sell across Kenya. In 2009 the daily turnover of the market approximated €90,000 (Context, 2010). Within the market, organization is tight and rules and regulations are observed. Young men collect tax payments from buyers and sellers alike, and security guards ensure that people can trade safely. In the adjacent village, a nursery school now operates, and work had started to dig a borehole. From the tax revenues generated by the market, some people had been supported to get further education and others to get medical attention.

Before the market was there, local communities would trek long distances to sell their livestock, often taking two to three days to reach any market. There were serious costs and challenges along the way including numerous district boundary taxes, risks of attack, and loss of livestock condition. Animals used to change hands many times before reaching any market. By and large, producers had no direct link or engagement with markets. This was the domain of traders. Even though there was strong demand in terminal markets, these high transaction costs kept prices very low for producers.

Intending to design an intervention that would help, SNV conducted a study of price margins along the value chain. With the new insights gained from this, they designed an intervention to increase sale prices. The idea was that if producers could add value to their cattle, they could get better prices. Before livestock from pastoral lands can enter national markets, they must be certified as disease free. Such certification requires livestock to be vaccinated and quarantined for approximately three months. This presented an opportunity for intervention, because prices in the national markets were considerably higher than in local ones. If a cattle owner wished to sell into the national market, they could use the quarantine time to fatten the cattle with purchase feed and forage. In collaboration with Kenyan District Livestock Marketing Association (DLMA), SNV proposed to use holding grounds close to the quarantine boundary to build a feed lot where recently vaccinated cattle could increase their live weight and be certified. Such a venture would cost the producer, but analysis of prices and costs indicated that this would yield a 29 per cent increase in gross margins for the producer. It appeared that these higher margins would attract many producers to this facility. In fact, the reality proved quite different. A few months after opening, the holding ground had only attracted about 50 cattle, far short of the expected 3,000. SNV and DLMA had assumed that pastoral producers were driven by economic returns and consequently price.

In a conversation with Stuart, Thomas Were – the SNV facilitator running this process – expressed his frustration that the scheme was not working. They agreed that Thomas should take time to drive out to producers directly, as opposed to the producer organizations that purported to represent them. Thomas visited them to find out why they were not bringing their animals to the feed lot holding grounds. Through these conversations it became apparent that economic yield was not the main driver behind producer action. Instead, maintaining herd integrity and survival underpinned key decisions. Thomas discovered that within the producers there was a collective resident perspective of what was wrong. They described this as follows.

A producer with a herd of 100 cattle passing through the Isiolo area would have approximately 5 head of cattle suitable for fattening and sale. For these to enter the holding ground, the herder would have to release a herd boy to remain with the cattle during the fattening process. This compromised herd management for the remaining 95 who would continue migratory grazing. In other words, the 95 were more important than the 5, so the opportunity was not attractive to producers. In the conversations that revealed this information, producers consistently expressed frustration about the way that local markets operated, and pointed to their inadequacy. They said that, here, they could only get throwaway prices because middlemen cartels controlled all purchases.

All district livestock markets were run by district councils. Taxation charged at every district border, informal fees demanded by police on the way to the market, insecurity, and robbery meant that a journey to market was an act of last resort. Deeper interior markets did not exist in any organized sense, in part because the local council and the veterinary department actively discouraged these on the grounds that their purview became overextended.

One conversation was held in an area called Lolkuniani. With a local organization, the Samburu Integrated Development Programme (SIDEP), SNV and a group of producers from the area gathered to talk about the market. They told how they could only get half the price that their cattle were fetching in terminal markets. There were layers of middlemen traders, long distances over difficult terrain to reach a market, high levels of animal mortality en route, high transport costs, local charges en route, insecurity, and theft of stock. They said that they were being cheated by more market-savvy traders. When they sold animals to an itinerant trader, they would walk to a market site, the nearest of which was about 50 km. Here, animals would be sold to another trader who would take the animals to a terminal market. They felt that with a local market in Lolkuniani, producers could cut out at least one layer of middlemen to get better prices. With enough volume they could be attractive enough to terminal market traders to attract them to send trucks and buy larger volumes. This would enable participation in the marketplace for even the poorest pastoralist producer.

The producers said that they really wanted to run an interior market. Although they had never done such a thing before, they felt that they could manage this better than the council was doing, and would create the right trading conditions. There had once been a market here, and occasionally sale days were arranged. On these days they observed that producers were effectively excluded from marketplaces, and that this was the domain of traders only. They said that they could establish separated selling areas, holding areas, and security services and proposed that, if they could secure access to some of the tax revenues, they could invest these in the market and make it work.

The Samburu County Council (SCC) is the local representative of the parent Ministry of Local Government and has jurisdiction over all markets in the district, including passing legislation with regard to animal movement and general security. A meeting was convened between the SCC town clerk in charge of council affairs, and the group of producers who wanted to operate as a collective local Livestock Marketing Association (LMA). The meeting was intended to enable these producers to put their proposition to the clerk, and see if there was any chance that they might be able to do this. The Lolkuniani market site was a name only, for there was no market there. The council occasionally allowed the sale of animals there, but this was always awkward for it was a long way for the council officer to travel for such a small tax revenue. The producers proposed that they could easily double traded volumes. If they were allowed to retain half of the taxation revenues collected, they would invest this in running the market. For the council, at worst this would be a zero-sum game the halving of tax would be offset by a doubling of volume.

The clerk was amenable to the idea, but was constrained by by-laws that determined that the council was the only body authorized to oversee such trading. He offered the nascent LMA a limited time period to run the site to see what would happen, perhaps feeling that the experiment would not work. A deal was formalized around managing the market and on equally sharing tax revenue.

This new space immediately presented an opportunity, and SNV worked in conjunction with SIDEP to assist the producers to form an LMA and to build their capability to run the market. This entailed systems of collecting tax on behalf of the council, keeping records and accounts, providing security, and organizing selling areas.

To assure ongoing support, a supportive line of work was undertaken to strengthen the national Kenya Livestock Marketing Council (KLMC) network, of which the DLMA and LMA were part. SNV felt that the chance of success for the LMA would be greatly increased if there was support from DLMA who could provide capacity building and support services, play a supervisory role, and audit the books of the LMA. Once this deal was agreed, news of this was carried through the KLMC network and traditional networks to producers and buyers in the province, and to distant terminal markets.

With this change in control of the marketplace, producers found that they had direct access and were no longer reliant on middlemen. A regular market day was established, and several areas were fenced off into pens using thorn bushes. As trading started, a representative of the council observed transactions. An appointed LMA member recorded all sales, and collected the standard local tax for each transaction. Some traders from Nairobi who had been apprised of the initiative arrived with trucks and bought livestock. The prices offered to producers were higher than they were used to and lower than what the trucking traders were used to. This created a mutual attraction for more business, and trade began to grow. Within a short period of time, daily market turnover reached €44,000 (Were and Dido, 2008), representing a five × increase in previous volumes. This represented a more than doubling of council tax revenues, and offered evidence to the council that this was an experiment that was working.

Around the site, security was tight. LMA members patrolled the area to ensure that bandits were kept away, and began to offer escort services for livestock buyers. With the increased flow of trade through the site, new opportunities and risks emerged. It opened up opportunities for small traders to service a new concentration of producers, and quickly sellers of medicines and dried food set up shop. Business was good because it meant that, for the producers, a trip to Lolkuniani also represented an opportunity to buy provisions. But there was also a risk. With the increased volume of transactions, there was more money floating around in this remote corner of Kenya, and this presented a security risk. Within Kenya, there had been the emergence of M-Pesa, a mobile phone money transfer system, and the establishment of banking and lending for low-income groups. For small transactions, M-Pesa proved to be an effective way for people to transact without handling money, and this decreased the volume of physical cash floating at the site. M-Pesa transaction limits, however, were capped at levels that were too low for many transactions. To address this, SNV brokered a linkage with K-Rep, a microfinance and equity bank, who saw a business opportunity in operating a mobile bank for the market. (Figure 6.1 shows the players and dynamics involved.) With this additional security, confidence in the market grew, and news of its success began to reach beyond the borders of the district.

When Stuart visited the market in 2010, he estimated that there was over €200,000 worth of livestock for sale. The market had expanded to deal with camels, cattle, sheep, goat, and donkeys, and was surrounded by approximately 300 small enterprises each selling provisions, food and drink, and animal health services. There was a sense of permanence in the way that the market was laid out, with alleyways, fences, holding areas, truck off-loading points, and yet the feel of the market remained as local as he remembered it. It was clear that trade was booming.

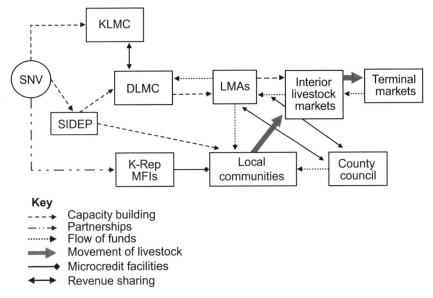

Key
- - - → Capacity building
— ·· → Partnerships
·······▶ Flow of funds
⟹ Movement of livestock
——◆ Microcredit facilities
◀——▶ Revenue sharing

Figure 6.1 Actors and dynamics in the Lolkuniani market
Source: Adapted from Were et al. 2008

In the nearby village, a nursery school had been established and work was underway to install a fixed water supply for the area. He heard stories of scholarship grants being awarded to students from the poorest households to enable them to attend school. In this location, the transformation was profound.

In an evaluation of this piece of work (Context, 2010), the evaluators note that

> Livelihoods are now more secure and ... vulnerability to environmental shocks and stresses has been reduced. Incomes for the 22 producer groups have risen by 40%. Livestock owners no longer need to walk 3 to 4 days to reach markets. Public bursaries resourced from the share of market-tax and managed by local communities have become available for children to go to school.

> Micro-finance institutions have taken advantage of the new business opportunities and now engage directly with the local communities, something that was previously unthinkable. Each of these group members now have active accounts with micro-finance institutions, where they also own joint accounts as a group. Over the last two years, K-Rep (Kenyan micro finance bank) has given out loans amounting to Ksh 18 million (about €184,000) with an average of Ksh 800,000 (€8,200) per group. Of this amount Ksh 13 million (€133,000) has since been repaid and members continue to service their loans.

The market had become a meeting place to discuss community issues. Inter-action between traders, producers, and other stakeholders boosted confidence and awareness of issues. The retained revenue from the market had functioned in part as a social protection net with funds used to help vulnerable people to access school and hospital. Local youth were employed in market tax collection, in the management of the sale yard, and in the provision of security. With the new connections to urban centres many young entrepreneurs started to bring in and trade supplies. This new involvement of youth fostered an increased sense of belonging to the community and was reported to have halted a trend of youth disenfranchisement and subsequent criminality.

Inspired by this experience, SNV used this market as an exemplar for other remote markets around the country. In 2010, seven other districts had engaged in similar experiments of producer-led market management. SCC proposed an amendment to local government by-laws to allow for such shared market management, an act that required endorsement by the Ministry of Local Government. This promised to change the policy landscape for all district markets. An evaluation of the intervention notes that 'perhaps the most significant result and impact of the capacity that has been developed is the fact that Lolkuniani Market is being used as a model to start similar markets in seven other Districts: West Pokot, Isiolo, Marsabit, Moyale, Narok, Wajir and Baringo' (Context, 2010).

The Lolkuniani experiment became regarded as a model by the Kenyan Ministry of Livestock and is being extended to other counties. The Ministry of Local Government has actively encouraged other pastoralist councils to follow suit. To this end, the Ministry is supporting efforts to review the Local Government Act so as to ensure that revenue collection and sharing agreements between councils and communities will be enshrined in law. Within their 2012 budget, the Ministry of Local Government invested €2 million to develop the model in six counties. What we see here is national policy created in response to bottom-up innovation rather than the other way around.

Reflections

Participation. The driver for change came from pastoralist livestock producers. The initial expert-led definition of issues and solutions clearly missed the mark, and it was not until producers were engaged that things began to move. It was their knowledge and understanding, their leadership in shaping the agenda, and their power to act and reshape that gave rise to action that worked. The growing story yielded evidence which was used to create new actions. SIDEP and SNV were deliberate in their actions to assure that participation was protected throughout. The engagement was one of facilitation of producer and wider stakeholder action as opposed to management. At the start, it was producers' concerns regarding how markets ran and their vision of what might be that drove the process.

Participation widened beyond producers. While they were the initiators of the first idea, the scope of action increased to encompass wider parts of society including youth, and market traders. Social concerns began to influence the way in which revenues were used, and we saw the development of set-aside funds to pay for education, hospital fees and water supply.

Learning. No one in this story had ever run a successful local market before. The council had run markets, but these were far from successful, and had overseen a marketing model that had become oppressive to the extent that it had effectively killed Kenya's pastoral livestock production base. Having identified the trigger to unlocking effective market access for them, the pastorialists proceeded to engage in running the market. Through a process of trial and error, they took steps to change things: starting with lobbying the council to organizing themselves, to running a market site, and through to persuading terminal market traders and service providers to join in. SNV assumed a role of facilitation here to make sure that the actions undertaken by various players were reviewed and assessed. This learning culture gave rise to a process of figuring things out as they happened as opposed to assuming an impact pathway. What caused one action to happen was the result of what happened before. SNV and SIDEP worked to help the LMA, the council, DLMC – and later traders, mobile banking, and other service providers – to reflect on what was working and what was not working.

The story exemplifies emergence of how one thing leads to another. The complexity of arrangements that grew could not have been foreseen. SNV took a facilitation role to assist people in learning their way through this to broker and connect players within this emergence. The story also shows how poor choices are corrected. At the beginning, SNV and its programme partners decided on a big and visible intervention. This design fitted well within the constructs of donor-funded programmes, and resonated strongly with a range of initiatives that had been conducted in previous years. It is likely that this initiative would have attracted donor funds had it worked for it would have been big and visible. Yet it was the wrong thing to do because it did not work. There is an element of humility displayed by SNV and DLMC to recognize their mistake and to correct this. This is an important element for learning without which arises a defensiveness that precludes change. SNV inculcated a culture and architecture of review and learning that enabled the process to tack towards success.

Network development. The confluence of energy that came out of participation and the learning that enabled this energy to evolve in response to that which worked was connected into a wider space through networks. We see these at two levels. Within the Lolkuniani catchment, relationships were used to communicate the market's presence, to attract terminal market traders and transporters, and through local community systems, to engage youth in providing key services. Beyond Lolkuniani, the KLMC network was invoked to provide support to this LMA. This had the effect also of carrying the story of change across a set of relationships that was interested in this story. SNV was deliberate in its role as a convenor at both levels, and took on a role to assist several of the players to engage with their own networks. Within the local government system, there were dynamics that were invisible to outsiders that only the council could deal with. In relation to the by-laws, it was the council that could credibly speak to the Ministry of Local Government to lobby for change. Clearly they were ultimately successful in this as evidenced by the spread of action and investment to new sites.

Appropriate action. Because this was an iterative process, innovations adapted over time to become fit for purpose. By brokering a conversation in a neutral space between the county council and the LMA, a solution was formed through engagement and was then tested in action. The establishment of the market started with a small and very low-cost action to build brushwood pens, and note-taking to record transactions. As time went on, this became more elaborate and actions evolved to meet new eventualities. The growth of the market meant that interventions had to change and we see this expand to incorporate financial solutions, brokerage, policy work, youth engagement, and social service provision. Linked to the learning culture described above, actions were altered by evidence.

Ownership. Participation created ownership. The facilitation of action around issues that people wanted created a buzz of excitement. As the actions began to deliver results, the commitment to act intensified giving rise to new and wider actions. SNV here exemplifies the principle of nurturing a process of organizing around enthusiasm by assuring that the support that was offered was what people wanted. The LMA did not see this as a project but as a new way to do things that prompted one national newspaper to comment that this was a 'customized model' that allows residents to form committees that manage markets and collect revenue (Wamanji, 2009). This was their process, their action, and consequently their commitment that transformed this market.

Scale. With the success at Lolkuniani, others followed suit, enabled also by the change in by-laws. These grew in their own unique ways building on the opportunities that came out of co-management. Scale came naturally with the national government willing to bankroll expansion because it made sense to them. SNV did not manage the scaling process. Rather, it selected groups to work with who had national reach. Through the use of formal and informal networks, SNV enabled scaling by connecting this experience to other markets around the country. In a similar way to their work in the market, they worked to connect markets in a process that supported natural scale.

Sustainability. The market transformation happened through natural and organic processes. It was not built through external intervention but was the manifestation of a changed system pattern. The act of co-sharing the management of the market resulted in the changes being persistent because they were natural emanations of that changed pattern. The emergence of events and subsequent actions created was complex and intricate with multiple strands of support and connection forming between actions. For instance, the increase in volume attracted trucks, which in turn increased volumes. This required financial services, and there were now enough market players to warrant a bank to establish a mobile facility. This in turn supported market stall transactions, and a well-equipped local market began to flourish. With this, the community living at the site could sink a new borehole and build a new school. The story extended to new areas and new markets in a way that was not planned. Yet it persisted and grew both in size and in complexity.

The consolidation of by-law change locked this system pattern into place, and created an environmental change which enabled further scaling.

Farmer participatory research and change at scale, Egypt

This is a story about the interaction of local knowledge with expert knowledge. Unlike the planned scientific roll-outs characterizing failed agricultural innovation, this process was rooted in participation and dialogue, ensuring that farmers could match their circumstances to potential technical solutions and then experiment with them and adapt them to ensure that they were the right solutions.

In 1991, the IMF and the World Bank engaged Egypt in a structural readjustment programme. Central to this programme was the liberalization of trade and payment policies. Domestic production had been protected and with liberalization tariffs were reduced and non-tariff barriers eliminated.

Up until this point, smallholder farmers in Egypt had operated within a very restricted and controlled space. Farmers were managed through a national agricultural extension system where farmers received instruction as to what to plant and when to conduct key husbandry tasks. This was accompanied by highly subsidized farm inputs. At harvest, all farm produce was purchased by the state at fixed prices that were well below world prices. Farmers could only vary their income through the management of yield.

With liberalization, all controls and guarantees were removed, and smallholder farmers found themselves suddenly exposed to free market dynamics. On the one hand, they were now free to grow what they wanted. On the other hand, exposure to market demand and prices introduced risk that farmers had not previously experienced.

In 1991, CARE responded to this change by expanding its flagship project, Village Self Reliance. This expansion was driven by CARE's goals for community organization and management, global reputation in agroforestry, and experience of promoting vegetable seedlings through agricultural cooperatives in Northern Sinai.

The new programme aimed at promoting technology transfer through farmer-owned-and-managed greenhouses. These were commercial enterprises intended as sustainable sources of improved horticultural varieties. After one year of establishment, most of these greenhouses had stopped functioning. Those that remained open were those that were providing local councils with ornamental plants. Greenhouse owners claimed that this was the only viable business option for them, for farmers seemed uninterested in buying seedlings and new varieties.

This stimulated an examination of the programme. The evaluator observed that farmer demands for change were much wider than the narrow options being offered by the project. The complexity of the system change in the Egyptian agriculture reform process required a wider menu of options for farmers to engage with. The programme was therefore redesigned to create an interface between farmers and technology sources. The new design was a farmer participatory extension service project named FarmLink.

This project employed a conversation-based methodology that used a participatory appraisal approach to find out from farmers what they wanted. A first meeting with farmers explained the project's limitations, stating that FarmLink was limited to work within horticulture. However, within that domain, FarmLink was interested in working with farmers to tackle any issue that they may have. With this understanding, a first conversation identified broad domains wherein work would be helpful. By and large these were defined by crops. Tomato cultivation was the single biggest enterprise nationally and was selected most often. Over a three-year period, 24 crop types were selected.

Once the crop had been selected, a conversation ensued around a timeline that started with a decision to grow that crop, and ended at the point when the revenue from the crop had been received. Along this journey, farmers were asked to identify issues that were important. This was graphically laid out using flip charts and pens, or floor-based models employing earth, sand, and paint powder. The exercise was always accompanied by a lot of laughter and debate as farmers became animated in describing what was important. This resulted in a series of issues from which key ones, that warranted attention, were chosen. The project asked farmers to prioritize these, and to do this using simple participatory ranking techniques.

FarmLink extension workers explained to the farmers that they proposed to take them on a visit tour to see other people who had worked, or were working, on these issues and who could offer them their knowledge. This would involve a two-to-three day visit to another part of Egypt where they would meet other farmers, input traders, crop buyers, researchers, and a range of relevant players. All farmers wanted to go on these visits, and it was clearly not cost-effective to do this. There was a need to make a choice as to who should go. In such a decision process, there were considerable power dynamics at play that did not correlate with the effectiveness of the link. A variant of wealth ranking was designed to select which of the farmers should represent the group in engaging in linking visits with sources of information.

Farmer groups were asked to define the characteristics of someone that they would copy agricultural ideas from for the selected crop, and someone who they would not copy ideas from. Collectively, definitions were offered, with each definition being unique to the group that offered it. At the positive end, criteria would include statements such as:

- is a full-time farmer who lives off of the land;
- has grown this crop for many seasons;
- always gets a good yield;
- whose crop does not suffer badly when other peoples crops do;
- is not rich, is not poor – but in the middle;
- can read and write;
- likes to do unusual experiments;
- owns his own land.

At the negative end, definitions would include:

- is very poor;
- does not invest in his farm;
- is a tenant farmer;
- illiterate;
- does not get main income out of farming.

These two sets of criteria bounded extremities and five or six volunteers from the farmer group were asked to rank cards with the names of interested farmers against these criteria. Normally four or five categories spanned these extremities, and scorers would simply place the name cards in the category they felt an individual belonged. Those that consistently scored highly were selected to join in on link visits.

The agenda of issues was used to craft a series of visits to technology sources and innovators who could offer insight into issues. The project employed a scout who would search for relevant information and make arrangements with these to receive a farmer delegation. With the use of databases, careful records were kept to keep track of these sources and initial farmer reactions.

These visits were named 'Links'. In general, 70 per cent of these were to other smallholder farmers, with the remainder being agricultural researchers, input traders, produce buyers, and, occasionally, specialist field trainers. FarmLink project extension workers would simply convene interactions between selected farmers and sources of information, and adopt a facilitation role. Within the project, the golden rule was 'provide no advice! Only link!' Following linkage visits, extension workers would record initial farmer reactions.

On their return from linking visits, there was considerable expectation from other farmers for linked farmers to share information. This curiosity was a considerable spur for the linked farmers to test new ideas in their fields and to talk about what they were doing. In most villages, an air of friendly competition arose between those that had attended links, with non-linked farmers actively observing what they were doing. In the village coffee houses and at mosque social events farmers would discuss what was happening.

FarmLink extension officers would visit linked farmers to see what they were doing, and would record who they said that they had spoken to about the visits, and who from these other farmers were copying them. This initially indicated a diffusion rate of three additional farmers for each linked farmer. Post-project external evaluation showed that this was a gross underestimation, and that new technology and practice had in fact been adopted by 29 farmers for every farmer linked. Moreover, the evaluation showed that for each household using new technology, income had increased by $300 per annum, compared with the prevailing per capita gross domestic product (GDP) of $1,250 (FAO, 2000).

FarmLink observed three different responses to linking visits:

- Farmers tested and then adopted technologies which provided direct solutions to identified problems.
- Farmers experimented with and adapted technologies before adopting them.
- Farmers developed new ways to engage with and address dynamic issues.

We will explore these in turn.

Adoption of specific technologies: citrus growers in Jazirat Tema

Jazirat Tema is a small island in the Nile in the northern part of Sohag Governorate of Upper Egypt. Many farmers here were orange producers. Through conversation-based participatory analysis, they described how blossom was falling off their trees before any fruit could set, and how they had very low production. During a linking visit to the Agriculture Research Centre in Giza, visiting farmers conversed with researchers and described how they were irrigating their trees during the hottest part of the day. Irrigation water in the village was allocated to farmers according to a schedule, and farmers had no apparent means to alter this. The researcher described how trees transpire and give off water. During intense heat, trees effectively pump water from the roots to the leaves. This makes the trunk of the tree wet, encouraging the growth of fungus that would cause blossom to fall. He proposed that, in the absence of the farmer's ability to change their irrigation timing to the night, that they instead make the trees work harder to get their water, and thereby reduce the flow of water through the trunks. He suggested that they build a circular bund around each tree, approximately one metre from the base. This he said would force the tree to obtain its water from its outer root zone, thus reducing water flow up the trunk, and removing the conditions that gave rise to the damaging fungus.

On returning to their farms, some of the farmers were sceptical and felt that this was risky advice and interfered with critical irrigation. A few farmers decided to experiment with the idea, and applied this to a few trees to see what would happen. As the season passed, treated trees significantly outperformed untreated trees both in terms of reduced blossom loss, and net yield. In the following season, many more farmers tried this out with a few trees, while those that had experienced the benefits increased their experimental areas. Within three years, the innovation had spread throughout Jazirat Tama, and into neighbouring areas, and had been adopted locally as standard cultivation practice.

This specific piece of knowledge had immediate effect. It spread with almost no modification of its original form. The testing process simply validated that this was a workable solution. Diffusion occurred when other farmers also tested the idea and personally validated the innovation.

Adaption then adoption: tomatoes in the Fayoum

Tomatoes are a staple product for millions of Egyptian smallholders. Three crops a year are normally grown, with many farms committing all of their land to tomatoes. Traditionally, cultivation entailed planting seed on a small patch of land, and then transplanting seedlings to their fields.

Farmers in the Fayoum were facing substantial crop losses to the tomato yellow leaf curl virus (TYLCV), a virus that was carried by the whitefly. Whiteflies feed on growing seedlings while they are young and succulent and, in doing so, transmit the virus. To counter this, farmers were using chemical control but still suffered significant losses.

On the basis of conversations that revealed this, FarmLink officers arranged for a selected group of Fayoum farmers to visit successful tomato growers in other parts of Egypt. One such visit was to a high-tech farm in the northern delta area. Here, a large commercial shade house grew expensive TYLCV-resistant tomato varieties in polystyrene seedling trays using the soil medium of Irish peat moss and vermiculite. Seedlings were sprayed with foliar fertilizers, automatically administered through electronically controlled booms. Seedlings were transplanted to drip irrigated field conditions once they had reached 10 cm in height. This level of automation and technology was about as far away from their farm reality as was possible.

During the visit, the farmers closely questioned the shade house manager, and one or two pocketed a small bag of the peat moss–vermiculite mix. On their return, several started to experiment. One farmer described how he tried to copy the principles of the shade house system on his own farm. He examined the peat moss and vermiculite sample he had taken, and based on a conversation he had had during the visit, determined that he needed a planting substrate that was soft, and that would hold water and nutrients. He therefore created his own version of this by using mature manure (soft and nutritious) and pellets of old newsprint (water holding). Without access to seed trays, he used cardboard egg cartons. In place of the automatic fertilizing boom, he used a tin with small holes carefully punched in its base. In place of foliar fertilizer, he steeped a cocktail of standard nitrogen fertilizer in water to make a solution. In place of the shade house, he made a small cubic frame from available wood, and draped this with net curtain material. He retained his current variety of tomato, and grew his seedlings within this shade house until they were 10 cm tall, before transplanting these to his traditional flood irrigated fields.

As a result of this experiment, this farmer's tomato crop yield significantly exceeded former levels. He had effectively circumvented the whitefly risk by keeping the seedlings behind a screen during their most succulent moment, and had provided husbandry that yielded seedlings with better survival and yield potential. Initially, he was viewed with some suspicion by his neighbours but this was accompanied by curiosity. His success stimulated imitation and within a year, his village was peppered with seedling cubes as others followed suit.

This example demonstrates how multiple pieces of knowledge gained from one source were combined and adapted through trial and error. Ideas were examined and reformulated within the specific context of the farm and household.

New ways of engaging with dynamic change: potato farmers in Sohag

Some years after conducting a series of linkage visits with citrus farmers in Sohag Governorate, FarmLink staff visited a potato research station in the Nile Delta in preparation for a group visit from a new group of potato farmers. While exploring with the research staff the issues that the upcoming visitors were facing, they were hailed by another group of visitors to the research station. These were former project farmers who had been linked in the past on citrus issues. In conversation, it transpired that they were now facing some difficult issues with their potatoes, and they wanted to find a solution. They told how they had discussed their experiences with FarmLink, and decided to try and do for themselves what the project had done. They made a phone call to one of the project staff who had given them contact details of this research station, and two of them had been delegated to find out what options there were. They were on a self-organized link visit.

These farmers demonstrated that the exposure to this visit process had changed the way in which they approached problems. They had moved to engage with the issues through proactive solution seeking.

Reflections

Participation. In this example, FarmLink built links based on what farmers wanted. This ensured that the starting point for action by the programme was based on articulated demand. Participatory approaches created conversations to yield actionable information and the project used this to enable such action. Information expressed by farmers framed a visit agenda. Farmers selected ideas that resonated with their issues. The FarmLink team saw links as being more important than the information. The 'no advice' rule assured space within which farmers could use their own knowledge and understanding while appraising options for action.

Learning. FarmLink fostered a culture of farmer experimentation. Okali et al. (1994) refer to the project as an example of farmer participatory research for it engaged farmers in experimentation to test innovations that they themselves select or create. The three stories above describe simple adoption; adaptation then adoption; and new ways to engage change. These are three different levels of learning. Farmers were encouraged to 'figure things out', test ideas, and use this evidence to shape new action. This connected experience over time to form learning strands that consolidated to become a changed approach to learning.

Network development. FarmLink was conscious in fostering networks between communities, farmers and sources of information. The farmer selection process identified trusted people within local networks. Linking these to sources of information used and strengthened network relationships by adding new value. New links opened up new network possibilities, with farmers self-organizing their own visits.

Appropriate action. Farmers experimented before adopting innovations. In the citrus case, this was straightforward – testing, validation, then adoption. In the tomato case, technology was first adapted to become fit for purpose. In all cases, farmers used testing to validate innovations before changing their farming practice.

Ownership. Participation engaged the knowledge and agendas of farmers to give strong ownership. FarmLink simply connected their demand with new opportunity, and left the rest to the interaction between farmers and information sources. Farmers focused where they chose to, and their choices were their own. There was considerable energy during experimentation. The tomato case shows dedication from involved farmers in adapting the technology. There was pride amongst farmers and communities as husbandry changes yielded significant results.

Sustainability. Changes made by farmers continued because they worked; this in turn was because innovations had been adapted to fit. Within the wider national context, these specific adaptations enabled local farming systems to more broadly adapt to the new reality. While the narrative describes three specific local adaptations, the many adaptations across smallholder farming systems together enabled farmers across Upper Egypt to produce and sell more, and engage in a wider diversity of cropping than had hitherto been possible.

Scale. FarmLink worked directly with 1,200 farmers with the intention of benefiting 6,000 households. In theory, for every farmer linked, four more would benefit through diffusion. The networked participatory learning approach enabled adapted innovations to spread across communities. A diffusion rate of 29 is remarkable in extension circles, and was six times the intention. Although further evaluation was not conducted in subsequent years, this rate alone indicated that FarmLink had triggered scalar effects beyond its control.

The new searching behaviour indicates a fundamental alteration in the way in which farmers were engaged with change. One might speculate that innovations adapted and adopted were profound enough so as to transform whole farming systems. Changed system patterns create the conditions for scale to happen. These two pattern change types, behavioural and technological, each offer the chance for transformational change at scale. It is noteworthy that such scale happened within the project life. This perhaps is indicative that the project had achieved a more profound system change, for scale happened without management. It was transformational, not a roll-out.

Community Led Total Sanitation: from Bangladesh to Africa and beyond

This is a story of the way in which one village-level intervention scaled up to become an international phenomenon. It raises complex questions about what is the necessary role of government when such initiatives reach a critical mass – opening up the potential spread across whole countries. Can this be done without undermining enthusiasm as we saw in the case of schools in Afghanistan?

CLTS is a facilitated, but community-driven, approach to improving sanitation that has rapidly grown from small seeds to an international phenomenon. It emerged from Bangladesh and has reached significant scale in Indonesia, Pakistan, and a number of African countries such as Zambia, Mali, Ethiopia, and Nigeria. In Bangladesh earlier attempts at sanitation solutions had focused on individual household hardware subsidies. These led to uneven adoption and showed no signs of sustainability. Ahmed (2009) describes the contrast between the successful introduction of handpumps to provide clean water in Bangladesh in the 1970s, and the complete failure to get any traction on sanitation. There was no demand because most people defecated in the open and there appeared to be no reason not to do so. Indeed, the assumption of many people in villages was that this was far more hygienic because the toilet was away from the house.

In the 1970s, approximately 1 per cent of Bangladesh's population had access to a form of sanitary latrine. At that time attempts were made by the Department of Public Health Engineering (DPHE) to introduce sanitary latrines on a limited scale, free of charge as demonstration models. This didn't work because they were too expensive to provide, and because there was no social movement behind them. In the 1990s much lower cost design had emerged and the government mounted a mass campaign for low-cost latrines, supported by UNICEF and various NGOs. This significantly increased the demand for sanitation, but as soon as funding ran out, the gains quickly began to regress. Ahmed describes visiting some of the locations where 100 per cent sanitation had been achieved to discover that latrines were all in a poor state of maintenance and that many people had reverted to open defecation. Change had not been sustained because it had been driven by the government and had not been internalized.

The big shift came in the late 1990s when Water Aid was reviewing its activities in Bangladesh. It was still trying to promote sanitation through subsidies with very limited success. They engaged Kamal Kar who was a participatory development practitioner in the tradition of participatory rural appraisal (PRA). Kar (2011) describes the way in which they came to the realization that something different was possible when he was carrying out an evaluation in a small village in Rajshahi, Bangladesh, in February 2000.

> A little boy, Mussaraff, who was wearing a pair of grubby shorts, his body sweating in the heat of the afternoon, brought our plates of rice and drinking water in greasy, yellowish glasses. I noticed the nimble fingers of Mussaraff dipping into the water when he grabbed the glasses. While eating our food, I asked Mussaraff where he had defecated that morning. Pointing at a bush behind another jhupri [makeshift restaurant] a distance of about 10 metres, Mussaraff showed us the places he usually did his morning business. None of us dared to ask if he had washed his hands with soap after defecating.

On that same visit 'The people of Mosmoil village community had just discovered that they were ingesting each other's shit at the rate of one or two tola per day.' At first they started blaming each other, then realizing that there was no external resource that was going to magically help them they started to self-organize local sanitation solutions. This offered a new way of thinking about how to combat the problem of open defecation. Chambers (2009: 11) describes CLTS as

> an approach in which people in rural communities are facilitated to do their own appraisal and analysis, come to their own conclusions, and take their own action. They are not instructed or taught. With CLTS in its classical form, a small team of facilitators conduct a triggering. The facilitators may be government, NGO or project staff, or Natural Leaders from other communities. The PRA (Participatory Rural Appraisal) principle that 'they can do it' is fundamental and PRA methods are used. These include participatory mapping on the ground to show where people live and where they defecate, transect walks to visit and stand in those places, calculations of quantities of shit (the crude local word is used) produced by each household and the community, and identifying pathways to the mouth leading to the shocking recognition that 'we are eating one another's shit'. This triggering is designed to lead to a moment of ignition and a collective decision to end OD [open defecation] followed by action to become ODF [open defecation free].

> When triggering is successful, Natural Leaders emerge. People dig holes and build latrines. There are no standard models and construction is by self-help with or without purchase of hardware from the market.

Kar, Water Aid, and their local partner, VERC (Village Education Resource Centre), developed this idea in a handful of villages in Bangladesh, where it flourished. In 2001 a review of Water Aid programmes revealed outstanding results in those villages in comparison with other localities. The news spread fast. According to Ahmed a critical factor in the spread was Water Aid's willingness to open up the approach to other stakeholders including Water and Sanitation Programme for South Asia (WSP) – 'this open source attitude let many partners join and own the CLTS approach'. Within two years of the introduction of CLTS into Bangladeshi villages, the message spread across the region with the aid of exchange visits and visits from other countries to local villages. CLTS was introduced India, Indonesia, and other Asian countries. In 2003 it was field tested and piloted in Kibale district of Uganda and began to take hold in East Africa in early 2007 when Kar ran a training workshop in Tanzania for Plan International staff in seven countries. CLTS has now been introduced in 28 countries in Africa and has been particularly successful in Nigeria, Ethiopia and Zambia.

> The adoption and spread of CLTS has been little short of spectacular. As of mid-2012 UNICEF estimates suggest that close to ten million people are living in communities that have been declared open defecation free (ODF) in Africa. This has happened in the context of an enabling environment which has been strengthened by the recognition, approval and support of CLTS by governments and external agencies. (Bongartz, 2014: 133)

From an early stage the basic principles of CLTS were:

- No external individual household hardware subsidy (IHHS). Communities install their own latrines or toilets with their own resources. Those who are better off help those who are too weak or poor to help themselves.
- No standardized top-down designs. People decide for themselves.
- Facilitation, not teaching or preaching. Appraisal and analysis are facilitated. But after triggering, information and encouragement can be provided.

More recently, two further principles that can be inferred from effective practice are:

- Creativity and innovation in approach.
- Review, reflection, learning, and change.

Chambers stresses the importance of methodological development and action learning; creative innovation and critical awareness; learning and action alliances and networks, with fast learning across communities, districts, and countries; and seeking to seed self-spreading or light-touch movements.

An important success factor also seems to be the identification and support of natural leaders on the ground and champions in organizations and policy arenas. This view is supported by various writers in Mehta and Movik (2011): 'without natural leaders the implementation of CLTS would not be as successful' (Priyono, 2011). Following the Water and Sanitation for Low Income Communities (WSLIC II) workshop in 2006, Chambers identified a set of critical factors in the spread and widespread adoption of CLTS (Chambers, 2009). The most unfavourable (in order of significance) were hardware subsidy, poor facilitation, unresponsive leadership, long-term habits, and difficult physical conditions. Those most favourable to the development of CLTS were team work, dedicated facilitation, natural leaders, tradition of self-help, and intensive-follow up.

One big enabling condition for CLTS has been the movement of people committed to CLTS into senior positions where they can work to reorient whole organizations and national policies. There is of course a danger with this as people who are good get promoted to positions where they are no longer involved. National policies provide an enabling environment and the engagement of national government can bring with it the people resources to reach the whole country. An important element of this approach has been NGOs handing over to governments, and the 'ownership' of governments themselves. Governments are able to create enabling conditions which allow significant spread. This includes 'making sanitation a political priority; mounting national campaigns; ensuring quality, inclusiveness, intensity, planning and timing of activities; and post ODF follow up' (Cavill et al., 2015). There is a common view that significant amounts of money are needed for training, facilitation, and capacity building as to do this work at scale has involved literally thousands of facilitators in some countries. There remains a debate amongst CLTS practitioners about whether hardware subsidies are helpful or detract from the process. Kar argues strongly that subsidy will undermine community ownership and momentum. This is reinforced by Mehta (2011: 9) who says 'where wide-scale subsidies have been doled out, toilet use is poor and worse than in areas where people have constructed their own toilets', but she also points out that the poorest of the poor may need additional help if they are not to be excluded. This is the view taken by Chambers, Bongartz, and others who argue that a more nuanced approach is needed when it comes to the poorest and most marginalized. They argue that different forms of support, for example in the form of vouchers such as those used in Pakistan and Bangladesh, could sometimes be needed in order to ensure inclusion of those who are least able. There seems to be strong consensus that blanket subsidy does not work, and many national governments have explicitly rejected funding of this sort from international agencies:

- In Ghana, the World Bank had sanctioned a project which included provision of subsidised sanplats, but after three months of Government resistance gave way and complied with the Government policy of no subsidy.

- States in Nigeria have been similarly successful. The AfDB negotiated with two states regarding support for rural sanitation, including subsidies for household latrine construction. Based on national adoption of CLTS in the scaling up strategy for rural sanitation in Nigeria, the states indicated that CLTS approach should be used instead. The AfDB representatives asked for official government documents stipulating the adoption of CLTS for rural sanitation. Presented with that evidence, it was agreed not to use the hardware subsidy approach.
- In Chad a similar situation occurred with the European Union in 2010. After the receipt of a letter from the Minister of Water, stressing the importance of community-driven demand-led approaches, the EU agreed to adjust its funding to support the CLTS initiative. (Community-Led Total Sanitation, 2011)

Finally Chambers points to the relationship between adaption and spread. Innovation in approach is crucial to ensuring that the initiative is appropriate to local conditions and thus sustainable. There has been a great deal of diversity in the way in which CLTS has been implemented. Some countries are driving the process through School-led Total Sanitation (SLTS); others have innovated around different aspects of sanitation and hygiene: for example by integrating menstrual hygiene management, finding more effective ways to trigger hand washing, adapting CLTS to the urban context, using participatory design for sanitation, incorporating new work on disability, and so on. This is clearly not then a form of roll-out. Each process is specific to each context, although it is happening at an increasingly larger scale, supported by government. The combination of innovation and diversity suggests the need for more extensive learning processes to help people navigate what is working and what is not. With this information people, organizations, and countries will move with their feet to where the strong attractors lie. Just as in the Lolkuniani case above, national policy is being created from the bottom up rather than the other way around.

Reflections

Participation. The whole CLTS model is built on PRA principles and uses PRA techniques such as transect walks, diagramming, and participatory analysis processes. It explicitly calls for the engagement of the poorest and most marginalized, and identifies natural leaders to carry the process forward. As we articulate in Chapter 8, participation is not confined to the analytical part of the process; participation lies in the practice identification of models of financing, and in the actual construction of different types of latrines.

Learning. It is important to be clear that the 'spread and scaling up of CLTS requires intensive expert facilitation' (Kar and Bongartz 2006: 8). Learning doesn't just happen. Opportunities for learning have to be created and delivered in ways which are both inclusive and encourage emergent thinking. This is a difficult challenge as the greater the scale the harder it is to maintain the quality of the facilitation. It is much more important that 'investment' goes into the quality of this learning process than into hardware which is quickly redundant if it is not supported by community understanding and ownership. As Kar Bongartz (2006) point out, 'early CLTS villages served as training and learning grounds and a live demonstration of what could be accomplished by communities'. The CLTS Knowledge Hub based at the IDS sees its central task as the brokering of learning and networks. Action learning is a core part of its methodology. Its bi-monthly newsletter reaches over 6,000 subscribers.

Network development. The emergence, nurturing, and support of champions at all levels has been key to the spread of CLTS. This is similar to the FarmLink example above. In some CLTS examples, children were explicitly identified as a crucial network channel. They were able to move messages very quickly through peer networks. Another key element of the networking strategy was that it was open source. People were invited to see what was happening, to talk it through in learning forums, and to adapt it to suit their circumstances. Critical to success has been changing the discourse about sanitation and associated social norms, and networks are an important vehicle for this. At a local level the most critical networking has happened within the villages. There are some good examples of peer-to-peer networking across villages. For example in Zambia, Chief Macha engaged extensively on these issues with a network of chiefs. But perhaps more significantly there have been the workshops and higher level NGO and government networking which have brought champions together to support the process. In many countries there are now national CLTS or Water, Sanitation and Hygiene (WASH) groups/taskforces/networks where representatives from different NGOs, agencies and government work together. This networking allows for sharing of experiences, innovations, challenges, emerging issues, and solutions.

Appropriate action. CLTS processes in rural areas have been evolving over some decades. The spread of CLTS occurred because local people generated their own solutions which were appropriate to their situations. This has led to many innovations being tested over many years. So as CLTS has become endorsed at government level, and its spread has become greater, the options that are available to people now are better developed to fit within specific country and cultural contexts.

Ownership. The CLTS case highlights the importance of enthusiasm. This amplifies the theme of 'organising around enthusiasms' (Hoggett and Bishop, 1986) which is one of the foundation stones of this book. It was also a strong theme in the growth of the PRA movement. Chambers (1990: 1) notes:

> I am amazed at how much I have had to revise these notes as a result of the experience of the past two months. People (villagers and outsiders), once unfrozen, enjoy improvising and inventing methods and variants on methods. The methods are now spreading rather fast as more people are trying them out and inventing their own variations. Part of the reason seems to be that they so often produce interesting and useful insights, and that they are often liberating and enjoyable.

As we saw in the example of Kisii in Chapters 3 and 4, when the community felt ownership of the local water and sanitation facilities they were protected and maintained. Prior to that when there had been no ownership a multimillion pound investment in the same place had been vandalized and destroyed within weeks. It is only when processes are owned that they continue to be used. This is particularly important viewed from the perspective of social norms. It is only when people have internalized the importance of, for example, washing with soap or not going to the toilet on open ground, that any hygiene gains are likely to be sustained.

Scale. For CLTS, scale has been built by extensive networking. We saw from the pre-CLTS attempts at large-scale sanitation in Bangladesh that change was not sustained because it was driven by government and subsidized. This is tricky because CLTS itself is now moving to the stage where to get the ODF message across in some countries the state has to be involved otherwise there will just be a series of local community initiatives and NGO projects that disintegrate when the funding runs out. CLTS is being institutionalized, and the danger ahead could be what happened in the case of the Afghan schools. The broad consensus on this seems to be that there comes a point at which governments need to invest in the enabling conditions, which include a supportive policy framework, incentives, and resources for facilitation, and so on. Local government plays a huge role in many places through integration of CLTS work into existing structures such as health extension workers, for example, who are active both in triggering and follow-up. What is important is that they do not 'educate', 'teach' or 'prescribe' in reality they often do a mix of participatory work and old-style community development.

Conclusion

In each of the narratives above there is a clear progression. Explicit learning, extensive participation, and intentional network development processes combine to create interventions and actions which are appropriate, and which are owned. Ownership combined with appropriate intervention creates the conditions under which scaling and sustainability are possible.

What we have tried to do in this chapter is offer clear examples of how this progression has been tangibly realized across a wide range of social change activities, and how local participatory activities have been scaled to both national and international levels: the examples include education; rights campaigning; market development; agricultural development; and sanitation. These are not fringe issues. They are mainstream development issues.

There are some important observations to be made by a number of these processes which describe the interaction between local knowledge and 'expert' or 'outsider' knowledge. Participatory processes are not a denial of expert knowledge. What they do is place the analysis and meaning making of that expert knowledge in the hands of the community. There is, for example, no doubt that open defecation leads to disease, but telling people that and telling them what to do about it doesn't work, because just like telling people not to smoke, there are many systemic drivers which will push them back in that direction. They have to understand these and it is their local knowledge that will enable the appropriate action. Similarly, participatory processes are not a denial of the role of government. We saw in both the Kenya markets story and the CLTS story the way in which bottom-up processes built a body of practice and learning about what worked and this was consolidated through the creation of enabling policy frameworks and resources to take the process to scale from government.

The role of government in scaling warrants reflection. In the case of Afghanistan, government action to scale CBE effectively quashed the movement that had given rise to scale. The government seems not to have bought in to community ownership of schools so much as to the fact that there were schools running that they could now formalize within a new political era of policy-endorsed secular education. Here, it was the presence of the schools that they bought into, and not the origins of those schools. They unwittingly killed the 'goose that laid the golden egg' through misinterpretation of the movement behind the schools in a reversion to expert-driven change. In the case of CLTS, some governments have sought to gain whole-country coverage of CLTS through the introduction of strong national policy, target setting, and building CLTS facilitation in to local government and school programmes, and so on. These programmes, though, still depend on local people coming to their own realization of the dangers of open defecation and buying into local and/or state supported action. Any government initiative must build on long-term contextual learning generated from the process as it goes to scale, and be continually alert as the process evolves so that it maintains the buy-in. This means that learning, participation, and networks remain central even in the final phases of scaling.

Reflecting on how to achieve scaling in relation to PRA Chambers (1995) highlights the importance of primary attention being focused on behaviour and attitudes; a process approach permitting continuous revisions to ongoing projects – one which doesn't get locked into pre-planned logical framework requirements; the importance of starting on an experimental basis in part of an organization, or in one geographical area; ensuring the direct engagement of the poor, women, and marginal groups in their own analysis, identifying their own priorities; and continuity of institutional engagement over years not just within short-term project cycles. These principles closely mirror the model that has been described in this chapter.

Note

1. A more detailed account of the growth of the anti-poll tax movement can be found in Burns (1992).

References

Ahmed, S. (2009) 'Community led total sanitation in Bangladesh: chronicles of a people's movement', Brighton: Institute of Development Studies.

Bongartz, P. (2014) 'CLTS in Africa: trajectories, challenges and moving to scale', in P. Cross and Y. Coombes (eds), *Sanitation and Hygiene in Africa: Where Do We Stand?* London and New York, NY: IWA Publishing.

Burns, D. (1992) *Poll Tax Rebellion*, Edinburgh: AK Press.

Cavill, S. with Chambers, R. and Vernon, N. (2015) 'Sustainability and CLTS: taking stock', Frontiers of CLTS: Innovations and Insights Issue 4, Brighton: IDS.

Chambers, R. (1990) 'Rapid and participatory rural appraisal: past, present and future', Paper for seminar at the University of Chiang Mai, 23 November 1990.

Chambers, R. (1995) 'Making the best of going to scale' *PLA Notes* 24: 57–61.

Chambers, R. (2009) 'Going to scale with community-led total sanitation: reflections on experience, issues and ways forward', Brighton: Institute of Development Studies.

Community-Led Total Sanitation (2011) 'Lukenya notes: taking CLTS to scale with quality'. <http://www.communityledtotalsanitation.org/resource/lukenya-notes-taking-clts-scale-quality> [accessed 8 July 2015].

Context, International Cooperation (2010) 'Evaluation of the Dutch support to capacity development (case study SNV, synthesis report)', p.25. <http://www.iob-evaluatie.nl/en/node/134> [accessed 28 July 2015].

Food and Agriculture Organization (FAO) (2000) 'Agriculture, trade and food security issues and options in the two WTO negotiations from the perspective of developing countries', Vol II, Chapter 4, Country Case Studies, Commodities and Trade Division, Food and Agriculture Organization of the United Nations.

Griffin, M. (1997) 'Aid agency outcry puts spotlight on girls', *TES*, 7 March. <https://www.tes.co.uk/article.aspx?storycode=64710> [accessed June 2015].

Hassan, M. (2006) 'Education and the role of NGOs in emergencies: Afghanistan 1978–2002, 2006, American Institute for Research.

Hoggett, P. and Bishop, J. (1986) *Organising around Enthusiasms: Patterns of Mutual Aid in Leisure*, London: Comedia.

Kar, K. (2011) 'Foreword', in L. Mehta and S. Movik (eds), *Shit Matters: The Potential of Community-led Total Sanitation*, Rugby: Practical Action Publishing.

Kar, K. and Bongartz, P. (2006) 'Update on some recent developments in community-led total sanitation', Brighton: Institute of Development Studies.

Mehta, L. (2011) 'Introduction: Why shit matters: community led total sanitation and the sanitation challenge for the 21st century' in L. Mehta and S. Movik (eds), *Shit Matters: The Potential of Community-led Total Sanitation*, Rugby: Practical Action Publishing.

Mehta, L. and Movik, S. (eds) (2011) *Shit Matters: The Potential of Community-led Total Sanitation*, Rugby: Practical Action Publishing.

Nolan, L. (2006) 'Afghanistan, education and the formation of the Taliban', Masters dissertation, January, The Fletcher School, Tufts University. <http://www.ariaye.com/english/b.pdf> [accessed June 2015].

Okali, C., Sumberg, J. and Farrington, J. (1994) 'Farmer participatory research: rhetoric and reality', London: Overseas Development Institute.

PACE-A (2011) 'Partnership for Advancing Community Education in Afghanistan', Final report, PACE-A.

Physicians for Human Rights (1998) 'The Taliban's war on women: a health and human rights crisis in Afghanistan' August, Physicians for Human Rights, p. 54.

Priyono, E. (2011) 'Institutional dimensions of scaling up CLTS in Indonesia', in L. Mehta and S. Movik (eds), *Shit Matters: The Potential of Community-led Total Sanitation*, Rugby: Practical Action Publishing.

Wadsworth, Y. (2010) *Building in Research and Evaluation: Human Inquiry for Living Systems*, Melbourne: Action Research Press and Allen & Unwin.

Wamanji, E. (2009) 'When traders become revenue collectors', Standard Media, 23 May. <https://www.standardmedia.co.ke/article/1144014916/when-traders-become-revenue-collectors> [accessed June 2015].

Were, T.O. and Dido, S.B. (2008) 'Lolguniani: a partnership for progress'; SNV. <http://ebooksgenius.com/pdf/lolguniani-a-partnership-for-progress-snv-world-27958041.html> [accessed 8 July 2015].

Wikipedia (no date) 'Community led total sanitation'. < https://en.wikipedia.org/wiki/Community-led_total_sanitation> [accessed 30 December 2014].

CHAPTER 7
Power in transformative change processes

In this chapter we look at some of the dilemmas and issues raised by power in complex systems. We argue that seeing power as a systemic property, rather than one which lies in the relationship between two or more conflicting protagonists, has a fundamental impact on how participation can be articulated, and how change can be enacted. Firstly we talk about the different ways in which power is manifest, and then we discuss the implications of this way of thinking for development.

Keywords: power; systemic change; occupation; facilitation

Inequality and injustice are constructed through power relations. By understanding how power works both generally and in specific contexts, it becomes possible to develop strategies for engaging with it, challenging it, and shifting it. As we have already outlined, the work of the Participate Initiative showed clearly that people living in circumstances of extreme poverty and marginalization see the biggest impediment to equality and access to services as power relationships expressed as discriminatory social norms and institutional discrimination. Power is writ large in the whole development enterprise. Logging, land grabs, restrictions to citizenship identity, evictions are all manifestations of power across the development landscape (Burns et al., 2013). Because power is a systemic property, and knowing that we must change system dynamics in order to achieve sustainable change, trying to create change without addressing power is like trying to swim across a river with lead weights tied to your feet. In this chapter we want to look at some of the dilemmas and issues raised at the intersection of participation and power. We argue that seeing power as a systemic property, rather than one which lies in the relationship between two or more conflicting protagonists, has a fundamental impact on how participation can be articulated, and this is at the core of the philosophy underpinning this book.

Power as a systemic property

Some exercises of power are simple and direct. People get killed in wars, children are taken and made to be child soldiers, women are raped. Some exercises of power are about controlling what is and what is not on the agenda (Bachrach and Baratz, 1962); some are about making people believe what they would otherwise not have believed (Lukes,1974). In each of these cases we emphasize the importance of the system. Even where power is expressed as a direct act of violence it is never solely about the relationship between two

http://dx.doi.org/10.3362/9781780448510.007

or more people or organizations. For anyone to exercise any power over any other, it has at some level to be legitimized or acquiesced in by the wider environment within which those players sit. Thus while Lukes (1974) frames his power analysis in terms of the power that A exercises over B, it is in fact a deeply systemic property. It is interesting that even Freire (1972: 31) in *The Pedagogy of the Oppressed* frames power in this way: 'any situation in which A objectively exploits B or hinders his pursuit of self-affirmation as a responsible person is oppression'. It is, ironically, earlier writings which begin to articulate a more systemic conception of power. Kurt Lewin who developed the notion of force fields in the early 1940s (Lewin, 1943) argued that all power relationships exist within a 'field' of multiple forces. At any one time there is a particular balance of power and within any system there are always multiple forces and multiple counterveiling forces. A number of important principles can be derived from force-field analysis:

- Many small forces in a system combined will create the same force as one big force.
- The small forces do not all have to be in the same place.
- A big force in a system is likely to attract as strong a countervailing force, so it is often more effective to catalyse multiple small forces across the system.
- Elements within the force field are interconnected so changes to any of them will have an impact on the system.

This understanding of power within systems was substantively advanced by Foucault. Foucault saw power as a dynamic process characterized by constant ebbs and flows. Power is never monolithic. People may have space to act within some arenas and not in others. People who are oppressed may be the oppressors of others; shifts in relationship patterns can change the entirety of the power relationships. A more recent version of this thinking conceives of power as a systemic property:

> Power's mechanisms are best conceived, not as instruments powerful agents use to prevent the powerless from acting freely, but rather as social boundaries that, together, define fields of action for all actors. Power defines fields of possibility. It facilitates and constrains social action. Its mechanisms consist in laws, rules, norms, customs, social identities, and standards that constrain and enable inter and intra-subjective action ... Freedom enables actors to participate effectively in shaping the boundaries that define for them the field of what is possible. (Hayward, 1998: 12)

The laws, rules, norms, customs, identities, standards, and so on are elements of a system dynamic which become crystallized like well-worn paths through a forest. Lukes' (1974) assertion that the most insidious form of power is that which makes someone believe that something is in their interest when it is not, is not usually some form of individualized brainwashing, rather it is established by deeply embedded norms. When we see the same patterns repeated every day we see them as normal. People who have been abused as children may see child abuse as normal; women who have had their lives constrained since childhood often come to see this as how life is (and how it should be). Power is held within social norms and deep structural patterning.

The key message here is that power does not exist in binary relationships. It exists within a field of relationships, and power relationships are constantly in flux. Even what appears to be a static equilibrium is effectively a balance of constantly moving forces. We have used this description from Foucault before (Burns, 2007) but it is worth repeating as it captures the essence of systemic power relations in just a few words:

> The multiplicity of force relations immanent in the sphere in which they operate and which constitute their own organisation; as the process which, through ceaseless struggles and confrontations, transforms, strengthens or reverses them; as the support which these force relations find in one another thus forming a chain or a system or on the contrary, the disjunction and contradictions which isolate them from one another, and lastly as the strategies in which they take effect, whose general design or institutional crystallisation is embodied in the state apparatus, in the formulation of law, in the various social hegemonies (Foucault, 1984: 92)

To shift the dynamics of these systems, we have to shift the balance of forces through action, and the action has to be focused on chains of interrelationships such as we have described earlier in this book. We also need to be aware that power is always and constantly contested. The balance of forces now, may be quite different in two months' time. Small changes in the system dynamics can create opportunities for those trying to create progressive change, but equally for those who are resisting those changes and advancing other world views. It is just as possible to go backwards as forwards. The current global situation with regard to lesbian, gay, bisexual, and transgender (LGTB) rights is testament to this with huge setbacks in Uganda, Russia, and India to name just the most high profile.

Now let's layer some complexity thinking into this. The notion of attractors is helpful here. Attractors can be envisaged a bit like magnets within fields of power. As latent attractors grow in strength they have the power to pull people into different configurations and relationships. People gravitate towards groups, activities, and positions that are 'attractive' to them, and which appear to give their lives some sort of coherence. Power can be expressed as shifting discourses which draw people into organizations and action around them. So the first critical step in challenging oppressive power relations is to build alternative attractors. Given that the whole concept of attractors is predicated on drawing support, and it cannot ever be known in advance what will draw support and what will not, this suggests the need to nurture environments in which multiple alternative attractors can be generated. But it is not as simple as to say, 'then sit back and wait to see where people go'. We also have to identify the system dynamics that are blocking people from shifting to that new attractor, or indeed pulling them back into the old system dynamics even when as individuals they have been able to move.

Understanding power relations as systemic allows us to look for interlocking chains of causality and then to intentionally act on leverage points that are manifest amid those chains.

Another defining feature of complexity is the way in which 'starting conditions' are critical. The starting configuration of relations substantively determines what is possible afterwards because what comes next flows iteratively from what started. Earlier we gave a simple example. If you set up a project based on a linear logic model and evaluate it against the log frame, then the possibilities for iterative learning, flexible programme delivery, and innovation are very slim.

Power through knowledge

System change becomes possible when system dynamics are revealed, and system dynamics are revealed through a process of meaning making. Knowledge that is generated in different parts of the system can be brought together to create collective knowledge. This is a route to concientization (Freire, 1972) where through inquiry we become aware of what is happening around us and to us. We become aware of how we have come to construct the knowledge that we hold and what the assumptions are that underpin it. Unlike the notion of consciousness raising or even of 'false consciousness', conscientization does not mean telling people how they are oppressed but creates the conditions for co-learning through which they can discover this. Through the same sort of processes people can learn what challenges oppression and what good solutions look like. This process can be connected to our thinking on innovation.

There are a number of ways in which we can generate knowledge which is intrinsic to the system that we are in, but it is also important to bring in external perspectives. As we have discussed earlier we have found the ATD Fourth World concept of 'merging of knowledges' helpful (Fourth World University Research Group, 2007). Here intrinsic knowledge interacts with external knowledge to generate new ideas and solutions that are adapted to local circumstances. There is some convergence here with Freire's notion of 'cultural synthesis': 'In cultural synthesis the actors who come from "another world" to the world of the people do so not as invaders. They do not come to teach or to transmit, or to give anything, but rather to learn with the people, about the people's world' (Freire, 1972: 147).

In Freire's conceptualization, those from 'another world' are 'bringing' knowledge, but framed in relation to themselves and their experiences, as resources with which to learn together. Freire argues that: 'Authentic education is not carried out by A for B, or by A about B, but rather A with B.' He refers to 'a movement of inquiry' where inquiring together is the main way through which knowledge is acquired and knowledge achieved. We have explored this idea in more detail in the VSO Valuing Volunteering project (Burns et al., 2015). It is an important conceptualization because it helps us to get out of the much discussed trap that is inherent in international development where, on the one hand, local knowledge is privileged and this allows long-standing oppressions to continue (e.g. the subjugation of women) and, on the other hand, external knowledge is privileged (e.g. wearing the burka is unacceptable), which brings with it a taste of colonialism and the privilege of Western perspectives (see also the chapter on participation that follows). One critical reflection on this discussion relates to the direction of travel of knowledge. It is easy to assume in this framing that Western countries are the outsiders. Clearly the 'developed' countries have much to learn from other countries across the world, two obvious examples being the way in which indigenous people understand land and the need to protect it, and the way in which many traditional communities care for their older people.

If, however, we see knowledge in the same way as we described power above, as held within fields of force and part of a constant process of contestation, then to bring new knowledge into a dialogue, or to model new norms and so on is a form of juxtaposition which allows for a merging of knowledges through learning. This enables people to see how others live, discern why they live that way, and to make choices for themselves. Being able to achieve those aspirations does not flow directly from having the knowledge. Thus, returning to the previous section, knowledge about how to change the dynamics of the system is as crucial as knowledge about collective circumstances and aspirations.

This is also what is happening in a self-organizing system. People encounter something new, they explore its relevance to themselves, they make judgements about its utility, and they adapt it to their needs. As the new encounters the old it is rarely adopted in the same form but evolves through the interaction. Self-organizing systems adapt to flows of discourse. As Foucault argued these cannot be seen in binary ways:

> There is not, on the one side, a discourse of power and opposite it, another discourse that runs counter to it. Discourses are tactical elements or blocks operating in the field of force relations; there can exist different and even contradictory discourses within the same strategy; they can on the contrary circulate without changing their form from one strategy to another, opposing strategy. (Foucault, 1984: 101–2)

The anti-poll tax story (Burns, 1992) which we told in Chapter 6 is a good example of this. The strategy was fashioned from multiple and contradictory discourses which interacted systemically in ways which were not visible to most of the actors.

One very specific issue about knowledge that we want to raise here relates to how meaning can be safely transferred across systems in a systemic inquiry process. There are dangers in moving knowledge across systems. In a conflict zone, or arenas where interests are contested (e.g. where people are held in slavery or bonded labour, or where mining companies are trying to take land etc.), risks are everywhere. In the work that Danny did in Ghana on the climate change project, there was a moment during a dialogue when powerful local officials who had the power to evict local villagers suddenly asked who had told a particular story (Harvey et al., 2012). The facilitators had to quickly divert the conversation and shut down that line of inquiry. It was clear that people were seeking knowledge that could put research participants at risk. Often it is not that obvious. This is a tricky issue for large-scale systemic work because we need to build pictures of the whole system, and test it across different localities, but we also need to avoid exposing people to danger.

We have found that stories and maps are not only a good way of generating meaning but they are also a good way of transferring meaning safely. The ethics of this are complex. In Danny's work in Myanmar this issue was highly visible. In October 2014 he was facilitating a combined workshop in Laschio, Myanmar. The team was working with NGO networks in Laschio, Laiza, and Hpakant in Kachin and Northern Shan states. When people arrived at the workshops with their stories, they didn't know who the other groups would bring. Laiza is located within the Kachin Independence Army controlled territories, Laschio is Burmese controlled but with a very diverse and conflicted population of Muslims, Buddhists, and Christians and a majority Chinese population. The Laschio group included some ex-Burmese military and police. This created a moment of tension in the wider group. Many discussions were had behind the scenes in response to people's concerns about the dangers of sharing information. It was decided that the stories were too sensitive to share in the whole group, despite being anonymized, but that the system maps could be used as a vehicle for transferring knowledge across the groups and for creating shared understandings about the system dynamics in different places.

The risks that relate to process, as well as risks related to the action that results from the process, must be debated closely with the participants. There are many situations where even inquiry can be dangerous. The process that people are engaged in must be clear and transparent, and proper time must be given to debating risk. It is not up to external facilitators to make the judgements on risks, but it is our responsibility to make sure that they are discussed. Equally, it is important not to be paternalistic about risk assessments. Local people are often making decisions everyday about risks that are far greater than external facilitators will ever encounter. Nevertheless a systemic analysis can bring into view more of the unseen risks. So assessing risk should be a continuous process which is not just confined to the beginning of a process.

Power as occupation

Power lies in the doing. In enacting things, they become real and have real presence and real force. The concept of fait accompli may be useful here. According to the Oxford English Dictionary 'fait accompli' is 'something that has already happened or been decided before those affected hear about it'. The effects of action are often not as clear-cut as this, but consider for a moment the idea of momentum. It is much easier to prevent a stationary bicycle from moving than to stop a moving one. This does not mean that it is impossible. If we know in advance that a bicycle intends to move we can stop it just by standing in front of it, or puncturing the tyres, or pushing the person off it, and so on. If it is moving it is much harder. The same principle applies to action. Once it is situated within a field of relations it has a presence. As soon as something happens it creates momentum and it occupies space that was otherwise unoccupied. The idea of a movement is closely allied to this thinking. It is through movement that space is occupied. As we have discussed in Chapter 6 much of our work is similar in form to movement building.

This observation is not exclusive to any particular value set. Regressive reactionary forces enact power through occupation as well. One extreme manifestation of this is rape where the body is quite literally occupied. The pain of violation and the range of reactions – from silencing and shame to defiance – mirror the ways in which, for example, indigenous lands are taken over by extractive industries, militaries, and so on. Lukes' notion of brainwashing is not only characterized by open debate but by the occupation of the mind. Occupation is power.

These forms of occupation should clearly be antithetical to those who value human dignity and freedom. Nevertheless, explicitly understanding occupation as a form of power is crucial to understanding how to engage with complex dynamics. We are not starting from zero here. All direct action is a form of occupation. People's occupation of land for shelter typified by informal settlements in large cities is a well-known form of occupation; the student occupations of the 1960s and 1970s were a manifestation of the same phenomenon.

Action research builds on the same philosophy. Rather than over-planning and analysing, action research encourages experimental action because it is often only possible to make something happen by seizing the moment when it is possible to make it happen. People talk about power and empowerment in terms of it not being a zero-sum game. But this is not entirely the case when it comes to space. Space is not instantly expandable so if I occupy a space you cannot occupy it. Every action that is taken opens and closes space for different actors. Effective change is often achieved through an awareness of the changing space and the capacity to move into it when it opens up.

Power in facilitation

Facilitation is not neutral. Facilitators have life experience, views, and vested interests just as everyone else does. Facilitators have the power to open up spaces and deepen democratic inquiry, but also to close down spaces, to manipulate processes, and even to expose people to danger. Facilitators can change the dynamics of a relationship – having a strong influence on, for example, deciding whether a group should be paid or not. Consequently, it is important that the power of facilitators is subject to critical scrutiny.

In a SAR process, facilitators may have even more power than in a more concentrated participatory action research (PAR) relationship (Burns, 2012). Because SAR process are not rooted within a single group, and because the participants may change as the inquiry evolves, there is no simple line of accountability, and SAR facilitators will form a bridge across different parts of the inquiry. Nevertheless, as we have argued, SAR is a critical evolution from PAR as it allows power to be addressed much more substantively because the inquiry is constituted across the system and is able to surface the system dynamics. As Burns has articulated in earlier texts, this opens up a trade-off between the sort of direct group ownership and participation that is character-istic of PAR, and a more diffuse participation which enables a stronger power analysis. Burns (2012) suggested four strategies for mitigating the dangers of this diffusion which ensure that there are multiple bridges across the inquiry:

- supporting and embedding distributed leadership where one or more individuals in inquiry strands work with an external facilitator to guide the whole process;
- locating responsibility for the processes with a widely trusted group on the ground;
- organizing regular cross-system events to bring the strands together, to test the resonance of emerging issues, to test existing interpretations, and to offer new ones of system dynamics, and so on;
- developing interactive spaces where information, knowledge, inter-pretations, and sense making is shared even though people may not meet face to face. International peacemakers have used this process successfully.

The first of these approaches was used in the Bristol Children's Initiatives process (Burns, 2007). The second strategy was developed in work with Ghana Community Radio Network (GCRN) and more recent work with the RANIR civil society network in Kachin, Myanmar. In these cases the external facili-tators provided methodological support and initially provided guidance on the overarching direction of the inquiries, but as the work moved beyond the first phase it was carried out entirely in the local languages and responsibility was taken by local civil society groups. While this strategy is one of the best for ensuring local ownership, it is important to ensure that these facilitators are sensitive to inclusion issues – local people are as capable of excluding members of their communities as anyone else. The third strategy is essentially a knitting strategy. It ensures that the inquiries don't go their own way without reference to each other, and that strategic decisions can be made by large numbers of actors across the inquiries. We have not used the fourth strategy – that is, an Internet facility – as articulated; however, we have used the large maps as a platform for shared dialogue. The important principle here is that inquiry in one part of the system is visible to people in other parts.

Underlying this analysis are two key messages: firstly that external facilitators have a role in constantly ensuring inclusion, and being self-reflective about the direction that the inquiries are going in (continuously checking whether they following their own biases or the flow of the inquiry) and secondly that they must explicitly build-in an architecture which locates local stakeholders as facilitators and co-leaders of the process. This ensures that the process is driven on the basis of local knowledge supported by external knowledge.

Conclusion

Changing system dynamics changes power relationships occupation allows control over spaces, places, and people; fait accompli sets up system dynamics which are hard to shift once they are in place; new knowledge opens up pathways which didn't appear to be there before; facilitation of relationships builds trust and solidarity and juxtapositions create social innovations that can transform power relations. Understanding power is crucial to understanding change in systems which are held in dynamic equilibrium by complex power relations. Understanding power also reminds us that everything is always contested. There is no room for complacency; yesterday's gains may quickly be reversed.

References

Bachrach, P. and Baratz, M.S. (1962) 'Two faces of power', *The American Political Science Review* 56(4): 942–7.

Burns, D. (1992) *Poll Tax Rebellion*, Edinburgh: AK Press.

Burns, D. (2007) *Systemic Action Research: A Strategy for Whole System Change*, Bristol: Policy Press.

Burns, D. (2012) 'Participatory Systemic Inquiry', *IDS Bulletin* 43(3).

Burns, D., Howard, J., Lopez-Franco, E., Shahrokh, T. and Wheeler, J. (2013) 'Work with us: how communities and organisations can catalyse sustainable change', Brighton: IDS.

Burns, D., Aked, J., Hacker, E., Lewis, S. and Picken, A. (2015) 'The role of volunteering in sustainable development', Brighton: IDS/VSO.

Freire, P. (1972) *The Pedagogy of the Oppressed*, London: Penguin.

Foucault, M. (1984) *The History of Sexuality: Part 1*, London: Penguin.

Fourth World University Research Group (2007) *The Merging of Knowledge: People in Poverty and Academics Thinking Together*, Lanham, MD: University Press of America.

Harvey, B., Burns, D. and Oswald, K. (2012) 'Linking community, radio, and action research on climate change: reflections on a systemic approach', *IDS Bulletin* 43(3).

Hayward, C.R. (1998) 'De-facing power', *Polity* 31(1).

Lewin, K. (1943) Defining the "field at a given time"', *Psychological Review* 50: 292–310. Republished in *Resolving Social Conflicts and Field Theory in Social Science*, Washington DC: American Psychological Association, 1997.

Lukes, S. (1974) *Power: A Radical View*, Oxford: Oxford University Press.

CHAPTER 8
Participatory processes in development

Participation is central to our understanding of how change can and should happen. Yet it has been extensively co-opted by the development industry and is thus contested by many who are cynical about how it has been utilized. Much participation is confined to 'invited spaces'; often it only engages those with more power in local communities; it can be extractive and legitimize development interventions which might otherwise be contested. In this chapter we confront these critiques. We offer some reflections on how to ensure that participatory processes are meaningful, and we advance an alternative model of participation allied to nurtured emergent development, which is rooted in action rather than deliberation and formal decision-making processes.

Keywords: participation; participatory development; participatory research; inclusion

Inclusion is the opposite of exclusion and can only be created through participation. We have put a lot of emphasis on participation in this book because we believe that everyone has the right to be properly included in society. Participation is also important because it generates realistic and appropriate solutions to the issues that people face on the ground. People will only sustain participation if they feel that action will result from it, and that they, and people that they care about, will benefit from it. 'Participatory Action research is an approach to inquiry which should yield results that are useful to the people who are researched. This begins with getting the right topics. If they urgently need to be investigated, shared, debated, spoken and acted on, good work will be taken up and acted on without delay' (Karamoja Action Research Team, 2013).

So the issue of participation is intrinsically connected to the issue of effectiveness.

There is always a danger that participation will be co-opted and used by those with vested interests in oppression, to legitimize that oppression. This no more undermines the importance of participation than the attempts of the radical right to hijack concepts like freedom. Rather the opposite, it creates an imperative to defend it, and to continuously re-articulate it as a progressive force for good in society.

So we will respond to the critiques of participation in two different ways. Firstly we look at the how to ensure that structured dialogue and decision-making processes (including inquiry and action research process) are genuinely participatory. Secondly we propose an alternative model for conceptualizing participation that challenges the idea of formal decision-making as the only or

http://dx.doi.org/10.3362/9781780448510.008

best vehicle for participation, and conceptualizes participation as action that creates changes in behaviours and attitudes which may then be legitimized by decision-makers.

Participation in structured decision-making processes

Where does power lie in participatory processes?

Perhaps the most fundamental questions which need to be asked about formal participatory processes are who frames them? Who participates in them? How participatory are they? And who controls the outputs? We explore some of the issues relating to these questions in this section.

Who frames the process and who initiates it? Yoland Wadsworth (2010: 53) describes how participatory processes tend to form. She says that it is all about questions:

> Interestingly we don't usually start with talking about methods or techniques; or even by going and reading the literature about what others have done or thought. We start in the middle of everyday life by noticing something, stopping, and 'experiencing' a question (one that might not yet even be consciously articulated). A kind of question mark appears over the discrepancy ...

Broad areas or specific foci for an inquiry can be generated from the inside or from engagement with facilitators or others from the outside. But it always involves those on the inside noticing a disjuncture between what is, and what they had previously thought; between what is, and what could be, and so on. It is only when the people who are at the heart of those questions articulate that they want to act on those questions that a legitimate process of inquiry and action can begin.

If a process is initiated from outside, there needs to be real transparency about what the motivations for the external engagement are, and where the interests of the initiating party lie. For example, as individuals we might want to explain our personal motivations for engagement; similarly we should be clear about our constraints (e.g. IDS is a self-financing organization and depends on project funding for its survival, so we cannot do this work without generating large project grants from donors).

In a group or single community-based action research process, building ownership can be straightforward because a relatively small number of people stay involved in the inquiry throughout its duration. In a more systemic process it is not straightforward at all because while the inquiry might begin with a linear sense of 'ownership', as it evolves and moves, it will often move beyond the originators of the process. As ideas are enacted they pick up momentum and draw in new people. New pathways are opened and new lines of inquiry may be opened that go in a different direction to the original inquiry. People with different positionalities, interests, and views to the originators become involved. As soon as the space is opened up in this way, the initiating groups cede ownership and become partners in shaping the direction of the process. This, as we saw in the preceding chapter, also raises questions about the power of facilitators who have greater scope to influence the direction of the process. So in systemic work, ownership will only ever be partial. For example, in the volunteering research described earlier, while VSO initiated the action research process, it was not initiated by their country offices, local volunteers, or anyone that VSO worked with on the ground. Their engagement was dependent on their interest in, and commitment to, a process that had been created elsewhere. The success of a process is determined by who engages with it, adopts it, and champions it. If we see power in a Foucauldian sense, what happens is the result of a balance of forces that are continually in flux. The legitimacy of an action (in this case a participatory process) is denoted by the extent to which it resonates with others, and is adopted.

What are people participating in? When assessing the extent to which processes are participatory, we start by looking at what people are actually participating in, and ask if they have meaningful engagement in the whole process or only parts. Within a cycle of action research we might consider:

- setting the questions;
- designing the methodology;
- collecting the data;
- analysing the data;
- taking action on the basis of the analysis.

As indicated above, the questions that underpin participatory research must be generated by participants on the ground. Designing the process is more complex as this is often the area where facilitators bring important expertise and experience. One of the paradoxes of participatory processes is that participatory facilitators often need to show great confidence and be quite assertive. This is because in many situations there is someone with a background in traditional research analysis who is eager to tell other participants that this is not a scientific process and that real research looks like something else. Local people may need a lot of methodological support and to trust a participatory facilitator until they are really familiar with the methods but at every stage they need to review whether it is working for them. Our experience is that once people have learned the different methodologies that are relevant to their situation, they quickly and creatively adapt them to their purposes.

Stakeholders are important in collecting the data. They know the local terrain and in most circumstances they are much more likely to be trusted. Sometimes, only local communities can meaningfully collect data because outsiders are not trusted, their presence may be seen as insensitive, or their methods may not uncover the reality of the situation. In our current work on slavery and bonded labour in India and Nepal we will support community participants in more than 60 hamlets to collect statistical data on the prevalence of slaves and bonded labourers in their community. They have a local knowledge, which will allow them to find out the numbers in a politically sensitive way.

If a process is truly participatory the people who are engaged in the research should do the analysis. There are many ways in which analysis can be carried out. People can do this within an action research meeting, or in a collective analysis workshop, or through system mapping, and so on. It is in carrying out the analysis that it is possible to see what action can be taken. What is worrying is that 'analysis' is the area that people are least likely to be engaged in – even in so-called participatory processes, yet as we have described in Chapter 4 there are many ways of doing collective analysis.

In an action research process, stakeholders engage not only in sense making and decision-making, but in designing, constructing, and enacting action. In this sense action research is an enactment of participation. It breaks down the distinction between policy, planning, action, learning, leadership, capacity development, and evaluation. These become integrated parts of the same process. This is important because even the discourse of democratic participation separates democratic decision-making from action. In this model the action research process *is* leadership. The action research process *is* capacity development. The action research process *is* evaluation. It does not lead to it, support it, develop it. It is it.

Who participates in participatory processes? One of the strongest critiques of participatory processes is that even when they work well, and have real decision-making power and influence on policy and practice, they only involve the 'usual suspects'. This can mean tribal leaders, or male heads of household, or CBOs talking on behalf of people, or relatives talking on behalf of disabled people, and so on. Genuinely participatory work must be able to meaningfully engage the poorest and most marginalized.

Within marginalized communities (just as everywhere else) people are divided and are not equally oppressed. A PAR group that is designed to advance the cause of workers may end up further oppressing women. In many societies children are excluded, but the effects of actions taken by their parents may have major implications for them. Participation of some usually excludes others. To say that something is participatory because it is driven by a particular ground-level group is problematic. Andrea Cornwall states clearly:

> Participation all too often boil[s] down to situations in which only the voices and versions of the vocal few are raised and heard. Women, many critics argue, are those most likely to lose out, finding themselves and their interests marginalized or overlooked in apparently 'participatory' processes. (Cornwall, 2003)

and

> unless efforts are made to enable marginal voices to be raised and heard, claims to inclusiveness made on behalf of participatory development will appear rather empty. (Cornwall, 2003)

There are good examples of how this has been done. As we discussed in Chapter 4 the Bangladesh 'we can also make change' community research teams were all disabled and older people – many blind and most illiterate with minimal if any incomes. The Ground Level Panels that were developed as part of the Participate Initiative (Burns et al., 2015) brought together 10–15 people across diverse marginalized communities to deliberate the sustainable development goals in Uganda, Egypt, India, and Brazil. Another good example of PAR that has been driven by people living in great poverty is the work of Patta Scott-Villiers and the Pastoralist Communication Initiative in the Karamoja, Northern Uganda. Scott-Villiers co-facilitated two pieces of work. The first, starting in November 2011, was a six-week process carried out over three months. The second was a much longer process carried out over a year. In the first, a team of 13 Karamojong researchers, young women and men aged between 20 and 29 of different groups, set out to research the situation of youth in their areas. They visited 16 settlements, conducted 378 interviews, and took thousands of photographs in two districts. They analysed hundreds of stories and discussions and drew conclusions, which they put into an illustrated book. The book was taken back to the places where they did the research, as well as shared with development agencies and officials (Scott-Villiers et al., 2012). In the second piece of work, which focused on peace, land and customary law, Patta worked with a mixed research team of 23 young men and women from Karamoja. Some were schooled and some were not. Some lived in towns and others in rural areas. At some points in the process they were paired – literate people worked with non-literate people. Each had different roles and different perspectives from which to challenge each other. The group worked across 14 sub-counties, visiting 89 communities (some of them three or more times), interviewing 527 people, and informally talking to many more. This is how they saw their work:

> we research contemporary issues and present the issues to people in Karamoja. We also seek to inform local government and NGOs and bring them into debate with citizens on the issues raised by the research. Using the findings we support action with Karimojong, government and NGOs. We are Karimojong working for Karamoja. ...
>
> The young citizen researchers used their unique position to explore and articulate modern-day dilemmas in Karamoja. They used qualitative research methods to collect a bricolage of material; conversations; interviews; observations; stories; opinions and images. Collating, triangulating, weighing and testing. They forged it into evidence. It took nine months of data collection, repeated analysis and feeding back to incorporate a broad variety of voices and opinions into the narratives, until the material had been refined into a single argument. (Karamoja Action Research Team, 2013)

While the earlier work had been framed in advance around youth, this work was constructed entirely around what the group themselves thought was important. The role of IDS and the Pastoralist Communication Initiative (PCI) in this process was partly to support the methodology but as significantly 'to keep on pushing away the people who kept on telling them what to do' (Scott-Villiers, 2015, personal conversation).

The assumption that people living in extreme poverty and with extreme marginalization cannot make complex analyses and develop sophisticated strategies for action is simply wrong. Their analysis is usually light years ahead of experts and researchers from outside.

Who controls the outputs? Another critique of participatory processes is that they can be as extractive as traditional research processes, but with a dangerous veneer of popular legitimacy that traditional processes do not claim. This perspective points to the fact that quotes from people are co-opted to support the things that they would not otherwise support. One example that is often cited is the process known as 'Voices of the Poor' or 'consultations with the poor', which was organized by World Bank (Rademacher and Patel, 2002). There has been a mixed response to this initiative. On the one hand, critics such as Rosie McGee argue that quotes were cherry-picked to support a neo-liberal agenda that could not possibly have been in the interests of those who offered their voices. On the other hand, advocates such as Robert Chambers argued that while this was true, the process nevertheless offered important insights to global policymakers (e.g. the importance of security to people living in poverty) and, despite its flaws, was the first major attempt to bring together a detailed analysis of life from the perspective of the poorest.

Our response to this is straightforward. Good participatory processes are more likely to create influence than traditional research process because they draw policymakers into making real human connections. However, it should never be assumed that any influence will occur. Thus it is important that whatever process is initiated has an integrity and utility within its own domain, and that people have the ability to determine how their voice is articulated. The Participate Initiative started with an analysis of the failures of other global processes which had tried to bridge the local global gap (Participate Initiative, 2012). This fed into a set of guidelines and principles which were designed to mitigate the problems.

Firstly, even though DFID was paying for the coordination which was provided by IDS, we invited people into the process as self-funded participatory research teams. This meant that because no one had rights over their work they could completely control what happened to it. Secondly, we ensured that the work done was rooted in longer term trusting relationships between local people, local community-based organizations, and local NGOs so was not subject to external researchers flying in and out with information. Thirdly, we insisted that all research that was part of the initiative should have an intrinsic value in its own right. In other words it must directly contribute to local learning and action and not be dependent on a successful global outcome. Fourthly, we made it a requirement of joining the Participatory

Research Group that the research analysis was done by the local people. Participatory research did not mean that data was collected by local people and then analysed by researchers, and it did not mean local people sitting in a focus group, which was later analysed by researchers. Local people determined the meaning of their research, the implications of that meaning, what they wanted to convey to a wider public, and in what form. In this sense it was an empowering experience for the participants long before it came into any policy arena. Chambers observed in relation to the Voices of the Poor initiative:

> Voices of the Poor opted for a standardisation of data to enable a comparative study (rather than a dynamic, open-ended research process which was tailored to local conditions). Participatory research emphasises exploring people's own categories and meanings and using these as an entry point for analysis.

> The methodology guide was comprised of pre-framed conceptual categories and questions (e.g. 'social exclusion', 'gender') and thus framed what was possible for respondents to say. This restricted 'the space for creative improvisation and iterative learning that has been deemed so important by participatory research'. (Chambers, 1997, in Cornwall and Fujita, 2007: 53)

The Participate Initiative research on the other hand was diverse. Local groups used the methods that they wanted to use and asked the questions that they wanted to ask. This created both authenticity and diversity. Methodologically what is powerful about this approach is that it enables an extraordinary triangulation of data. If similar messages emerge from completely different communities, that asked different questions and used different methodologies, then we can safely conclude that these collective findings are robust.

Finally, we were prepared to challenge our funder. There were two moments where this came to the fore. As we discussed in Chapter 1, the first moment was when the early participatory research showed that people living in extreme poverty and marginalization were more concerned about 'how' development was done rather than 'what' development was done. This was presented to the High Level Panel on Post-2015 Development and worked through in a two-hour workshop. DFID was not happy, because they wanted us to focus on what the 'priority issues' were for the poorest. This made no sense for two reasons. Firstly because the research was showing clearly that, for the poorest, health, education, incomes, security, and so on were even more interconnected than more well-off families. Secondly participants were saying that many services were available but that they could not access them because of power, local social norms, institutional discrimination, and so on. This required a focus on process, behaviours, and attitudes, not on 'what' was delivered. We held our nerve and diversified the spaces that we put this message into. We found over time that it started to resonate with other consultations coming from the United Nations Development Programme (UNDP). The second moment was our critique of the HLP report itself. We had thought that we had been constructively critical by highlighting major progress and also big gaps from the perspective of the poorest and most marginalized. According to the prime minister's special advisor on the post-2015 process, this was the second most critical response of all 80 or so that they reviewed. We are not convinced that this was actually the case, but it does demonstrate that as long as the research itself has integrity it is possible to stand up even to the political positions of your funders. This does not mean that the perspectives of the participate network will have more than a small contributory influence on this global process, but without building the integrity and legitimacy of the participatory process, it would have had none.

The important message from this is to make sure any participatory work has integrity in its own right. The issue of extraction and manipulation should be put into perspective. Powerful players constantly take excerpts from published reports, and so on and use them to justify their own interests. These should not be afforded legitimacy. Now, it is much more possible with social media to rapidly and visibly challenge claims of legitimacy made by power-holders.

Participation as action

Dominant models of democratic participation centre around a right to be consulted and engaged, creating spaces within which voices can be heard, and mechanisms (e.g. voting) through which opinions are simplified, aggregated and decisions made. In participatory democratic processes, accountability typically lies in the voting system and in the mandate given to representatives. But systems thinking and complexity lay down some challenges to this way of thinking, because if prediction is limited then manifestos and plans against which representatives are held to account have limited value. They also challenge the assumptions of much participatory practice such as the aspiration for consensus. In complex systems mediated by power, consensus is often unattainable and systemic work requires multiple workstreams allowing different stakeholders to work separately. This signals a shift away from consensus toward shifts in system dynamics catalysed by small changes across the system.

The idea that participation in decision-making must precede participation in action is linked to the idea of accountability. Unless we decide on a course of action collectively, then the protagonists cannot be held accountable to the collective. Complexity thinking takes us on a different course and sees people operating in a dynamic field where things are constantly happening doors are continuously opening and closing. Just to walk through a door opens up a set of possibilities that were not there when the collective decision-making process took place. Within a field of relations many different things will be going on at the same time, emanating from different sources. People act on the things that make sense to them. They could be encouraged by something that their neighbours are doing; see something on the television; know someone who is involved; go and look at a demonstration. Whatever it is that draws them in, they then start to support and engage in the activity, and the primary indicator of their support is that they do it. They are drawn toward what appears to be coherent in the moment. If this does not work, then they change direction. Action helps us to guide them to where they want to go. This then is a model where the action generates momentum and from the action sense-making processes are activated. It is not the dialogue and formal decision-making process that generates momentum, although dialogue will be important in helping to ensure that people make quality choices. In this conceptualization of participation, agreement is signalled by engagement not by vote.

M-Pesa didn't take off because lots of people sat in groups and said it was a good idea; it took off because people started to use it. If they didn't like it they would have used something else. This form of democracy is also incredibly powerful because it inherently resists both a majoritarian and a consensual positioning. People can congregate around what works for them. People can still transfer cash by hand, or go to the bank and get a wire transfer, or barter goods, or go through a middle person or ... They do what works for them.

This approach can be characterized by the following features:

- Alternative attractors are built and people gravitate to and adopt the ones that work best for them.
- Because they are adopted they automatically have ownership. There is no risk that people say they support something but then don't actually engage.
- This is a highly dynamic process where changes in the levels of participation are constantly adjusting.
- Modern technology makes these approaches more powerful. Feedback mechanisms on what works and what doesn't in addition to the knowledge we get from our peers allows a high level of triangulation.
- These processes are characterized by continuous adaption. The form something starts in is unlikely to be the same as that in which it spreads.
- One thing leads to another. Relationships happen, and people take steps together; things can move quickly. Very often they move more quickly than any formal 'democratic process' can pick up. The alternatives are some sort of retrospective endorsement or to let the process be what it is.

This might be conceived as a form of democracy by attractor.

Without the ability to predict or control change, real power lies in innovation combined with mobilization. Here action and reflection will often happen in real time as people make real-life decisions. As we showed in Chapter 6, Yoland Wadsworth (2010) articulates action research as analogous to the day-to-day way in which we make decisions in life. In this scenario, legitimacy is constructed through action. Imagine a local community in which women have been discriminated against for years. Girls are not allowed to go to school; women have no say in who they are married to, or indeed whether they get married or not. Imagine over time that this begins to change. Family by family, girls get sent to school. Perhaps this is through home schooling or defiance of local norms or some other means that people have begun to converge on. After a while schooling for girls becomes a norm. This is an expression of the democratic will of the people. The participation is in the doing and the democratic legitimacy lies in their convergence on this form of activity. It does not require a vote or a consensus decision-making process. This is democracy in action and represents a distributed form of accountability which is not controllable or malleable in the same way as formal democratic deliberation. Predictive accountability in which actors are accountable to predetermined decisions is a myth because the future can never be adequately predicted. Furthermore, because those with less power are constantly under the surveillance of the powerful, who seek to shut down any dissident action as soon as it emerges, this approach to transformative change has a greater chance of success. It is much easier to close down ideas that are on paper which have been signalled in advance, than to stop collective action that builds traction. Giving actions the opportunity to grow and gain support, form latent attractors, and build the critical mass necessary to surface them as attractors is a powerful strategy for radical change.

In Chapter 3, we demonstrated the close analogy between political movements and social change processes. We depicted scaling up as akin to a process of movement building. We are describing very similar dynamics when we look at the adoption and implementation of technical knowledge, as we are when the focus is social norms, or political positioning. Scaling is a result of participation in action. It is about consolidating and extending an alternative attractor.

The formal democratic process is usually a retrospective reflection of these processes on the ground. It is rarely possible to get legislation passed unless people have already started to change their opinions and their actions. It was possible to introduce smoking bans in public places and plain packaging for cigarettes with extreme health warnings because there had already been a shift in public opinion and in behaviour. A decade earlier it would not have been possible to introduce this. Similarly when a politician pushes through legislation that is unpopular, it either attracts support and therefore becomes sustainable, or it loses support and is vulnerable to repeal. In this way politicians are enacting leadership, and the accountability processes lie in the ways in which people are drawn to or repelled by the attractors.

The difference then between the two forms of democracy – dialogic versus action oriented – is summarized in Table 8.1

Participation is absolutely fundamental to inclusive sustainable change, but it must move beyond 'invited spaces', and be inhabited by those in the margins who are not normally engaged. Meaningful participation means engagement in analysis, decision-making, and action, and cannot be restricted

Table 8.1 Dialogic versus action-oriented democracy

Representative and participatory dialogic democracy	Democracy by attractor
Predictive logic	Iterative steps based on experience, and modified by what works
Accountability to agreed decisions or manifestos	Accountability through support and withdrawal of support
Information and ideology	Trust and experience
Agreement, consensus	Convergence around action that shifts system dynamics
Orchestration of outcomes	Interventions that open up new pathways and contribute to shifts in direction of travel

to data collection and dialogue. Participation for social change is ultimately about movement and movement building.

References

Burns, D., Ikita, P., Lopez Franco, E. and Shahrokh, T. (2015) 'Citizen participation and accountability for sustainable development', Brighton: IDS.

Chambers, R. (1997) *Whose Reality Counts? Putting the First Last*, London: Intermediate Technology Publications.

Cornwall, A. (2003) 'Whose voices? Whose choices? Reflections on gender and participatory development', *World Development* 31(8): 1325–42.

Cornwall, A. and Fujita, M. (2007) 'The politics of representing "the poor"', in J. Moncrieffe, and R. Eyben (eds), *The Power of Labeling: How People are Categorized and Why it Matters*, London: Earthscan.

Karamoja Action Research Team with Patta Scott-Villiers (2013) 'Ekoi and Etem in Karamoja: A study of decision-making in a post conflict society', Brighton: IDS.

Participate Initiative (2012) 'What do we know about how to bring the perspectives of people living in poverty into global policy-making?', Brighton: Institute of Development Studies.

Rademacher, A. and Patel, R. (2002) 'Retelling words of poverty: reflections on transforming participatory research for a global narrative', in K. Brock and R. McGee (eds), *Knowing Poverty: Critical Reflections on Participatory Research and Policy*, Chapter 6, London: Earthscan.

Scott-Villiers, P. with Scott-Villiers, A. and Wilson, S. (2012) 'Action research. How a group of young people did it in Napak and Moroto in Karamoja, Uganda. A method paper for research: "Strength, Creativity and Livelihoods of Karimojong Youth"', Restless Development Uganda and the Institute of Development Studies.

Wadsworth, Y. (2010) *Building in Research and Evaluation: Human Inquiry for Living Systems*, Melbourne: Action Research Press and Allen & Unwin.

CHAPTER 9
Implications for development

Lasting change that benefits people who are marginalized and live in poverty requires external development actors to understand and work with people, their issues and the power dynamics that they face. This means challenging oppressive power relations and not framing political issues as technical issues. Development interventions require constant reflection and continuous planning, not fixed plans. As dynamics change, development policy that nurtures space for emergence will enable flexible responses that lead to ownership and adoption. Scale will follow organically through movement-based spreading. Policies of roll-out miss the point completely by assuming that success in one place translates to success in another.

Keywords: power; planning; emergence; scale; system dynamics

Don't treat political issues as technical issues

Poverty is caused more by power imbalance than a lack of technical know-how. While technical solutions can offer important opportunities, these will always be operationalized in the context of local power relations. The quickest way to understand the political issues is to engage people. High-yielding seeds in the hands of a farmer who cannot afford the other required inputs will not improve yields. The reasons behind poor nutrition may relate more to land rights than the availability of agricultural inputs. The fact that tenant farmers have to give up half of their produce to landowners in Afghanistan is probably a greater cause of hunger than is the availability of good seed. It is hard to address land politics where people with power will fight ruthlessly to protect their vested interests. Inquiry-based techniques of the type described in this book enable the political as well as the technical issues to be surfaced and offer insight into where effective action might be taken.

Don't act for people; act with them!

Trusteeship is the dominant principle underpinning development action. It is the claim to know how others should live, to know what is best for them, and to know what they need. In certain circumstances, where crisis is acute and the pain of others is manifest, it is a human virtue to offer a helping hand, and compassion should continue to be an important driver for development. However, charity as a framing for intervention has failed, because by acting for the poor, development actors take away their ability to act for themselves. It also fails to recognize and often undermines the assets that they have.

http://dx.doi.org/10.3362/9781780448510.009

Working with people and investing in their agendas, using the approaches to participation that we have articulated, significantly reduces costs and increases efficiency because it harnesses the interest, enthusiasm, intelligence, and ownership of society. Not only does the rhetoric of participation need to change to become a reality, it needs to be re-conceptualized as action and not restricted to dialogic spaces.

Don't make plans; never stop planning

The context within which development processes occur is complex, multi-faceted and dynamic. The specific manifestations of system dynamics within which poverty flourishes are impossible to predict although, like rivers, they can be navigated. We have shown that plans frequently don't work because their assumptions are flawed, they are driven by ideological frameworks, and they are framed, as technical responses. By contrast, we have shown that by nurturing an environment within which learning is captured from action, as the action unfolds, it enables development practitioners to be reflective, smart, agile, and responsive. What is needed is the continual scanning and reassessment that prompts acceleration or braking, a swerve to avoid a pothole, or a change of direction when faced with new evidence of traffic build-up. This is planning in the moment that allows context to inform and guide. A sensible driver will stop to ask for directions in a new place. When they are on the wrong track, they can use this information to redirect themselves. They may also discover new information that changes where they want to go. What people imagine might be an attractive future will change with experience as reality unfolds.

Currently, development assistance is financed in line with priorities defined by experts. These are locked into policies and long-term contracts for programmes. Because complex systems are emergent and unpredictable, what is actually needed is the ability to adapt and allow room for manoeuvre; yet changes of plan require such inhibiting negotiation with contracting donors that this becomes almost impossible. *Flexibility is not a weakness, it is strength.* Poet Ella Wheeler Wilcox (1916) notes, it is 'the set of the sails and not the gales, which tell us the way to go', indicating the need to adapt ourselves to the specifics of changing momentary context. While external knowledge is important in the creation of options, it is specific and contextual evidence that most effectively determines what works. Local learning creates room for the effective use of external knowledge. For development processes to achieve sustainable change at scale, they need to be able to track dynamic system patterns. This requires a new form of management practice. Allana (2015: 4) notes that:

> Adaptive management is defined as 'a structured, iterative process of robust decision making in the face of uncertainty, with an aim to reducing uncertainty over time via system monitoring. Adaptive management is

a tool which should be used not only to change a system, but also to learn about the system.' In essence, managing adaptively means: (i) a high level of experimentation, where some initiatives will work while others will not; (ii) excellent monitoring processes feed a continual flow of information that sheds light on the operating environment (e.g., gathered from successful and failed experiments); and (iii) the ability of the organization to change strategies, plans, and activities rapidly in response to this new information.

Plans need to be replaced by the generation of real-time evidence, enabling the continual generation of theories of change which can be tested and modified through action.

Plans are held up as an instrument of accountability and management to ensure that what was intended was done. Yet, what is intended always misses the mark because systems never stand still. If there is to be sustainable change at a scale that is worth the investment, the role of plans as the overarching framework for action needs to be rethought. It needs to be replaced with an embracing of continual planning, shaped and managed as locally as possible. The creation of development investment funds that are contingent on participation, learning, and networking would enable plans to give way to planning.

Prioritize sustainable change over financial accountability

When donor funds are properly used in accordance with a plan that does not work, accountability may be upheld, but actual return on investment is zero or negative. As we noted in Chapter 1 in relation to water and sanitation around Lake Victoria, the strenuous enforcement of such policy caused the local businesses who were supposed to be implementing the programme to go bankrupt because they could not withstand the length of time that it took to fulfil procurement policy guidelines. Similarly we showed in Chapter 2 how monitoring processes drive programme managers toward programmes that they know they can deliver on – simultaneously managing risk and innovation out of the equation. This effectively means that we never learn how to do what we don't know how to do. Being accountable for resource use or even for delivery of outputs does not equate with impact. Yet this is probably the strongest value at play in development financing today. Conversely, resources that are agile enough to quickly flow in response to evidence or towards actions that work to generate evidence will attract investment to things that work and away from things that don't. Action-based learning and research can reveal important evidence that makes further investment smart and more sustainable. This requires patient investment mechanisms that support iterative evidence gathering to underpin emergent action. This will require courage by governments to defend public spending that involves risk.

Scale up – don't roll out

We have shown how scale can be achieved by nurturing emergent processes. Using participatory systemic inquiry, systemic action research, and nurtured emergent development, development practitioners and researchers can navigate complex systems and through learning that comes from action, reveal underlying system dynamics. While the idea of taking things to scale by 'cranking things up' is alluring, it does not last. Development interventions that seek sustainable scale must shift system dynamics. This is a function of innovation, adaptation and adoption, and movement building – not of roll-out. The form of these processes is closer to the scattering of many seeds, the creation of a rich environment within which the seeds can grow, and the nurturing of emergent seedlings to growth. Once nurtured, the young sapling becomes strong enough to grow into a tree and ultimately a forest on its own. This sort of process has carried many important issues to scale. The M-Pesa mobile phone banking system in Kenya is an example of facilitated organic process which developed from an early initiative to transfer credit between phones to become one of Kenya's most widely used financial instruments. Mobile phone banking has not taken root in the same way in other countries where attempts have been made to transplant it.

Conclusion

Clothed in arguments of accountability and stewardship, the ever-increasing imposition of tight controls on development investment ensures that development programmes will never deliver results where they are really needed. Successful development practice requires a fundamental change in thinking and behaviour. It requires development investors and actors to navigate complexity through engagement with people, in ways that are responsive and emergent. This requires new levels of flexibility, a willingness to stop pushing top-down change agendas, and an acceptance that sustainable change within complex systems will result from good process rather than detailed plans. Building trust and fostering movement through participation is essential. Learning from local experiences, and linking these within networks offers a rapid and sure way to find solutions, build movement, secure changes in system dynamics, and achieve sustainable change at scale.

References

Allana, A. (2015) 'Navigating complexity; adaptive management at the Northern Karamoja Growth, Health and Governance Program', Engineers Without Borders and Mercy Corps.

Wheeler Wilcox, E. (1916) *World Voices*, New York: Hearst's International Library Company.

Index

Page numbers in *italics* refer to figures and tables.